The Reform Debates

The Reform Debates
An agenda for a better democracy

Ken Ritchie

With Lewis Baston, Andrew Blick, Chris Frost,
Tom O'Malley, Robbie Parkin, Alexandra Runswick,
Paul Salveson and Damien Welfare

The Reform Foundation
2016

All rights reserved. This book or any portion thereof may not be reproduced or used in any manner whatsoever without the express written permission of the publisher except for the use of brief quotations in a book review or scholarly journal.

The rights of each chapter author to be identified separately as authors of this work have been asserted by them in accordance with the Copyright, Designs and Patents Act, 1988.

First Printing: April 2016

ISBN 978-1-326-59748-1

The Reform Foundation
37 Kilsby Road, Barby, Rugby. CV23 8TU

www.reformfoundation.com

Cover design: Tom Carpenter

To Aharon Nathan

A democrat without whose encouragement this book
would never have been written

Contents

Foreword by Polly Toynbee		ix
Acknowledgements		xi
Author and Guest Contributors		xiii
Preface		xvii

1 WHAT'S GONE WRONG WITH OUR DEMOCRACY?

1.1	Introduction	3
1-2	Political turn off	7
1-3	The rise of democracy	18
1-4	Democracy in decline	23
1-5	Cracks in the mould	46

2 PROSPECTS FOR REFORM

2-1	Lessons from history	67
2-2	Lessons from abroad	75
2-3	A roadmap to reform	82

3 THE DEBATES

3-1	How we elect our MPs	99
3-2	Cleaning up politics	
	Alexandra Runswick and Ken Ritchie	119
3-3	Holding our politicians to account	140

3-4	Reforming the House of Lords		
		Damien Welfare	152
3-5	Politics and the media	*Chris Frost*	173
3-6	Broadcasting reform in an age of digital communications	*Tom O'Malley*	189
3-7	The dog that needs to bark: the case for regionalism	*Paul Salveson*	203
3-8	No short cuts to democracy – the problem with referendums	*Lewis Baston*	211
3-9	Political parties that serve democracy		224
3-10	An elected head of state		243
3-11	Engaging young electors		255
3-12	Running better elections		271
3-13	Should voting be compulsory?		289
3-14	Defending rights and liberties		
		Robbie Parkin with Ken Ritchie	293
3-15	A written constitution for the UK		
		Andrew Blick	311
3-16	An agenda for debate and action		322

APPENDIX:
Organisations engaged in the reform debates   327

Foreword

Polly Toynbee

Not since the universal franchise has there been such a great need for reform of our political system. Citizens are profoundly disaffected with the two main political parties, alienated and often disgusted and yet they find themselves locked into choosing the least worst of these two to form any future government.

Both main parties are more profoundly split than for over a generation: Labour is torn between its socialist and its social democratic wings, while the Conservatives are deeply divided over Europe and should split, as the EU symbolises deep differences in their world views. But the iron law of our electoral system forces these unnatural bedfellows to stay together, fumbling and stumbling over their messages as everything they say is an unhappy compromise between opposites. Voters want clarity, sincerity and choice restored to their politics.

Freedom for new parties to emerge with a chance of being heard at Westminster is essential to democracy: locking out all other voices is anti-democratic. Voters dissatisfied with this narrow choice should be able to express their feelings in a vote for, say UKIP, or a socialist party or a Green party, without certainty that their vote will be wasted. If the voter were sovereign, the two old parties would be broken apart by a fairer proportional system.

This book looks at all the many great dysfunctions in our democracy in urgent need of reform. The House of Lords is a bizarre anachronism that makes foreigners laugh at us. The symbolism of monarchy distorts the people's perceptions of where power lies and who is truly sovereign: the people or unelected other forces?

The overt corruption of party funding sees large donors rewarded with a seat in our legislature, while the government of the day cuts off the funding stream to the main opposition from trade unions and reduces 'Short' money – public funding intended to help hold the government to account – all without consulting the electorate.

Dictatorship of the ruling party needs to be moderated. It's high time to raise questions about how our national discussion is warped and distorted by a biased media, mostly owned by a handful of non-UK tax-payers. The powerful lobbying of politicians by global corporate interests needs strong scrutiny.

The plea in this book is for a constitutional convention to engage the public in a serious national debate. That would surely be welcomed by all. It's time Britain had a written constitution to radically reform a system that no longer fits the country we are or the rainbow of political opinions in a diverse society. How much longer will Britain tolerate a political system that no longer reflects its voters?

Polly Toynbee
March 2016

Acknowledgements

In my 13 years as Chief Executive of the Electoral Reform Society, it became increasingly clear to me that, while changes in our voting systems were necessary, a much broader raft of reforms would be needed if we were ever to achieve the sort of democracy many of us want. It was in discussion of these ideas with Aharon Nathan, with whom I had worked on electoral reform, that the proposal emerged for a book which brings all the debates on constitutional change together. At all times during its preparation he has been a source of encouragement and support and without his help the book would never have been written. The book is therefore as much his as mine – although he may disagree with much of what has been written!

Causes need champions, and the campaign for a better democracy – and, indeed, a better society - could not have been better served by Polly Toynbee. For many years she has been commenting on the state of our politics with such clarity, good sense and passion that her articles have been a source of inspiration for those of us who want to see change. I am therefore hugely grateful to her for providing the foreword to this book.

The chapters on some the 'debates' in the third part of the book have been written by some of the leading experts on the topics - Lewis Baston, Andrew Blick, Chris Frost, Tom O'Malley, Robbie Parkin, Alexandra Runswick, Paul Salveson and Damien Welfare. They have analysed issues and contributed their expertise in a way that greatly adds to the arguments of the book. That they have given their time freely to this project demonstrates their commitment to a better democracy, and I am immensely grateful to them.

There are numerous others who, through my discussions with them and through their own writing, have contributed many of the ideas contained in this book. They include colleagues, past and present, in organisations including the Electoral Reform Society, Unlock Democracy and Republic, as well as all those whose published works I have quoted. I am particularly grateful to Professor Natalie Fenton for allowing me to use material from her forthcoming book (with J Curran and D Freedman) on 'Misunderstanding the Internet' (Routledge) in chapters 1-4 and 2-2, and to Tamasin Cave and Andy Rowell for permission to use examples from their work on lobbying, 'A quiet word' (Vintage, Penguin 2015) in chapter 3-2.

In preparing the book I received much assistance from friends and colleagues, including Bryan Blears, Jamie Cooke, Fay Dabbs, Lisa French, Owain ap Gareth, Annabelle Harle, Liam Howley, Roger Mendonca, Sue Myers, David Orr, Tom Pratt, Chris Terry, Daniel Vince-Archer and Rebecca Williams. Not only have they proofread and corrected chapters, but they have checked facts, commented on arguments and offered ideas. Junade Ali has helped on IT matters and Tom Carpenter has contributed his professional skills in designing the book cover.

Finally, thanks are due to my fellow trustees of the Reform Foundation for their enthusiastic support for this project. They have been provided encouragement and advice at all stages in the writing and publication of the book.

Ken Ritchie

The author and guest contributors

Principal author and editor

Ken Ritchie
Chair of the Reform Foundation. Dr Ritchie was Chief Executive of the Electoral Reform Society from 1997 to 2010 and has written extensively on elections and voting systems. He is a member of the boards of both the Electoral Reform Society and Republic. Previously he held senior positions in voluntary organisations concerned with human rights, refugees and international development. He was a candidate in the 1987, 1992 and 1997 general elections and remains active in local politics.

Guest contributors

Lewis Baston
Writer and analyst on history, politics and elections. Lewis Baston was principal researcher on the authorised biography of John Major and author of *Reggie* (2004), the biography of Reginald Maudling. From 2003 until 2010 he was Director of Research for the Electoral Reform Society. He has written several books on history and electoral studies, including guides to recent UK elections and, with Ken Ritchie, *Don't Take No For An Answer* (2011), on the electoral reform referendum of 2011. He has also been published and broadcast on a wide range of media outlets.

Andrew Blick

Lecturer in Politics and Contemporary History, King's College London, and Director of History & Policy, a UK-wide initiative that brings together historians and policy-makers. Dr Blick has advised numerous democratic reform groups around the world. From 2010-15 he was research fellow to the first ever parliamentary inquiry into the possibility of introducing a written constitution for the UK. Since 2015 he has been expert adviser to the All-Party Parliamentary Group on Reform, Decentralisation and Devolution.

Chris Frost

Emeritus Professor of Journalism at Liverpool John Moores University. Professor Frost has been a newspaper journalist, editor and journalism educator for more than 40 years. He is member of the National Executive Committee of the National Union of Journalists, a former union president and chair of the union's Ethics Council. He is Chair of the Association for Journalism Education and sits on the national council of the Campaign for Press and Broadcasting Freedom. He has written several books about Journalism as well as many book chapters and papers.

Tom O'Malley

Emeritus Professor of Media at Aberystwyth University. Professor O'Malley is co-editor of the journal *Media History* and a member of the Campaign for Press and Broadcasting Freedom. He publishes on press and broadcasting history and policy. His publications include: *Closedown? The BBC and Government*

Broadcasting Policy, 1979-1992 (1994); with Clive Soley, *Regulating The Press* (2000); with Siân Nicholas (eds) *Moral Panics, Social Fears, and the Media* (2013).

Robbie Parkin

A public and constitutional law specialist solicitor-advocate based in London, and a departmental head of a London law firm. He regularly advises clients on the day to day implications of the Human Rights Act 1998 and the European Convention across a broad range of topics, including immigration and asylum, housing and welfare, medical ethics and diplomatic law. Away from work, he provides legal research and advice to 'Republic' and is their current (2016) national campaigns volunteer of the year.

Paul Salveson

Convenor of the Hannah Mitchell Foundation, formed in 2012 to work for a fair and prosperous North of England in a federal Britain. He has written extensively on politics, including 'Socialism with a Northern Accent' (2012). He has a senior management position in the rail industry and is Visiting Professor of Transport and Logistics at the University of Huddersfield. He is an advocate of the development and use of local and regional railways: his book on 'Railpolitik – bringing railways back to communities' was published in 2013.

Alexandra Runswick

Director of Unlock Democracy which campaigns for a vibrant and inclusive democracy. Following work on feminist and environmental issues and public participation in health care, she moved to democratic reform, campaigning on issues such as lobbying transparency, party funding, freedom of information, House of Lords reform, electoral reform, women's representation in politics and participatory democracy. She has published a number of pamphlets on party funding reform including *Party Funding - Supporting the Grassroots* and *Life Support for Local Parties*.

Damien Welfare

Barrister and Co-ordinator of the Campaign for a Democratic Upper House, a Labour grouping supporting a second chamber which is wholly or mainly elected. He was Special Advisor to the Leader of the House of Lords, Lord Richard QC, in 1997-98, and co-wrote 'Unfinished Business: Reforming the House of Lords' with him. He also worked with MPs and peers opposing local government bills in the 1980s and 90s. He is a former parliamentary and council candidate, Council member of the Electoral Reform Society and executive member of the Labour Campaign for Electoral Reform.

Those who have contributed to this book believe in the need for changes in the way we conduct our politics. In should not be assumed, however, that views expressed are necessarily shared by all contributors or are the views of any organisations to which they are affiliated.

Preface

In the middle of 2014, with a general election still a year away, it appeared that Britain was heading for another hung parliament. Labour and the Conservatives seemed neck and neck, but neither with enough support to give them an outright majority in the Commons. Hung parliaments are of course moments that constitutional reformers wait for as it then that smaller, more reform-minded parties can push their agendas as the price of their support. It was at that time, with a sense of impending opportunity, that this book was conceived. If there were to be a government prepared to consider constitutional change, what should be on its agenda and what opportunities would there be for citizens to have a say in how their country is governed? There therefore appeared to be a need for a book which set out the issues and the arguments.

Back in 2014, few political commentators, if any, foresaw the scale of the events which would follow. Scotland almost voted to leave the United Kingdom and in the general election of May 2015 the SNP almost wiped out all opposition. Nearly 4 million people voted UKIP, partly because of its populist approach on immigration and EU membership, but it appears partly as a sign of disaffection with Westminster politics. In spite of the unpopularity of many of its policies, the Conservatives won 37% of the votes which, with our First-Past-the-Post electoral system, proved enough to enable them to form a government on their own. For reformers, the victory of a party which had have little interest in constitutional change seemed to be bad news.

However, we live in interesting times. The Chinese may regard that as a curse, but for us it is an opportunity. The extent to which voters expressed their dissatisfaction with mainstream politics, as manifest by the numbers voting for the SNP and UKIP, and even the Greens, indicates that many are looking for new style of politics. The Scottish referendum has made the UK into, in the words of the academic and veteran commentator Peter Hennessy, 'a constitutional building site', and the changes needed to accommodate Scottish aspirations will have implications for England, Wales and Northern Ireland as well as Scotland. More recently, the Labour Party has been shaken, and perhaps re-energised, by an astonishing leadership election in which members voted not just for a new leader but for a new direction for their party. The appetite for change is therefore there.

The circumstances in which this book was originally planned have changed, but the need for a reform agenda and a broad movement to call for a new style of politics is if anything stronger.

However, even if popular support for reform has increased, we have yet to find the means to convert support into a movement capable of articulating its demands and with the political leverage to effect change. A possible way forwards might be the establishment of a citizen-led convention to examine constitutional issues and make recommendations, and it is encouraging that this idea has received support from all parties other than the Conservatives. While the logistics of a convention on a scale sufficient to adequately deal with all the issues raised in this book are challenging, such a convention would enable us to look at the state of our politics in a holistic way, recognising not just the case for particular reforms but the whole package of measures needed to change politics in a way that gives citizens more control over their politicians and their political institutions.

What we strive for is a politics that not only enables people to be involved, but makes them want to be engaged. Thus while the establishment of a citizens' convention could be an important step forwards, it should not just be a group of people discussing on their own but the centrepiece of a national debate involving people and organisations across the country. It is my hope that this book can help set the agenda for that debate and provide some possible solutions to the problems of our democracy.

The book is in three parts:

- The first part looks at what has gone wrong with democracy, identifying some of the changes that have moved politics further from the people it is supposed to serve.
- The second part looks at the prospects for change. Although the obstacles may seem formidable, taking lessons from history and from other countries, as well as recent developments in the UK, that all is not lost and there are still grounds for hope.
- The third, and major, part of the book discusses some of the principal areas where reform is needed and proposes measures which the chapters' authors believe will at least contribute to building a better politics in which citizens are sovereign.

Not everyone will agree with all the arguments and recommendations of the book, but it is hoped that all will agree on the importance of debate on the issues. Some may want to read the book from cover to cover while others may want to focus just on chapters of special interest them, but it is hoped that all will recognised the inter-connectedness of the issues and the need for reform on a wide range of fronts.

However, books alone will not bring about political change – that requires people. And if we want a politics which engages people in discussions about how society can be made better, a starting point must surely be to engage citizens in discussing how the country is run. If this book can contribute to their debates, then it will have done its job.

Ken Ritchie
March 2016

Part 1

WHAT'S GONE WRONG WITH OUR DEMOCRACY?

INTRODUCTION

1-1. Introduction

We live in a representative democracy. People elect their representatives, to whom they entrust the business of government. They do so in anticipation that these representatives will take account of their views and act in their interests and with the knowledge that, if they fail to do so satisfactorily, they can be replaced at a future election. Politicians are accountable to the people and it is the people who are ultimately sovereign.

That, however, may be the theory, but there are few who believe it is how the system actually works. Most people do not feel that they are represented or that their politicians act as their agents in parliament, and they have good reason to be cynical about the representative nature of our democracy. The word 'democracy' means the rule of the people, but we are a long way from a situation in which citizens, collectively, are in charge of how the country is run.

We do have elections to elect our representatives. These elections are fair in the sense that they are generally free of fraud, intimidation and other malpractices which undermine democracy in too many other countries, but they neither produce politicians whom we feel belong to us nor a parliament which truly represents the views of the electorate. Politicians are perceived to be a class apart from ordinary people, operating in a separate world, remote from the everyday concerns of their constituents, and engaging in acrimonious debates conducted according to obscure

THE REFORM DEBATES

rules. Consequently many have lost faith in democracy and see politics as having little relevance to their own lives.

Our democracy has never been perfect. Politicians have always been regarded with suspicion and it is of course healthy that people adopt a questioning attitude to those who want our votes and claim to speak on our behalf. In recent times, however, trust in politicians has sunk to a new low – politicians and the parties they represent are viewed by many not just with cynicism but with contempt. Even more troubling than people's distrust of politicians is that many have lost faith in democracy itself – they are contemptuous not just of politicians but also of politics.

Our democratic institutions are no longer serving us as they should. They have been put under strain by changes in the nature of politics and in the nature of society itself and their legitimacy is being questioned. Our attempts to reform them have done little more than paper over the cracks rather than tackling the much more fundamental repair job needed to build the sort of democracy we now require.

It is the contention of this book that what we must aim for is a form of democracy based on the concept of 'popular sovereignty' – the idea that politics must belong to 'the people'. Politics must no longer be what politicians do, but an activity that involves us all and in which we all, irrespective of our wealth, positions in society and circumstances of our births, have an equal share of political power. It should be the way in which communities, and the nation as a whole, reach decisions about what sort of society we want to live in, what services the state should provide and how we pay for them, how we generate wealth and tackle poverty, what role we play in international affairs, etc. It must therefore engage people in

INTRODUCTION

decision-taking, and it should do so in a way that empowers them and enhances their sense of citizenship.

That requires a change in the way we think about politics and the part it plays in our day-to-day discourse. It does not, of course, mean we all need to be full-time politicians involved in debating every issue that arises – good representative democracy does not require that – and few if any want to be involved in debating the details of every aspect of government policy. It does, however, mean that we must all be more conscious of our political rights and collective responsibility for the affairs of the nation. Politics must become our business and not just that of an elite group at Westminster. Politicians take decisions on our behalf, but in doing so they should be acting as our servants and not our masters, and they need to be accountable to us in a more meaningful way. How decisions are reached should be more transparent and there should be more opportunities for people to have their say on whatever issues concern them. Gerry Stoker, in his excellent book, 'Why politics matters', concludes:

> My solution to the problem of disenchantment with politics is ... deceptively simple. We need to change our political institutions to 'give people more opportunities to have a say about the issues they care about'.[1]

However, not only should people have such opportunities, but when they express their views to their political representatives they should be able to be confident that the points they make will be heard and considered.

What we need is a whole change in the culture of our politics. That is not something that can be achieved overnight. Political culture is not something on which government can legislate, but it

THE REFORM DEBATES

can introduce reforms to our institutions and political practices which encourage a different culture to develop. There is no reform that on its own can bring about the changes we seek, but this book explores a whole package of measures which could go a long way towards giving us the sort of democracy our country needs.

---

[1] Gerry Stoker, *Why Politics Matters: Making Democracy Work*, Palgrave Macmillan, 2006

1-2 Political turn-off

Most people have lost faith in politics. They see politics as being remote from their everyday concerns and something over which they have little or no influence. They have little respect for politicians and they don't trust them to serve their interests rather than the politicians' own. These negative views, which are not always unreasonable, are fuelled by the tabloid press which treats our politicians with derision. Very few belong to political parties and those who do have are too often regarded by their leaders as donors and leafleters rather than as contributors to debates on policies.

Elections provide the main opportunity for people to have their political say, but an increasing number of people have come to the conclusion that voting doesn't matter. They may not feel that any of the candidates are likely to represent them, or they may think that the outcome, in terms of things that matter to them, will be the same whoever wins.

Elections, however, are important, and general elections are particularly important. They determine what party, or parties, will form the government and what the policies of government are likely to be. Choosing a government should be a matter in which all electors have a direct, personal interest: the choices involved can affect everything from health services – whether we have more doctors and nurses or longer waiting lists – to whether there will be more jobs or houses built for those who need them, and of

THE REFORM DEBATES

course how much tax we will need to pay. We might therefore expect that everyone would want to have their say on issues which will have implications for them and their families. But they don't: in recent general elections, many more electors have stayed away from the polling stations than the numbers voting for the winning parties.

In the 2015 general election, only 66.1% of electors voted. That was a slight increase from 2010 when only 65.1% voted and certainly better than the miserable turnouts of 61.4% in 2005 and 59.4% in 2001. Nevertheless, again more than a third of electors did not feel sufficiently motivated to cast their votes in spite of the apparent salience of the main election issues, including austerity measures and Britain's relationship with the EU. In Scotland, where politics appeared to have been re-energised by the independence referendum only eight months previously, the turnout of 71.1% was above average, but only modestly so.

The real situation is even worse than these turnout figures suggest: turnout is calculated as the percentage of registered electors who vote, but it does not take account of the growing number of people who do not even bother to register. Research in 2014 suggested that 7.5 million people were not registered, although by the time of the 2015 election that number may have dropped to around 5 million. If we were to take them into account in our calculations, the turnout in 2015 was probably under 60%.

In local elections, which are often about issues people see around them and services they use on a daily basis, the problem is even worse. Very rarely do local elections produce turnouts even approaching 50% - on average less than a third of electors have voted (other than when local elections are held on the same day as

POLITICAL TURN-OFF

general elections) and there are too many cases when turnout has dropped below 20%. In spite of the attention given to the arguments over our relations with the EU, when it comes to electing MEPs, only around a third of electors bother to vote (less than a quarter in 1999), and UK turnouts have always been well below the EU average. Less than a quarter have voted in mayoral elections and the first elections of Police and Crime Commissioners in 2012 attracted only 14.7% of electors.

There have always been people who, for one reason or another, decide not to vote (or just forget to do so) but for general elections, the scale of non-voting is a relatively new phenomenon. Historical accounts of early election campaigns describe vast crowds at meetings and halls crammed with people wanting to hear what the candidates had to say. Churchill, for example, filled the Caird Hall in Dundee when he fought his first election campaign there in 1908, and Charles Bradlaugh, the radical Liberal and proponent of both secularism and republicanism, attracted thousands to his campaign meetings in Northampton in the 1880s - over 4,000, including many constituents, travelled to his funeral in Woking in 1891. Nowadays candidates struggle to attract audiences and generate interest in elections, and around 70% of electors cannot even name their MPs.

The first half of the twentieth century saw the rise of the Labour Party and political opinion was split between left and right. It was a time when the economy was dominated by heavy industry and organised labour was strong. In these days Labour and the Conservatives were more clearly representative of class interests, and people were perhaps more conscious of on which side of the ideological divide they stood. General election turnouts were far from perfect, but they were generally well above 70%, reaching

THE REFORM DEBATES

83.9% in 1950. The period that followed saw the political gap between the major parties narrowing (the so-called post-war consensus of 'Butskellism') and it could be argued that the political choice offered in elections had also narrowed, but nevertheless turnouts remained over 70%. The battle lines of politics did not of course disappear, and whatever consensus had existed was truly over when Margaret Thatcher was elected in 1979, beginning a new era of more adversarial politics: although this might have given people more incentive to vote, in the elections from 1983 to 1992 turnouts changed little, averaging around 75%.

Blair's victory in 1997 was seen by many as a watershed. The story of that election was that voters, fed up with eighteen years of Conservative government, turned out in force to vote for a change. The reality, however, was rather different. The 1997 turnout was only 71.4%, the lowest since 1935 – in spite of the prospect of getting rid of an unpopular government, 3 electors out of every 10 stayed at home. Any disappointment at the turnout was drowned in the euphoria of those who had waited so long for an end to a period of Conservative governments which had waged war on the unions, introduced the poll tax and privatised many public services, and no Labour supporter was likely to be unhappy with an election that had delivered a thumping great majority.

It was the following election, in 2001, however, that demonstrated in dramatic fashion that there were problems. Only 59.4% voted. The result produced no end of studies and seminars on what had gone wrong, but none came up with any clear answers. The government responded with a series of pilots of new voting methods and introduced postal voting on demand (previously postal votes had only been available to those who required them for medical or other reasons). But the reason for the fall in turnout was not that voting had become more difficult, and making it easier was not therefore a solution. Turnout, as has been noted, has risen in subsequent elections, but only slightly and in each the number of non-voters has been more than a third of the electorate.

Why, then, are there so many people who do not make use of their votes in elections? The right to vote was, after all, something that people had fought and suffered for, and the act of voting is our most important opportunity to have our say on how the country is run.

Each year the Hansard Society produces its 'Audit of Political Engagement'. These excellent and detailed reports measure the extent to which people participate in politics and, by asking similar questions each year, they can chart the changes that are taking place. They make depressing reading. The Audit for 2014 reported that:

- For the third year running, less than 50% said they would be certain to vote if there were an immediate general election;
- Only a third of people think our system of governance works well;
- A third of people say they do not support any political party;
- 21% have no desire to be involved in local decision-making locally and 25% have no desire to be involved in decision-making nationally;
- Only a third think Parliament holds government to account, and less than a quarter think it encourages public involvement in politics.

THE REFORM DEBATES

This, however, was an improvement on the previous year when the Audit painted a particularly gloomy picture with the authors observing:

> Trends in interest and knowledge declined dramatically, the number of people who had discussed politics or participated in some form also dropped and the number of people certain not to vote increased to its highest ever mark ...
>
> Alarmingly, there has been a further collapse in the public's certainty to vote; only 41% now say that in the event of an immediate general election they would do so ...
>
> If turnout at the next general election is realised along current certainty to vote lines then the credibility and viability of conventional politics as we know it may increasingly be called into question.[1]

Given the results of these surveys, the 66.1% turnout in the 2015 election appears a lot better than might have been expected. It would be a mistake, however, to think the 2015 turnout means things are getting better. That more people voted in 2015 than in any of the three previous elections was good news, but it did not mean that more people felt satisfied with politics, felt they had any meaningful voice in how the country was being run, or had respect for their political representatives. People don't just vote to express support for one party or another – they may also vote to express their anger at their political leaders and in 2015 there was a lot to be angry about.

Political disengagement amongst younger people is particularly worrying. In all the measures of engagement used by the Audits, there is a marked age gradient: younger electors show much less knowledge of, and interest in, politics than older voters and, while many of the older generation still regard voting as a public duty, few in the 18–24 age group share this view. Back in 1964 the number of young people voting was almost the same as for other age groups,[2] but it has been on a downward trend and in 2005 sunk to only 38%. Although it recovered in 2010, the Audit Report for 2013[3] found that a staggering small 12% of the under 25s would be certain to vote if there were an immediate general election: by the time of the 2014 Report, this had doubled to 24%, but it was still an alarming figure.

Estimates of the 18-24 age group turnout in 2015 vary widely. Shortly after the election, British Election Study statistics suggested it might have been as high as 58%,[4] but Ipsos MORI later estimated only 43%.[5] It thus appears that more young people voted than had been predicted but, as figures are percentages of registered electors and voter registration levels for this age group are lower than average, these estimates disguise the extent of the problem.

Whatever the 2015 turnout of younger electors might have been, the evidence of their attitudes and understanding of politics reported by the Audits of Political Engagement shows that there are no grounds for complacency. It is of course possible that when many of these younger people start families, set up homes and start paying more taxes they will take greater interest in the alternatives offered by the parties, but there is a danger that if they remain non-voters our election turnouts will fall to new lows, threatening the legitimacy of government. Unless greater political engagement comes with age, the prospects are dire.

A second concern is the marked differences in attitudes, understanding and participation levels between social groups: people

THE REFORM DEBATES

in the AB category are on average nearly twice as likely to be knowledgeable and interested in politics than those in social group DE, and they are much more likely to vote (63% of ABs would be certain to vote in a general election compared to 38% of DEs). The 2014 Audit found that while 52% of the white population was certain to vote, for BME voters the figure was only 31%. Thus those people who may have most need of a strong democracy to protect their interests are those least likely to participate in it, and those who are more comfortably off will have a stronger voice in determining what government we have and what policies it will follow.

Given the decrease in political engagement, it is not surprising that the membership of parties has decreased dramatically. While the Conservative Party had 2.8 million members in 1946, it now has only around 150,000, and Labour dropped from a peak of about one million in the late 1940s to only 200,000 at the time of the 2015 election. As Jess Garland and Will Brett have noted in 2014, 'there are more people who identify their religion as 'Jedi' than there are members of the Conservative Party – and almost the same as the number of Labour members'.[6] The Liberal Democrats could now be accommodated in a major football stadium. Now less than 1% of the electorate belong to one of these parties compared with 3.8% in 1983.

There have, however, been exceptions to this trend: membership of the SNP tripled to over 100,000 following the 2014 independence referendum, the Greens and UKIP have seen significant growth through disenchantment of people in the larger parties, and the Labour leadership election of 2015 has brought about a dramatic surge in members seeking more influence on Labour's direction: in the space of a few months, its membership doubled to around 400,000. However, it remains to be seen whether these recent surges in membership are transient or permanent: will the SNP maintain its level of membership when the euphoria of the independence referendum and the 2015 election subsides, and will all Labour's new recruits remain members now that the excitement of the leadership election is over and the limitations on what is possible become apparent?

Does all of this matter? Unfortunately it does, because if our democracy is not working as it should, we cannot be confident that our government is truly representative and acting in the national interest. Greater participation in our elections might have produced a different government with a different approach to solving our problems, such as how to revive the economy and maintain services for the vulnerable in society when there are demands for austerity. That the less-affluent and members of ethnic communities do not engage to the same extent as others, the representativeness of our government is skewed in favour of the interests of the more wealthy. The policies we've got are in part a result of the state of our democracy.

When democracy is weakened by a lack of participation, there is a danger that space is created for the rise of extremist and anti-democratic views. To adapt Edmund Burke's famous quote: 'The only thing necessary for the triumph of evil is that good men and women don't vote'. Many of the BNP's successes in local elections have been in areas where there is a strong perception that politics has failed to deliver what people want. Many of the riots and street protests of recent years have not been manifestations of democracy but of people's loss of confidence in democracy as the way of taking decisions. As Derry Irvine, when Lord Chancellor in 1998, put it:

THE REFORM DEBATES

> We should not, must not, dare not, be complacent about the health and future of British democracy. Unless we become a nation of engaged citizens, our democracy is not secure[7]

It also matters for those who regard democracy as not just a means to an end (the election of those who run the country) but an end in itself. Our citizenship is more complete if we are able to meaningfully participate in the affairs of the nation. Not only should elections offer us real choices, but our citizenship is also more fulfilled if we are able to respond to debates between elections in the knowledge that our views matter. Being able to play a part in shaping our own futures is something to which we should all aspire, but if politics is failing we can be reduced to mere subjects rather than active citizens.

Good politics should give us all a sense of having a stake in the nation, and that stake can give us a sense of ownership and responsibility for the society we live in. Thatcher declared "There is no such thing as society", and increasingly it is becoming true. People have become more insular in their views: the concept of 'the common good' is rarely heard in our political discourse and concern for the vulnerable has decreased. The socially and economically marginalised are talked about rather than with (and often talked about as problems rather than as citizens). Their sense of powerlessness makes them less likely to vote and consequently they have little voice in our national debates. Is it too much to hope that a better politics – one which places greater emphasis on the rights and roles of ordinary citizens and their effective ownership of the state – would give us a society that is more inclusive and cohesive and in which people live in greater harmony with each other?

[1] *Audit of Political Engagement*, Hansard Society 2013

[2] In 1964 the voting age was 21, and 76.4% of 21 – 24 year olds voted.

[3] *Audit of Political Engagement*, Hansard Society 2013

[4] E.g. Sky News, *Six out of 10 young voters turn out for election*, 9 May 2015

[5] Ipsos MORI, *How Britain voted in 2015*, 26 August, 2015

[6] Jess Garland and Will Brett, *Open Up: the future of the political party*, Electoral Reform Society 2014

[7] Quoted in *Education for citizenship and the teaching of democracy in schools: Final report of the Advisory Group on Citizenship*, Qualifications and Curriculum Authority, 1998.

THE REFORM DEBATES

1-3 The rise of democracy

The first half of the twentieth century saw the rise of democracy in the UK: the second half saw its decline and fall.

The Reform Acts of the previous century had greatly expanded the franchise – in 1900 most men could vote, provided that they were over 21 and had lived at the same address for at least a year. The 'rotten boroughs' had given way to constituencies that took account of population, and the Ballot Act of 1872 had introduced the secret ballot. Women, however, were still without a political voice and both the Commons and the Lords were all-male.

The Lords was, and would remain for many years, a chamber of hereditary peers and bishops, and had real clout. In 1909 it voted down a Liberal budget and only in 1911, when George V agreed to back Prime Minister Asquith in threatening to create more Liberal peers to counter the Conservatives' Lords majority, did the Lords accept the primacy of the Commons (kings were important players in those days – the previous king, Edward VII, had refused Asquith's request).

It was the Commons, however, that started to change. Keir Hardie had won his first seat in 1892, and in 1900 the Labour Party was born to seek representation for working people. In the 1906 general election, it won 29 seats and from there it rapidly grew in strength. In 1922 it replaced the Liberals as the second largest

THE RISE OF DEMOCRACY

party, and in 1924, with Liberal support, it formed its first government, although it lasted for only nine months. However, Labour returned to power in 1929 as the largest party but, faced with the pressures of the Great Depression, it soon disintegrated, giving way to a 'national government', headed by former Labour leader Ramsay Macdonald until 1935, but essentially a Conservative government.

By this time the franchise had been extended again, and women were now included. It was women who, through the suffragette movement, had been in the forefront of the campaign for a fuller democracy – in 1918 women over the age of 30 were given the vote (subject to a property qualification), and ten years later all over 21 were allowed to vote, as was the case for men.

Labour at this time could claim to be truly representative of the working class. Not only was it backed by the trade union movement, but its MPs were largely people who had risen from humble origins. Keir Hardie had worked from the age of 10 in the mines, Aneurin Bevan was a miner at 13, and Ramsay Macdonald grew up in rural poverty in Scotland.

Labour's big breakthrough, however, did not come until 1945. Labour politicians had been members of the wartime coalition, but there was an assumption that, Churchill, who had inspired the country as a war leader, would become prime minister of a Conservative government. But it was not to be. As in 1918, those who had sacrificed so much in the war years were not going to be satisfied with a return to the status quo, and Labour won by a landslide: it won over 61% of the seats with nearly half of the votes.

The Labour government of 1945–50 was the most remarkable one that Britain has seen. It was, in the words of Jeremy Paxman,

THE REFORM DEBATES

'packed with people who had a passion to build the new Jerusalem'.[1] Although the country was bankrupt from years of war, facing huge problems in rebuilding industry and infrastructure, and still with food rationing, Labour took control of the country and used its power to transform the nature of the state. It abolished the 'poor law' and created the Welfare State to tackle Beveridge's five 'Giant Evils' in society: squalor, ignorance, want, idleness and disease. The NHS was created to provide free medical care; unemployment, sickness and other benefits as well as universal state pensions were introduced through the National Insurance Act; in response to the need for more homes, many council houses were built; and about 20% of the economy was taken into state control, including all major industries. Whatever view one might take of the 1945–50 government's policies, the scale of the changes it introduced was truly impressive (and, for reasons we will return to in Chapter 1-4, was something it would be very difficult for any present-day government to even contemplate).

This was a time when politics was important. Although it lost the 1945 election, in 1946 the Conservative Party's membership reached 2.8 million, while Labour's was around one million (it also had the support of trade unions with a combined membership of 10 million): even the Liberals, who had been reduced to a fringe concern, had 250,000 members. Although turnout in the 1945 election was only 72.8% because of number of men still returning from war service, by-election turnouts in 1945-50 averaged 67.2% (in more recent years they have been well under 50%), and in the general election of 1950, 83.9% voted – the highest turnout Britain has seen.

THE RISE OF DEMOCRACY

The Labour government's achievements of 1945-50 have been celebrated in Ken Loach's brilliant film, 'The Spirit of 45', in a way that leaves few dry eyes, but what the film does not remind us is that the story finishes with Labour only narrowly winning the 1950 general election, going to the country again in 1951 and then, in spite of receiving more votes than the Conservatives, narrowly losing in terms of seats. Why was such a successful and transforming government rejected by the voters? As a party, the Conservatives were much stronger in 1950 than they had been in 1945: while Labour was nationalising, the Conservatives were re-organising, recruiting and fundraising and in 1950 and 1951 they had well-run campaigns which successfully exploited discontent at the privations of the post-war economy. Labour was not helped by splits in its ranks, and although Labour had used its power to make a real difference for working people, it had done so by controlling from the centre without sufficiently involving people in shaping the new Britain. It had certainly been a government for the people, but whether it had been government by the people was less clear. There were also criticisms that Labour had not involved trade unions more in its policy-making (although unions were far from models of democracy), and the 1945–50 cabinet only had a single woman (who died in 1947).

The period 1945–50 was nevertheless the high point of British democracy – Britain had a government focused on delivering what people, and in particular working people and the vulnerable, needed, membership of political parties had reached its zenith and the numbers of people participating in elections were at record levels.

Colin Crouch has written about 'the parabola of democracy'[2]: in most Western countries, democracy developed in much the

THE REFORM DEBATES

same way as it did in Britain but, after reaching the top of the curve, it started to decline. In Britain we were on top of the democratic hill around the middle of the last century and for a few decades that followed we appeared to remain on relatively high ground, but we are now well on our way down the other side and we appear to have encountered a rather steep gradient. However, while we re-cross the same contour lines we passed on our ascent, we are now in a different place – one in which the terrain is more hostile to democracy. If we are to regain height, we need to understand what has changed and how democracy must be redesigned to survive in a new environment. In the following chapter we will examine some of the changes that contributed to our democratic problems

---

[1] Jeremy Paxman, *The Political Animal: An Anatomy,* Michael Joseph(Penguin Books), 2002

[2] Colin Crouch, *Post-Democracy*, Polity Press, 2004. Crouch is a political scientist: a mathematician would have compared the trajectory of democracy to a Gaussian (bell-shaped) curve and not a parabola!

4. Democracy in decline

Democracy in 1945-50 was far from perfect, but it was much healthier than it is today. In this chapter we will look at some changes that have undermined democracy and reduced politics to something many regard with contempt.

Changes in society

When democracy was gathering strength in the first half of the last century, class divisions in society were much more pronounced. It was a time when the economy was dominated by heavy industries such as mining, manufacturing and ship building and organised labour was strong. The Labour Party had been formed to give representation to the working class, while the Conservatives could be seen as the party which stood for the interests of the middle classes and the more wealthy. That, of course, is a simplification but, generally speaking, the two major parties were positioned on different sides of an ideological divide, and people were perhaps more conscious of on which side of the divide they stood. Social status was, to a much greater extent than it is today, the main determinant of how people voted. In 1882, W S Gilbert had written:

> That every boy and every gal,
> That's born into the world alive,
> Is either a little Liberal,
> Or else a little Conservative![1]

THE REFORM DEBATES

In the first part of the twentieth century, although there were many middle-class people on the left (some of whom rose to prominent positions in Labour) and many working class voters who subscribed to Conservative values, Gilbert's satire, but with 'Liberal' replaced by 'Labour', remained apposite.

In the decades that followed 1945, however, many traditional, heavily unionised, industries began to decline. There were more educational opportunities and more could aspire to home ownership and white-collar jobs, and consequently there was a growth in the middle class. For Labour this presented a difficulty as unionised labour had been the bedrock of its support. The party could no longer win elections with the votes of the down-trodden poor and had therefore to appeal to those who had started to climb the social ladder, and those who had aspirations to do so.

Labour had already accepted the 'post-war consensus' of Butskellism – an unwritten cross-party agreement between the parties on the direction of government, based on Keynesian economics and the state's responsibility for meeting the needs of the disadvantaged and vulnerable. Thus, the differences between what the parties were offering, although still significant, were not so acute and the electorate not so clearly divided between opposing camps. The political choices for voters had become less stark and party support less entrenched. Not so many electors were ready to vote Labour or vote Conservative just because that was what their parents had always done, and the numbers who described themselves as 'strong Labour' or 'strong Conservative' in opinion polls decreased: in 1964 44% strongly identified with one party or another, but by 2001 it was only 13%.[2]

It was never possible to plot people's political views on a single axis between left and right, but other dimensions of politics have become increasing important, such as where people stand between liberalism and social conservatism. There has also been a growth in identity politics with many people regarding their positions as feminists, as people of LGBT sexuality and as members of ethnic minority communities, as more important than their positions on the left-right divide of the two main parties. Parties, to a greater or lesser extent, have attempted to embrace these new movements, but they cannot assimilate them.

These changes only happened gradually, but increasingly parties could not expect people to support them on the grounds of loyalty alone – they had to appeal for votes. That people were more likely to vote on their assessment of parties and their manifestos was, of course, good for democracy, but if electors did not think what was on offer was sufficiently attractive, their likelihood to vote was reduced. Fewer people were participants in politics and for more people deciding how to, and whether to, vote was like examining the products on a supermarket shelf to see if any were worth buying. As Jeremy Paxman has remarked, 'ideological division has been replaced by consumer choice'.[3] In many ways, politics has become less important.

Political engagement has also been affected by changes in life styles, in the nature of work and workplaces, which have made society more atomised. The American sociologist, Putman, has written of people 'bowling alone', noting that many do not socialise in groups to the extent which they did so in the past. With the advent of television, and later the internet, people could entertain themselves in their own homes without needing to go out to meetings and events. But political activity is social in nature – it is the way in which people take decisions collectively.

That many people are now more mobile and have less attachment to the areas in which they live has also had an effect on politics as a collective activity. Local communities have become weaker – those who live in a neighbourhood may sleep there, but they may work and socialise elsewhere and consequently their interest in local affairs is weak. Research[4] has shown that where more people identify with their local area and are engaged in its community, electoral turnouts in local elections are likely to be higher, particularly when there are local candidates.

Many have come to see themselves as observers of society rather than participants, and that has had an effect on people's willingness to engage in politics. It does not mean that people have become less concerned about what is happening in the world, but they don't see involvement in politics as way of expressing that concern or contributing to the search for solutions. Rather than joining or supporting parties, more now prefer to seek change through single-issue organisations campaigning on issues such as human rights, the environment, tackling poverty worldwide and animal welfare (the Royal Society for the Protection of Birds now has more members than all the parties put together). These organisations do valuable work and they have an important part to play in democracy: they offer a form of political participation but, unlike parties, they do not aspire to represent people, other than their own supporters on their very specific demands, and they do not need to address the much more complex questions about how the country should be run. Their work is based on issues which can be presented in black and white terms, and they do not require people to make political choices between alternative policies on matters such as taxation and spending priorities, and they do not need to deal with the tricky business of negotiating compromises between the different interest groups in society. Consequently, they cannot be seen as an alternative to politics. As Jess Garland and Will Brett have put it:

> Politics requires parties to aggregate interests as well as articulating them. Whilst interest groups are able to articulate citizens' views, they do not perform the task of mediating between them. They can campaign on their chosen issue or group of issues without the need to balance competing demands.[5]

For many, the nature of political engagement has been changed by the internet. Never has it been easier for those who want to know about what is happening in politics to keep abreast of issues and debates. The ease of sending an email, posting on a website or 'tweeting' allows much more communication between politicians and electors (or at least those electors prepared to receive communications or inclined to contact their representatives) and enables campaign groups to mobilise support and lobby government in a way that was not before possible. It has allowed the creation of organisations such as 38 Degrees, Avaaz and Change.org which enable people to show their support for a cause and convey it to their MPs with the click of a mouse: by September 2014 Avaaz had nearly 40 million 'members' worldwide, while 38 Degrees had 3 million in the UK[6] – twice as many as the total 'likes' of the Facebook pages of the major parties. Perhaps even more important is the way the internet, particularly through social media sites, allows 'horizontal' rather than 'vertical' communication: people can exchange their views with others and share bits of news they have found interesting without the need for a political party – a modern version of the nineteenth century coffee houses where people met to discuss the issues of the day, but one that is open to all parts of society (other, of course, than the declining number who are not e-connected).

However, while a lot of internet communication is about politics, it is rarely real politics. More often it is the politics of protest. Its language is often more likely to fuel disenchantment with politics than encourage engagement. While the contribution of Avaaz and 38 Degrees is valuable, Natalie Fenton notes that:

> Campaign populism is a trap that is hard to avoid for many such organisations that are undoubtedly challenging the powerful and making public concerns heard but nonetheless run the risk of producing a form of radical politics that favours gut reaction and quick fixes over long-term struggle. One that is all about the short, sharp referendum, a tick-box politics that prefers to avoid the complicated, drawn-out assessment of social and political systems and their consequences. One that is more likely to lead to sticky-tape solutions than genuine political alternatives.[7]

This new, individualistic, on-line form of political engagement is better than no engagement, but is a poor substitute for debates on 'genuine political alternatives': it can only be effective when it leads to people getting together, organising and working for change. Although it may have its successes in influencing politicians on particular issues, on-line politics that does not connect with our political system and institutions in a deeper way cannot be a wholly adequate way of involving people in debates and decisions on the sort of society they want.

DEMOCRACY IN DECLINE

Many of the changes that have taken place in society are of course good. We still have, for example, too many who are poor, but not as poor as some were in the past; housing standards are generally much better than they were in the past; and we now have more educational opportunities even if they are not always of the quality we would like. While we are far from achieving gender equality, we have made progress; racism, sexism and homophobia still exist but we have anti-discrimination legislation and have recognised the rights of gay and lesbian people. However, although Margaret Thatcher was wrong in declaring 'there is no such thing as society', in many ways the fabric of our society is weaker and that has had consequences for political engagement.

Changes in the political class

As well as changes in society, we have seen changes in the nature of those who represent us at Westminster and particularly in Labour's ranks. In the early years of the Labour Party most of its MPs were from the labour movement, but by the middle of the last century this was changing. There were still people like Manny Shinwell, George Brown and Callaghan who had risen from humble origins, but many of its leading figures, including Attlee, Castle, Crosland, Crossman, Gaitskell, Wilson and Healy, were all Oxford graduates, while Dalton was an old Etonian, Cripps and Foot the sons of MPs, and Crossman's father was a judge. The change in the Parliamentary Labour Party was not, however, too surprising: with the expansion of educational opportunities, able people were more likely to find their way to universities, and a present-day Keir Hardie would be more likely to go to Oxbridge than down the mines. Nevertheless, the numbers from upper middle class backgrounds and public schools meant that the nature of Labour was changing and the leadership of the party was further from its roots.

The Conservatives were changing too. A century ago their MPs were largely upper class, many with aristocratic connections, and almost all were products of top public schools. Over the years Conservative MPs gradually became more diverse, with more MPs from the world of business and from the wealthy elite – a land and title-based aristocracy was being replaced by a financial one. Although there are some Conservative MPs who have risen from ordinary backgrounds, many of its leaders are still from extremely privileged backgrounds: in 2014 the Prime Minister and many of his inner circle, as well as the Mayor of London, attended Eton and other top public schools where the annual fees are well above the average wage, and even Michael Gove, when Education Minister, commented 'it's ridiculous ... I don't know where you can find some such similar situation in a developed economy'. Some might argue that MPs who know about money and business, and who have been successful in it, are a good thing, but being millionaires, as many are, sets them as far apart from their constituents as the landed gentry were in the past.

More recent years have seen the rise of a new class of MPs – people who have spent their entire lives in politics and have no work experience outside it. They may have started as student politicians, holding office in the National Union Students or in their own universities, before becoming MPs' researchers and graduating to ministers' SPADs (special advisors) and then MPs, often with considerable help from their party machines in getting selected as parliamentary candidates. Such people cannot be criticised for their commitment to politics, and many of them are exceptionally talented, but if too many of our politicians have no real experience of working environments outside Westminster, questions must arise over their ability to understand the lives and concerns of their constituents, and the extent to which our parliament represents the electorate.

That our politicians are not 'like us' and that, even if they represent us, are not representative of us, undermines our confidence in them. Poll after poll tells us that people don't trust their MPs. They are trusted no more than second-hand car dealers and only slightly more than journalists.

People have always been cynical about politicians, but in a democracy it is not a bad thing that people treat the claims and promises of those who want their votes with some suspicion. In earlier periods, however, that suspicion did not deter people from voting or turn them off politics, at least not to any noticeable extent. Now, however, many voters are not just cynical but contemptuous and it appears that the level of distrust of politicians has led to distaste for politics and disengagement from it.

Politicians must take much of the responsibility for this state of affairs. They have made promises they have not kept, often they offer us only half-truths and are evasive when questioned, they often appear as badly behaved public-school boys (and of course many were just that), and they spend much of their time isolated from real people in the Westminster bubble with all its bizarre procedures and protocols. Tony Wright, the former chair of the Public Administration Select Committee, has remarked that: 'The real discontent with politicians turns on how they behave, and the sort of people they increasingly are...'.

THE REFORM DEBATES

In 2009 trust in MPs took a hard knock when the Daily Telegraph published the full list of expenses they had claimed. It was truly shocking. As well as loads of claims for minor expenses which most people outside politics would meet from their salaries, there were the exotic claims for a duck house and the clearing of a moat. More devious were claims for second homes which did not appear to be necessary, and the switching of main homes and second homes needed for parliamentary or constituency duties in order to maximise the claims MPs could make for mortgages. Some even continued claiming for mortgage premiums after their mortgages had been paid off and ended up behind bars as a result. Not all MPs were, of course, expenses cheats, but all MPs, including the honest ones, were tarred with the same brush. However, while the expenses scandal was damaging, it only added to the distrust which already existed.

A poll in 2013 found that only 21% of people trusted their MP to tell the truth, while 72% did not trust them.[8] In 2014 a further poll[9] found that only 24% trusted their MPs to represent them in parliament, while another poll conducted at the same time found that 86% of MPs thought their constituents trusted them – clear evidence of the extent to which politicians are out of touch with the views of those they should represent.

The 2013 poll also found that two-thirds of people think that at least half of politicians use their power for their own personal gain. Public concern may not be misplaced: in the same year the Guardian reported that 20 MPs earned more in outside interests than their parliamentary salaries and that:

> Conservative MPs declared more than £4.3m in earnings from outside directorships or jobs, against £2.4m for Labour

DEMOCRACY IN DECLINE

– more than half of which was Brown's £1.37m. More than 50 MPs had directorships of at least one company, while 295 declared at least some kind of minimal earnings from outside parliament.[10]

To be fair to Brown, however, he used his earnings to support his 'involvement in public life' and £600,000 went to charity.

To add to the concern, recent years have seen MPs being exposed for offering to ask questions for cash, and to introduce clients to ministers for huge fees. In February 2015, for example, two senior politicians, Malcolm Rifkind (Conservative) and Jack Straw (Labour) were caught in a media sting offering their political services to a fictitious Chinese company for £5000 per day. Rifkind claimed that it was 'quite unrealistic' to expect MPs to exist on their (then) salary of £67,000 without looking for extra income.[11] In May 2015, while the government was busy cutting benefits, MPs' salaries were increased by over 10% to £74,000 – nearly three times the average salary.

That distrust of politicians is undermining faith in politics does not, of course, mean that today's politicians are any worse than those of days gone by. Throughout the history of parliament, it has always had its rogues, and, while MPs should be expected to lead by example, they are people nevertheless and vulnerable to the temptations of quick money that might come their way. What has changed is our expectations of them. Lack of respect for politicians has made us less deferential and more prepared to make demands of our political leaders, while greater transparency in MPs' affairs and a more intrusive media has allowed much greater public scrutiny of their conduct.

However, the directorships and consultancies of some MPs as well as their relatively large salaries puts them in a class apart

THE REFORM DEBATES

from the great majority of their constituents. In some ways this is a relatively new development – in 1990 MPs' pay was only 42% above national average earning, rising to over twice average earnings in 2000, and to more than two and a half times average earnings in 2014 (until 1911, MPs received no payment for their services, which was as bad, if not worse, as it made it difficult for people without independent means to stand for parliament). But many MPs are still not content with their salaries: a survey in 2014 found that some felt they should be paid £100,000, which would then have been a 50% pay rise, when the salaries of many people were being capped or cut. There are therefore good grounds for the common complaint that politicians are not "people like us" and that they are becoming more remote from us.

The number of MPs with a background in manual work has now shrunk to only 25 in a Commons of 650 – they include a few who have risen to cabinet office, such as Labour's Alan Johnson and the Conservatives' Patrick McLoughlin – and the prospects for this number increasing are not good. With changes in educational opportunities, it is now likely that most young people with the aptitude to become MPs, whatever their social background, will have benefited from college or university training and progressed to white-collar jobs without getting experience of the sort of environments in which many electors must work. That parliament must take decisions that affect shop-floor workers and those on benefits without any of them being in the Commons and being able to directly contribute to debates is a problem to which there is no easy answer.

In 2014 the Fabian Society brought together a group of non-voters and swing voters by to discuss how politics might be improved.[12] What they asked for were:
- 'Politicians who are more like one of us'
- 'Politicians who listen to people'
- 'Politics that makes people feel they have an impact'
- 'Politics that is led by issues, rather than people and parties'

However, while people want their MPs to be 'like them', it is unlikely that they mean it literally. In 2013, a poll found that only 22% agreed that 'a person like me could do a good job as a local MP',[13] suggesting that what people really want is an MP who, even if not 'like them' in many respects, is someone who speaks to them in a language they can understand and with whom they can identify. That may mean someone from a similar background and with similar life experiences, but it certainly means that people want a representative who relates to them and who is committed to serving their interests.

Doorstep canvassers of all parties are frequently frustrated by finding people who maintain that 'you're all the same'. All party activists know that this is nonsense – parties have different policies and candidates spend time finding things to disagree about – but there is a sense in which the doorstep respondents are often right. As members of an elite political class, or as people who aspire to belong to that class, they may have more in common with each other than with the people they want to represent.

THE REFORM DEBATES

Money and politics

The political power of money is not new. The rich and privileged have always had more influence than others over political decisions. They no longer run the country in the way they did in earlier centuries, but the extension of the franchise to all adult citizens did not in practice mean that everyone had an equal political voice. Money talks, and in politics it talks loudly, posing a challenge to the democratic control of the nation's resources. As the economic historian, R H Tawney, put it in 1938:

> That democracy and extreme economic inequality form, when combined, an unstable compound, is no novel doctrine. It was a commonplace of political science four centuries before our era. Nevertheless, though a venerable truism, it remains an important one, which is periodically forgotten and therefore requires to be periodically rediscovered ...[14]

Tawney's 'truism' has not so much been forgotten as ignored. Since his time, inequality has grown and the way in which economic power exerts its influence on politics has become almost institutionalised.

Globalisation, and the emergence of huge companies, many operating internationally and some with turnovers which exceed the GDPs of many small states, have had an impact on economies which national politicians cannot ignore. These giant corporations have enormous power and influence, reducing the ability of politicians to shape events. Even if we had a government that really wanted to make radical changes, it would be hard for it to do so if it meant seriously challenging their corporate interests. Alas, however, we have too many politicians who simply accept a world in which corporate power holds sway and consequently democracy has been diminished.

Politicians, whatever their political colours, need these companies to provide jobs and generate revenue, making it all too easy for major companies to bully government. They can oppose policies they don't like by claiming they will lead to dire consequences (take, for example, the energy companies' response to Ed Miliband's proposal in 2014 for a price freeze) and they can even threaten to relocate their activities if they don't like decisions that are, or might be, taken (as some did when Scotland was considering independence). Their lobbying power is formidable: they spend fortunes employing highly professional teams of lobbyists to persuade ministers to follow their advice, and their importance to the economy gives them access to senior politicians – something that is seldom possible for interest groups of citizens, the people whom the politicians are supposed to represent.

The political power of 'the City' has become huge. Its financial institutions are of great importance to our economy, particularly with the decline (some would say neglect) of our manufacturing industries, making politicians wary of challenging their views and practices. Nevertheless, the city leaves nothing to chance: in 2011 the financial sector spent £92m lobbying politicians and policymakers, successfully fighting off proposed regulations which would have interfered with its ability to make large profits, and in 2010 more than half of the donations to the Conservative Party came from City sources. In the case of the banks which the government had to bail out to enable them to survive the financial crash of 2008, the government has not even used its power as one of their major shareholders to change their policies: they have con-

THE REFORM DEBATES

tinued to pay massive salaries and bonuses, making the handwringing by some leading politicians seem rather insincere.

The increasing practice of contracting-out services, at local as well as at national level, has also weakened the democratic control of them. When public services are provided by private companies, our politicians may retain control of the broad policies, but not necessarily of the way they are implemented, and if people are dissatisfied with the services they received, it is more difficult for politicians, unless something has gone very seriously wrong, to intervene. (This, of course, may be to the liking of some politicians as it removes from them the responsibility for service delivery, allowing them to pass any blame to the contractors.) While contractors are responsible to politicians, even if only for meeting the detailed requirements of their contracts, they are also responsible to their shareholders, and it is inevitable that situations will arise when the two are in conflict. Then there is the danger that the nature and quality of a service is not determined by the needs of citizens but by the demands of investors. The problem is not just privatisation, but that what should be political decisions become commercial decisions.

Some argue that private sector involvement in public services improves their quality by opening them up to competition, but this is not a free market that Adam Smith would have recognised. There is only one buyer – central government or a local authority – and with large contracts there are generally only a small number of companies capable of bidding. These include giants such as Capita, G4S and SERCO, companies which already have multi-million-pound government contracts and a cosy relationship with the departments concerned. Neither does the argument that these companies provide expertise hold much water. Some appear to go for any contract on offer: for example, Capita's portfolio ranges from contracts with schools and hospitals to providing the Ministry of Defence and BAE with 'IT capability for its submarine solutions business' while SERCO manages the UK Atomic Weapons Establishment, prisons and OFSTED inspections. Their expertise appears to lie more in winning contracts and making money.

Democracy has been even more undermined by the direct political power exercised by the media industries. Press barons, such as Rupert Murdoch, have used their papers to present the world as they want it to be, castigating politicians who dare to disagree with them and advising readers, sometimes subtly but sometimes quite directly, how to vote. Political leaders cannot formulate policy without keeping an eye on how it will be reported, and winning the support of the tabloids has become an important part of winning elections. The Leveson Enquiry brought to light the way in which political leaders cultivate their relationships with tabloid editors. These people are not in the business of illuminating political debate or even holding politicians to account – their aim is profit and their agenda is that of corporate power and politicians who get in their way can expect no mercy.

The anti-politics of much of the press has spread to broadcasting. That our journalists no longer feel the need to show deference towards politicians is positive, but showing disdain is not. It is right that interviewers should press politicians for clarity over their policies and intentions, but the aggressive manner in which people like Jeremy Paxman and John Humphries have used their formidable skills to grill politicians does nothing to improve politics. If Paxman and Humphries, who have never stood for public office themselves and have never needed to take the difficult decisions faced by politicians, make their dislike and distrust of politicians all too clear, their listeners are left with the view that politics is a sordid business run by scoundrels.

The influence of large corporations on politics is made worse, however, by the extent to which politicians collude with them. As we have noted, more than 50 MPs are directors of companies, and many more have accepted consultancies with them. These companies do not employ MPs because of their business acumen, but for their inside knowledge and contacts. Conservative MP, Tim Yeo, for example, was a director of energy companies while chairing the Energy and Climate Change Select Committee, and only resigned when it emerge that he had coached a company representative on how to present evidence to the Committee. Jack Straw boasted to undercover reporters that he influenced EU rules for a company that paid him £60,000 pa, and Geoff Hoon, on leaving politics after having been exposed for appearing to be willing to accept thousands for giving companies access to policy-makers, was given a job by a company that was given a controversial £1.7 billion contract when he was Labour's Defence Secretary.

Many MPs, including the former Liberal Democrat leader, Nick Clegg, have backgrounds in lobbying. In 2010, the pressure group, Spinwatch, revealed that 19 of the 143 new Conservative MPs elected that year, and 11 out of 67 new Labour ones, had been employed in lobbying,[15] and some were even working as lobbyists during their election campaigns – without, of course, revealing it to voters. To Spinwatch it suggested a 'revolving door' between parliament and industry. Owen Jones has revealed another 'revolving door' between the big accountancy firms and the

Treasury, with company employees being seconded to the Treasury to help formulate tax legislation while their companies advise their clients on tax avoidance.[16] (Revolving doors, and how to close them, is discussed in chapter 3-2.)

It is therefore little wonder that many people believe that MPs are in politics for themselves. People have every reason to think that politics is no longer about the national interest, and certainly not about their interests. It is therefore hardly surprising that many shun political involvement and see little point in voting.

People v. the Establishment

The Labour Party's mission is to ensure 'power, wealth and opportunity are in the hands of the many not the few', but:

> In Britain today, power is definitely not in the hands of the many. Our country is one of the most centralised in the world, with a shocking proportion of decisions that affect daily life taken by an insular ruling elite of politicians and unaccountable bureaucrats in London... At best, it can lead to stale thinking and shuts out innovation. At worst, it breeds corruption.

These words, written in 2015, are not from any Labour policy paper, but from Lynton Crosby, the Australian political strategist who has advised the Conservative party on campaign tactics over the past ten years. To the ruling elite of politicians and bureaucrats, he might have added the business leaders, the press barons and the establishment figures (often political appointees) who control our national institutions.

There has always been an 'establishment' – people with power and influence and with insider connections – which effectively runs the country. What it is, and who it is, may be difficult to define but that does not mean it does not exist, and too often those we elect are co-opted into it and accept its values: as Kingsley Martin wrote in 1962, 'One way of making sure that an influential politician will not revolt against it is to make him a Privy Counsellor'.[17] In Victorian times the establishment was dominated by people with land, wealth and titles and those linked to their interests, and although financial and industrial power became more important in the 20th century, in 1959 Hugh Thomas maintained:

> Now it is ... Victorian England, with all its prejudices, ignorances and inhibitions, that the Establishment sets out to defend. The Establishment is the present day institutional museum of Britain's past greatness.[18]

The Establishment may have evolved since 1959, but Thomas's point – that the Establishment is a force that will strenuously oppose progressive reform and anything that threatens its vested interests – remains valid.

Owen Jones has written of the Establishment which runs the country as being a financial and professional elite of people who run our major companies and institutions and whose interests are closely tied to their corporate interests. In the main, he argues, they accept the values of a relatively free market in which the pursuit of wealth is much more important than the alleviation of poverty. For Jones, the Establishment is:

> powerful groups that need to protect their position in a democracy in which almost the entire adult population has a right to vote. The Establishment represents an attempt on behalf of these groups to 'manage' democracy, to make sure it does not threaten their own interests.[19]

DEMOCRACY IN DECLINE

Jones goes on to quote the right-wing blogger and columnist Paul Staines:

> We've had nearly a century of universal suffrage now, and what happens is capital finds ways to protect itself from ... the voters.

In other words, those with power and privilege have learnt how to manipulate democracy for their own ends. Our challenge is to build a democracy which is not necessarily hostile either to the corporations on which our economy depends or to those who, on merit, occupy positions of influence, but is strong enough to ensure that politics belongs to the people and that it is their concerns and aspirations that will determine the policies of the country.

Politics has thus moved a long way since the high point in the middle of the last century. We still have the formal institutions of democracy – we have elections in which people can vote, and vote freely, and we have an elected parliament of MPs who engage in vigorous, even if sometimes pointless, debates. As well as local elections, we elect our MEPs, members of devolved bodies in at least some parts of the country, and we even elect Police and Crime Commissioners giving us more opportunities to vote than ever before. Nevertheless, there is now something hollow about our democracy – Anthony Sampson referred to its 'humbug and deceptions'.[20] Politics has lost its importance and many of us have lost faith in its ability to change things for us. It has become corrupted, not necessarily in a legal sense (although it has been marred by too many cases of fraud and criminal wrong-doing), but in that it has lost its values and in that many of those we elect are no more our representatives standing up for our interests that

THE REFORM DEBATES

were the aristocratic MPs of the nineteenth century. The Establishment is firmly back in control.

---

[1] W S Gilbert, *Iolanthe*, 1882

[2] British Election Studies, 1964 and 2001

[3] Jeremy Paxman, *The Political Animal: An Anatomy*, Michael Joseph (Penguin Books), 2002

[4] C Rallings and M Thrasher, 'Local electoral participation in Britain', in *Parliamentary Affairs*, Vol 56 issue 4.

[5] J Garland and W Brett, *Open Up: the future of the political party*, Electoral Reform Society 2014

[6] Natalie Fenton, 'The Internet of Radical Politics' in J.Curran, N.Fenton and D.Freedman, *Misunderstanding the Internet,* Routledge (2016, forthcoming)

[7] Natalie Fenton, ibid

[8] Ipsos MORI, June 2013

[9] YouGov, October 2014

[10] Guardian, 27 May 2013

[11] Daily Telegraph, 24 February 2015

[12] *Back to Earth: Reconnecting people and politics*, Fabian Society 2014

[13] *Audit of Political Engagement*, Hansard Society,, 2013

[14] Quoted in Paul Foot, *The Vote: how it was won and how it was undermined*, Penguin, 2006

[15] Guardian, 3 June 2010

[16] Owen Jones, *The Establishment*, Allen Lane, 2014

[17] K Martin, The Crown and the Establishment, Hutchinson, 1962, quoted in P Hennessy, 'Establishment and Meritocracy', Haus Publishing,, 2014

[18] Quoted in Hennessy, ibid

[19] Owen Jones, *The Establishment*, Allen Lane, 2014

[20] Anthony Sampson, *Who Runs This Place? The Anatomy of Britain in the 21st Century*, John Murray, 2014

THE REFORM DEBATES

1-5   Cracks in the mould?

The downward slide of democracy might suggest that people power has lost the struggle against the influence of money and the establishment and is no longer able to hold any meaningful sway over our politicians. Democracy, however, at least offers people the opportunity to use their votes to fight back against a system they don't like and recent years have seen three significant challenges to the prevailing political order. The first is the rise of UKIP – not a challenge that has democratic values at its heart but a challenge nonetheless; the second is the huge success of the SNP and its threat to the integrity of the UK; and the third is the astonishing result of the 2015 Labour leadership election. Is it just possible that the mould of British politics is beginning to crack?

Ever since the 1920s when Labour replaced the Liberals as the major alternative to the Conservatives, Britain has had an essentially two-party system. This pattern was nearly broken in 1983 when the newly formed SDP-Liberal Alliance won almost as many votes as Labour, but the electoral system came to Labour's rescue by giving it many more seats, and in future elections the Liberal Democrats, formed from the Alliance, were relegated to being a small third party. Although the combined Conservative-Labour vote, which was 96.8% in 1951, dropped to only 65.1% in 2010 and 67.3% in 2015, the voting system maintained the hegemony of the two main parties in terms of seats: the British experience appeared

CRACKS IN THE MOULD

to support Duverger's Law, formulated by a French political scientist who observed that the First Past the Post voting system favoured two-party politics.

UKIP and the SNP have been the first parties to break through as serious new forces in politics since the rise of Labour a century ago. UKIP and the SNP are of course very different but, while it is possible that opposition to the EU and the demand for Scottish independence might have resulted in their growth even if there had been broad satisfaction with the political system, the success of both parties is at least in a large part a protest against Westminster politics.

The third challenge has not come from a new or a minor party, but from within a party, with people, mainly on the broad left, reclaiming a party which they felt had lost its sense of direction and its radical edge. Those who gave their support to Jeremy Corbyn were not necessarily voting for a new democracy, but they were expressing their dissatisfaction with a style of politics which did not seem to address their concerns adequately.

UKIP

Although UKIP has only become a force in British politics relatively recently, it was formed about 20 years ago as an anti-EU party. It first stood candidates in the 1997 general election, but at that time it was eclipsed by James Goldsmith's Referendum Party which only wanted one thing – an in-out referendum on EU membership – and with around £20 million of Sir James' fortune it managed to get 3% of the votes. The Referendum Party, however, collapsed with Goldsmith's death shortly after the election, leaving space for UKIP to grow. In its earlier years it needed, however, to

THE REFORM DEBATES

compete with the more extreme and overtly racist BNP which was gaining ground, particularly in local elections. The BNP reached a high point in 2009 when it had 2 MEPs and 55 councillors, but it then collapsed with internal conflicts, controversies and financial problems. This left UKIP as the only serious anti-EU and anti-immigration party.

As UKIP's focus was on opposition to EU membership, it was always likely to do better in European Parliament elections than in others fought on wider, domestic issues, and its number of MEPs increased from 3 in 1999 to 24 in 2014. In the 2014 European election, it received more votes than any other party – the first time since 1910 that neither the Conservatives nor Labour had topped the poll in a national election. That something had changed in British politics was further underlined in November 2014 when UKIP won its first two seats at Westminster. Both by-elections were forced by Conservative MPs who resigned on switching to UKIP, but in a third by-election UKIP came very close to taking what had been a safe Labour seat.

As the 2015 general election approached, opinion polls showed support for UKIP running at around 14–15% and there was much speculation that UKIP would become a force to be reckoned with, especially if, as was widely forecast, no party won a majority of seats and a coalition would need to be formed. When the election came, their 12.6% of the vote put them in a clear third place in terms of vote share, but they only won a single seat: a strictly proportional result would have given them around 80 seats and a strong voice in the Commons. Never before had a party been so disadvantaged by our First Past the Post voting system.

In spite of UKIP's failure to win more seats, it made its presence felt in the election. Their strong showing in terms of votes, largely taken from the two major parties, may well have affected who won and who lost in a number of constituencies but, more importantly, the threat they posed forced others to take stronger lines on immigration and whether the Conservatives would have given such a clear commitment to a referendum on EU membership without UKIP breathing down their necks is questionable.

That winning only one seat with nearly 4 million votes was a great injustice is something with which few would disagree. For many, however, UKIP's failure to win more seats was a great relief: some of course were just worried by its threat to the established parties, but there is a wider concern that UKIP's success has arisen from a failure of politics. A closer look at UKIP suggests that its popularity demonstrates the extent to which many electors feel unrepresented and alienated by the major parties.

UKIP began as an anti-EU party on the right of the Conservatives, and indeed some of its early members saw it purely as way of hardening the Conservatives' stance on Europe. Immigration is just one area in which British policy must take account of EU treaties, but it is a toxic one and an issue on which UKIP found it could easily win support. Opposition to the way people could come to Britain to work and use public services enabled UKIP to attract many disaffected voters – people who felt their living standards were stagnating and who saw their job prospects threatened by workers from other parts of Europe who were as well qualified as they were and who would work as hard, if not harder, for modest wages. Although starting as a party on the far right of politics, the support it could easily win was amongst electors in Labour's traditional heartlands – blue-collar workers, people with limited qualifications and therefore limited job prospects, men more than women, and middle-aged and older electors who felt a sense of superiority in their Britishness. Such people in the past might have been regarded as part of Labour's constituency, but politically they were not of the left and have been better described as the 'left behind' – people who feel they are no longer represented by a Labour Party that has moved to the centre and become professionalised.

Immigration policy is a legitimate topic for debate. Concern arises, however, from the way UKIP has portrayed the issue, including scare stories about the extent of Britain being 'swamped' by an influx of millions of Romanians and others and the use of language likely to foment prejudice and even racism. UKIP claims that it is not a racist party, and it can point to members from ethnic minorities to support that contention, and quite a number of UKIP candidates, both for national and local elections, have been expelled for racist remarks. However, this raises the question why such people were selected in the first place. Others have been exposed as racist without action being taken against them: in March 2015, six UKIP candidates were found to have circulated racist material from far right groups, but none of them were removed as candidates. MEP Janice Atkinson, who in 2011 expressed support for "elements" of the BNP, was not suspended when she referred to a Thai constituent as a 'ting-tong from somewhere' but, following her expulsion when an aide was caught making a fraudulent expense claim, joined Le Pen's group in the European Parliament. The Scottish MEP, David Colburn, was not expelled for comparing an MSP to Abu Hamsa but a general election candidate, Tim Wilson, to his credit, resigned over his party's failure to take action. Not only have many UKIP politicians and candidates used racist language, but a poll in February 2015 found that half of UKIP's supporters admitted to being racially prejudiced: that is not surprising given that opposition to immigration has been a key policy of UKIP – what is surprising is that so many were willing to admit to their views.

It is not just on race, however, that the views of UKIP supporters differ from those of other parties. Most are quite illiberal in their attitudes, with a large majority wanting more respect for 'traditional British values'. Three quarters of them favour the death penalty, and 90% want stiffer sentencing; about half disapprove of children being born to unmarried parents; and less than half are in favour of gay marriage. Although UKIP has gay members, it has consistently refused to support gay rights and in February 2015 the chair of the UKIP LGBT group resigned from the party in protest at its policies.

The rise of UKIP does not therefore represent a resurgence of democracy, but is more an ugly manifestation of the degeneration of politics. UKIP has certainly given a voice to elements in society who feel other parties have not been listening to their concerns but, in attempting to portray immigration as a principal source of most economic and social problems, it has sought their support by playing to irrational fears and xenophobia.

Although UKIP only won a single seat in the 2015 election, it remains serious threat to the mainstream parties. It has more MEPs than any other party and nearly 500 local councillors. In elections it has demonstrated that it is a professional and effective campaigning force, and the near 4 million people who voted UKIP in the

THE REFORM DEBATES

2015 election are unlikely to change their allegiance just because electoral system denied them a fair result.

UKIP may be seen as a party of protest. Polls suggest that most who voted UKIP did so because of their opposition to EU membership and to immigration (and, of course, the two are linked because of the EU requirement that people can move freely between member states). These are serious issues which cannot be ignored, but it would be a mistake, however, to assume that the protest which UKIP represents is just based on these issues. As has been noted, changes in the nature of politics have eroded the way in which the established parties relate to their traditional constituencies of support and parties efforts to capture the 'centre ground' (something that parties must do to win elections under our present voting system), have left many feeling unrepresented. Unless politics can change in a way that allows the 'left behind'[1] to feel that they a voice in mainstream politics, that they are being listened to and that their concerns are being addressed and that they are respected as having an equal voice in the nation's affairs, then UKIP (or some other party of the same nature) will continue to flourish.

UKIP will not just disappear. It does however face challenges – its reliance on a few very wealthy donors and the privileged backgrounds of many of its leaders sit uneasily with its considerable working class support, and it faces difficulties in deciding where it stands on issues other than immigration and the EU. Many who have joined from Labour's ranks, for example, want the railways renationalised, while those from the Conservative Party favour a more right-wing agenda, and while in 2015 UKIP argued for more investment in the NHS, UKIP leaders in the past have argued that people show pay for health care through insurance. Ironically, if

UKIP had won more seats in 2015 it may have been forced to face these contradictions sooner rather than later. However, even if UKIP were to collapse, without a change in politics the space would still be there for another party to exploit the concerns of the 'left behinds' in a populist way.

SNP

Unlike UKIP, the SNP has been around for a long time. It was founded in 1935, but there were only 3 months in its first 32 years when it had an MP. It sprung to prominence, however, in 1967 when Winnie Ewing sensationally captured a safe Labour seat in a by-election with an astonishing 38% swing. From the time of that by-election, the SNP has always had MPs at Westminster, but until April 2015 the most seats they ever held were the 11 won in the general election of October 1974. That election, however, put them in a strong position: the slender majority Labour had won was soon lost through by-elections, and the government had to offer a referendum on Scottish devolution in return for SNP support in the Commons. In that referendum, held in 1979, 51.6% of voters voted 'yes' but it was not enough: a Labour backbencher had successfully moved an amendment requiring the support not just of a majority of voters but also of 40% of electors (whether or not they had voted) and the devolution proposal was thus defeated. As a consequence, the SNP withdrew its support in the Commons for Labour, the government fell, and the election that followed was won by Margaret Thatcher's Conservatives.

Although the 1979 election reduced the SNP to only 2 seats, the ball that the referendum had set rolling was not going to be easily stopped. Scottish resentment of Westminster rule was fu-

THE REFORM DEBATES

elled by Thatcher's use of Scotland as a testing ground for her hated poll tax and it was not just in the SNP that support grew for some measure of Scottish self-governance. In 1997 the new Labour government responded quickly to the pressure by holding another referendum on whether Scotland should have its own parliament. This time the vote was much more decisive and the first elections to the new body followed in 1999.

The voting system chosen was the Additional Member System (see chapter 3-1), a broadly proportional system which, its proponents argued, would ensure that the SNP never gained a majority. They were to be proved wrong.

The SNP got its first taste of power in 2007. In the Scottish Parliament elections that year, Labour fought a negative campaign on the dangers of independence, but it was the SNP's more positive messages about how it would run the country that won the day. It ended up with just one more seat than Labour. Although the SNP had far from a majority and was unable to find coalition partners, it formed a minority administration which, in spite of predictions that it would last only a matter of months, demonstrated a considerable degree of political maturity and competence. It was, however, helped in its task by the problems of Scottish Labour which, following the resignation of the popular and effective Jack McConnell, was never able to find a leader with either the political skills or charisma of the Alex Salmond, the leader of the SNP. Salmond maintained that Scotland now had a parliament in which decisions would be made 'by the force of the argument, not the argument of force', i.e. votes in the parliament would need to be won through debate rather than the power of the party whips. This was perhaps putting on a brave face in a difficult situation,

CRACKS IN THE MOULD

but many who wanted a more effective parliament at Westminster were envious.

If an SNP minority government was a surprise, it was nothing compared to the shocks that were to follow. In spite of the broadly proportional voting system, the 2011 Scottish Parliament elections gave the SNP an outright majority on 45% of the votes. Now the SNP was in a position to push for its ultimate goal – independence – and the Westminster government had little option other than to agree to a referendum in 2014.

The referendum campaign set politics in Scotland alight. Whether or not Scotland opted for independence was an issue that affected most people, in many cases profoundly, and discussion of the pros and cons reached parts of Scottish society that had never for a long time taken any real interest in politics. In village halls, work places and bus queues people exchanged views on what independence would mean for them and on how they would use their votes. It appeared that Scotland had rediscovered politics in a way that Britain had not seen for generations.

This political re-awakening was largely a result of the 'yes' campaign. It had the positive messages about what a new Scotland would look like (leaving aside some of the more troublesome details), and in Alex Salmond it had an astute leader. The supporters who joined the cause were recruited as activists in unprecedented numbers, and although the 'yes' side began as the underdogs, they not only closed the gap but in one opinion poll appeared to have taken the lead.

The 'no' campaign attempted to dampen this outburst of enthusiasm, but with little success. It suffered from being a coalition of parties that were at war with each other on almost every issue other then independence, and it was seen as Westminster's negative response to the demands of the Scottish people. A problem with referendums is that they are often decided as much by voters' views of the politicians and parties leading the campaigns as by their positions on the referendum question, and a campaign backed by the Conservatives and Liberal Democrats was always going to face difficulties.

Many good things can be said about the 'yes' campaign and the way it galvanised debate, but claims that it represented a democratic revival in Scotland need to be treated with care. Although the campaign was undoubtedly popular, it was also populist in style and some have questioned whether the quality of the debates matched their quantity. Part of the problem may have arisen from the nature of referendums: people were required to vote 'yes' or 'no' on questions of considerable complexity, and campaigners on either side felt compelled to present their arguments in black and white terms when the issues were all shades of grey. No sensible opponent of independence could seriously argue that independence would be an unmitigated disaster, and no intelligent supporter could have failed to recognise the risks, but the take-it-or-leave-it nature of the referendum left little space for serious debate.

Moreover, while the great majority of campaigners acted with propriety and good humour, it was perhaps inevitable that a campaign which unleashed so much passion would have a darker side: there were serious complaints of harassment, with some who did not accept the independence argument being accused of being anti-Scottish traitors, with one commentator complaining that 'non-believers were treated as Quislings'. A hostile crowd forced Ed Miliband to abandon a walk-about in Edinburgh and the then

CRACKS IN THE MOULD

Scottish Labour leader, Jim Murphy, was pelted with eggs. However, it would be wrong to tar the 'yes' campaign with antics of some of its more exuberant followers and the 'Yes' leadership did condemn these excesses.

When it came to the vote, the 'no' side won with 55% to 45%. Nevertheless, it was a moral victory for the independence campaign – from a weak beginning it had steadily built its support to a point at which the outcome was difficult to predict, and the possibility of a 'yes' victory had forced Westminster politicians of all parties to promise more devolved powers for Scotland if it were to remain part of the UK. Although the Prime Minister had overruled offering a 'Devo-max' option in the referendum (a half-way house between the status quo and full independence), Devo-max had effectively been won.

The vote did not end the headache for the Westminster parties. In the months that followed the referendum, the SNP acted as victors and they recruited new members by the thousands. With the Scottish Labour Party effectively leaderless and without any real alternative vision, Scotland belonged, politically, to the SNP. When it came to the 2015 general election, they wiped the board, winning 56 of the 59 seats, some with unprecedented swings, leaving each of the main three Westminster parties with only a single seat each.

The SNP, which wants to leave the UK, has become the UK's third largest party in the Commons and a force to be reckoned with. The constitutional implications are enormous – although Scotland remains part of the UK, no party other than the SNP appears to have much mandate for speaking on Scottish affairs, and the possibility of another referendum, which might produce a different result, cannot be discounted. Moreover, as the devolution of more powers to Scotland has created resentments and demands

THE REFORM DEBATES

for more local decision-taking in other parts of the UK, the referendum and election results have consequences for the whole country. These are matters which will be considered in the chapter 3-7.

If we are to understand these events in Scotland, we need to ask why so many people switched to the view that independence was their preferred option. Scottish nationalism had been around for a long time, but erupted in the space of only a few years. From the 2010 general election to that of 2015, they nearly tripled their vote and moved from 6 seats to 56. One reason for this extraordinary increase in support must lie in the SNP's dominance of the political debate in Scotland as the governing party in the Scottish Parliament since 2007, but the extent of their dominance was no doubt made possible by the ineffectiveness of their opponents. Since losing to the SNP in the Scottish Parliament elections of 2007, Scottish Labour never managed to find a leader who could match the political skills of Alex Salmond and worse, it was never able to articulate a specifically Scottish vision. Labour had devolved power to the Scottish Parliament, but it was reluctant to devolve power to its Scottish party: as Johan Lamont remarked on resigning as leader in 2014, Labour had treated Scottish Labour 'as a branch office of London'. Just six days after the referendum, Labour finished its annual conference in Manchester by singing Parry's hymn about building 'Jerusalem in *England's* green and pleasant land': as Ed Miliband liked telling his opponents, 'They just didn't get it'.

However, the SNP's pre-eminence in Scotland alone does not explain the rise of the SNP, and neither do the merits of their case for independence (they did not even convince all their supporters -

one in seven voted 'no' in the referendum). A poll by Lord Ashcroft found that 74% of those who voted gave 'Dissatisfaction with Westminster politics' as one of their main reasons for doing so. Thus while the idea of independence undoubtedly was attractive to many people, the referendum result, and no doubt the SNP's subsequent general election success, was to a large extent a rejection of national politics.

If UK politics had been more engaging and if democracy had been working as it should, would so many people have voted for opting out of the UK? It appears that the answer is 'no'. Support for independence was undoubtedly based on the premise that Scotland could better manage its own affairs, but it also demonstrated the extent to which people wanted a different sort of politics. If Scotland is to be kept within the UK, it will not be enough for unionists to convincingly counter the arguments for independence – they must also address the causes of dissatisfaction with politics in the UK.

Although it was only in Scotland that there was a real chance of breaking free from the Westminster system through independence, it must be assumed that many electors in other parts of the UK share the Scots' political disaffection. The rise of the SNP, whether or not one regards it as a good thing, must serve as a warning to politicians that things must change.

Labour's 2015 leadership election

In September 2015 Jeremy Corbyn won Labour's leadership contest in dramatic fashion. He started as a 100/1 outsider and got his name on the ballot paper with only minutes to spare thanks to the help of other MPs who were not even prepared to support him.

THE REFORM DEBATES

No-one, and not even Corbyn himself, foresaw what was to happen after that. He did not just win, but won with more than three times as many votes as his nearest rival. While the other three candidates had their own manifestos, they were candidates of continuity and not of change. Corbyn, however, seemed to speak for the many members who felt their party had lost its way – many were still angry over Blair's support for war in Iraq and many felt Labour had been weak in defending its record and had not done enough to oppose the Conservatives' austerity measures. Corbyn was different: he was not a character polished by Labour's spin doctors and was certainly not a careerist. He was clearly someone driven by a sense of political conviction and was prepared to challenge rather than compromise with vested interests.

While the extent of Corbyn's victory was magnified by changes to Labour's rules which allowed a new category of 'registered supporters' to vote on payment of a nominal amount, he would have been a clear winner even if only members had been entitled to vote: it is evident that his campaign galvanised many members whose involvement in the party had in the past been minimal, as well as many former members who returned to the fold. Although former prime ministers, Blair and Brown, along with a host of Labour notables, warned that Corbyn would make Labour unelectable, a majority of members and supporters were not prepared to accept the advice of former Labour grandees and decided to follow their own instincts.

It remains to be seen whether Blair and others were right but, whatever happens, it appears that the nature of the Labour Party has changed – members have rediscovered the power of their votes. Unsurprisingly, the schism that opened up during the leadership contest between Corbyn's supporters and more moderate voices in the party was not healed by Corbyn's victory. Serious divisions remain between those impatient for radical change and those who believe a more measured and pragmatic approach is needed if Labour is to win the power it needs to improve the lot of those it claims to represent. Debates of this nature should be the stuff of politics, but the manner in which they have been conducted suggests that Labour still has work to do in developing an internal culture of democracy. Both sides share a desire for a fairer society but, in the exchanges between them, there has been too much aggression, too little respect for the views of others and too little sign of the sort of political behaviour that will make politics attractive to the wider electorate.

At the time of writing it is not clear to where these tensions in Labour will lead, and whether a stronger voice for members in the party will result in demands for political reform that go beyond the party's internal affairs. However, Corbyn's campaign has demonstrated that political passions can be reawakened and that can only be encouraging for the prospects of revitalised democracy. If the political mould of Labour can be broken, then surely the same is possible for the entire political establishment.

Conclusions

The examples of UKIP and the SNP show us that politics must change. Although the Conservative-Labour hegemony survived the 2015 election in spite of the two parties together winning only 67% of the votes, it appears that we have entered a period of multi-party politics. In 2015 only the SNP made a breakthrough in terms seats, but UKIP, and to a much lesser extent the Greens, have

THE REFORM DEBATES

demonstrated that they too could be significant players in future elections, particularly if we ever achieve a change to a fairer voting system.

However, these two examples demonstrate that even if many people appear to have opted out of mainstream politics, when there are opportunities for them to influence policies and events which matter to them, and when they perceive that voting might actually change things, they are ready to engage. To a large extent UKIP and SNP voters were voting against Westminster politics, but they were also voting for something. Although in the case of UKIP it was something that many would regard as distasteful and although UKIP's appeal was unashamebly populist, they were nevertheless willing to turn out to support candidates who appeared to be addressing their concerns in a way that made sense to them. That other parties were unable to attract their support in the same way raises questions about the efficacy of our politics and its institutions.

Whilst support for Scottish independence and the SNP was also to a great extent a rejection of Westminster politics, it was nevertheless also support for something more wholesome. Many local debates during the referendum campaign were not just about how to answer the referendum question, but also about how Scots could run their own affairs better, with or without an attachment to Westminster. Amid the discussions, often acrimonious, on the pros and cons of independence, it emerged that many had a real thirst for a better democracy. In that respect the referendum campaign provides encouragement for those who want political reform.

There are many ways in which Scottish independence would have been good for democracy in Scotland, but even the defeat of the 'yes' campaign in the referendum leaves us, and not just the Scots, with new opportunities for pushing the reform agenda. The concessions offered by the Westminster party leaders shortly before the referendum have raised questions about how people in other parts of the UK might be given more control over their affairs. English-votes-on-English-laws was a simplistic reaction to events, but it does not provide answers to what powers should be devolved and to whom. In the aftermath of the referendum and the SNP's sweeping election victory, the integrity of the UK can no longer be taken for granted: some hoped that a referendum defeat would take the wind out of the SNP's sails, but the opposite appears to have happened, and unless a settlement which satisfies the aspirations of most Scots can be reached, it can only be a matter of time before the SNP demands a further referendum. An essentially independent Scotland in a federal UK may be an option that could satisfy many SNP leaders (even if not all of their rank and file), but what place would there be for not just Wales and Northern Ireland but also England's regions in a federal structure? The Scots may have given us an opportunity to debate the whole constitutional architecture of the UK.

The revolt of many Labour members in their choice of leader has happened within a single party, but what it has in common with the rise of UKIP and the SNP is that it shows the extent to which people are disenchanted with the state of politics. Given a chance to make a difference – a chance which the Labour hierarchy did not expect them to take – they used the power of their votes.

THE REFORM DEBATES

Ken Livingstone once wrote 'If voting changed anything, they'd abolish it', but voting was not abolished and Labour's members and supporters have proved voting can change things.

---

[1] Robert Ford and Matthew Goodwin, *Revolt on the Right: Explaining Support for the Radical Right in Britain*, Routledge, 2014. This book looks in depth at the nature of UKIP's support.

Part 2

PROSPECTS FOR REFORM

2-1 Lessons from history

Throughout the history of our democracy, the major reforms have been citizen-led. There have been politicians who have been given credit (and some are entitled to credit) for the abolition of slavery, the Great Reform Acts that expanded the franchise, votes for women, and more recently LGBT rights and freedom of information legislation, but these reforms were only introduced by politicians in the face of pressure from concerned and active citizens. Before considering the prospects for present-day reform, it is therefore worth reflecting on some of these past struggles by people to win their political rights.

The title of this book pays homage to those who demanded their rights in the Putney Debates of 1647. Five years earlier war had broken out between parliament and Charles I. The conflict followed a long period of hostility between the two over issues including taxation, the king's promotion of his own brand of religious orthodoxy and his disregard of the role of parliament - in 1628 he dissolved it and ruled alone until 1640. That year he recalled it in order to raise funds to suppress a rebellion by Scots who opposed his interference in their form of worship, but the parliament (the 'Short Parliament') would not support military action in Scotland and was dissolved again. The 'Long Parliament' which was then formed proved to be even more hostile, seeking curbs on the monarch's power. In 1642 Charles responded by en-

THE REFORM DEBATES

tering parliament with 400 troops in an attempt to arrest five parliamentarians, but when this was unsuccessful the king left London in fear of his own safety. In the months that followed both sides started preparing for what was to be a particularly bloody war. The forces of parliament, led by Cromwell and largely composed of commoners, gradually got the upper hand and in 1646 Charles put himself in the hands of the Scots, but they had little sympathy for him and he was handed over to his enemies.

The king was in prison, but his captors were divided over what should happen next. Many of its leaders were not opposed to a monarchy and sought to negotiate with the king, but many who had endured years of battles were unwilling to accept the restoration of a monarch who had caused so much suffering. Within Cromwell's 'New Model Army' there was dissent, particularly over the parliament's refusal to give them either adequate recompense for the sacrifices they had made or the rights and freedoms for which they had fought. However, some, both within the army and without, did not just demand that their grievances should be addressed, but that there should be a constitution which protected their rights and gave people a say in the election of their representatives. They became known as 'The Levellers'. They wanted democracy. Their movement was fuelled by pamphlets from 'Honest John' Lilburne and others who feared that the tyranny of the king would be replaced with that of parliament. More than four centuries before it had been the barons who confronted their king and forced him to sign the Magna Carta, but this was the first major demand for political reforms by ordinary people.

In September 1647, when representatives elected by the regiments presented their commanding officer with a pamphlet calling

LESSONS FROM HISTORY

for dissolution of the parliament and constitutional changes, they were, remarkably, given an opportunity to state their case in a series of meetings with their leaders, chaired by Cromwell himself. These meetings, which began in St Mary's Church in Putney, have become known as 'The Putney Debates'. The transcripts of the debates show that the army's 'agitators' and their civilian supporters were not just protesters but high-minded people advocating democratic principles in a way that shames most present-day political discussions. In a statement they prepared for the opening of the debates, they called for:

1. Liberty of conscience in matters of religion ...
2. Freedom from conscription (since 'money – the sinews of war' is always at parliament's disposal, it should never force citizens to fight).
3. A general amnesty to all who had fought on either side in the civil war.
4. That all laws should be 'no respecter of persons but apply equally to everyone: there should be no discrimination on grounds of tenure, estate, charter, degree, birth or place'.
5. Parliament could pass no law 'evidently destructive of the safety or wellbeing of the people'.[1]

A major point of contention was the 'Heads of Agreement' which Cromwell hoped to negotiate with the king, but having fought a war, the agitators were not prepared to see Charles restored to his throne. Another was the franchise: while Cromwell and his deputy, Ireton, wanted it to continue to be restricted to those with freehold worth more than 40 shillings, a Levellers' pamphlet had argued that all freeborn men (it was long before the days of gender

THE REFORM DEBATES

equality) over 21 should be entitled to vote. For the agitators, Colonel Rainsborough famously stated:

> The poorest he that is in England has a life to live, as the greatest he; and therefore truly, Sir, I think it is clear, that every man that is to live under a government ought first by his own consent to put himself under that government; and I do not think that the poorest man in England is not at all bound in a strict sense to that government that he has not had a voice to put himself under ...[2]

Government, it was argued, had to be government by popular consent. These demands of the agitators, revolutionary at the time, were not, of course, accepted. Cromwell remained intent on doing a deal with Charles, but his plans were overtaken by events. The king was already preparing for a new military offensive against the parliament – one that led again to his defeat and this time his execution. Cromwell was not going to tolerate the Levellers' challenge to his authority and in the years that followed many were imprisoned and some were executed.

At the time, the Levellers' demands came to nothing. They had courageously demanded their rights and democratic reform, and they had suffered as a result. Their example, however, provided inspiration for reformers in generations to come.

Two centuries later came the Chartists, the largest popular movement for political and economic reform the country has seen. Angered at the failure of the 1832 Reform Act to extend the franchise beyond those with property and at the New Poor Law, which cut aid to those in poverty and established workhouses for them, the Chartists launched their movement in 1838. Branches were formed around the country, rallies attracted tens of thousands of supporters, and a petition signed by 1.3 million working people was presented to parliament in 1839: parliament, however, refused to listen to them. Three years later came a petition with over 3 million signatures (and that was long before the time a petition could be signed with a click of a computer mouse). Nevertheless, it was again rejected, and in places the refusal of politicians to consider their demands almost led to popular uprisings. These demands were summarised in their 'People's Charter':

- A vote for every man twenty-one years of age, of sound mind, and not undergoing punishment for a crime.
- The Secret Ballot – To protect the elector in the exercise of his vote.
- No Property Qualification for Members of Parliament – thus enabling the constituencies to return the man of their choice, be he rich or poor.
- Payment of Members, thus enabling an honest trades-man, working man, or other person, to serve a constituency; when taken from his business to attend to the interests of the country.
- Equal Constituencies, securing the same amount of representation for the same number of electors, instead of allowing small constituencies to swamp the votes of large ones.
- Annual Parliament Elections, thus presenting the most effectual check to bribery and intimidation, since as the constituency might be bought once in seven years (even with the ballot), no purse could buy a constituency (under a system of universal suffrage) in each ensuing twelve-

THE REFORM DEBATES

month; and since members, when elected for a year only, would not be able to defy and betray their constituents as now.

The following years saw further protests and a wave of strikes throughout the country: in response the government imprisoned hundreds, and some were transported to penal colonies. The movement was not, however, crushed. It continued to make its demands, and in 1847 a Chartist leader, Fergus O'Connor was even elected as an MP for Nottingham. However, with the government's refusal to make concessions and the difficulties of maintaining strikes which resulted in extreme hardship for working people and their families, the movement petered out.

Although the movement did not produce immediate political results, it had political impact. The Reform Acts that followed were not passed because a majority of politicians wanted reform, but because they had seen the dangers of insurrection and wished to avoid the unrest that was sweeping across many other parts of Europe. Change eventually came, although it was a long time in coming, but by 1918 the first five of their six demands had been met.

The Chartists had demanded a vote for every man, but by the end of the century it was women who were demanding their political rights. The National Union of Women's Suffrage Societies, formed in 1897 by Millicent Fawcett, set up groups of women around the country to lobby for votes for women. As women paid the same taxes as men, why should they not have the same political rights as men, and if women had to obey the laws passed by parliament, why should they not have a say in the process? Such a reasoned approach won some support in an all-male parliament, but progress was slow.

That changed, however, when Emmeline Pankhurst set up the Women's Social and Political Union, an organisation of women who were not prepared to wait. Although they were in the main educated and accustomed to the comforts of middle-class society, they were the British pioneers of direct action. About a thousand were arrested for public order offences and, rather than paying a fine, many chose prison where some successfully used hunger strikes to gain publicity and put pressure on a parliament that feared having a death on its hands.

The militant wing of the movement seemed quite unrestrained - they burnt down churches, vandalised buildings in the centre of London, fire-bombed politicians' homes, set fire to mail boxes and even blew up part of Lloyd George's house. Whilst these extremist tactics generated publicity, they were not necessarily helpful to the cause: not only did they split the movement by offending the great majority of suffragettes, but they also have strengthened the hands of the opponents of women's suffrage. In a democracy, winning should be about winning the battle for public support, and the militants were not going to achieve that through arson attacks.

Most suffragette activity was brought to an end not by political reform but by the declaration of war in 1914. The mainstream of the movement decided to focus its energies on supporting the war effort, and the government offered an amnesty to those in prison. Four years later women over 30 were given the vote, provided they met a minimum property requirement, and legislation opened the way for women to stand for parliament. Ten years after that, women were allowed to vote on the same basis as men. As with the Chartists, the suffragettes' campaign did not culminate in

THE REFORM DEBATES

the passing of legislation they wanted, but unless very determined and very courageous women had been prepared to challenge their exclusion from politics, votes for women might have been a lot longer in coming.

The likes of the Levellers, the Chartists and the suffragettes have not been seen since, but is a similar movement of people in defence of their rights inconceivable in present times? Certainly austerity measures of the governments elected in 2010 and 2015 cannot be compared to the callous indifference to poverty of the governments of the 1830s and may not generate the level of popular resentment that fuelled the Chartists' protests, but we still have a lot to be angry about. Moreover, nowadays citizens have many more tools to effect change than their predecessors. We now have more rights and freedoms and, above all, the power of our votes, but we appear to have lost the appetite to use them.

Could that appetite be refreshed, and is a new, popular demand for a better democracy too much to hope for? The way in which people of previous generations fought for their political rights and freedoms, often at great personal cost, should be a source of inspiration for us, and inaction would surely be a betrayal of their efforts and sacrifices.

---

[1] As summarised by Geoffrey Robertson *The Levellers: The Putney Debates*, Verso, 2007

[2] ibid

2-2 Lessons from abroad

We appear to be living in a new age of protest against unpopular, undemocratic and corrupt governments. In many countries new popular movements have shaken politics and have shown that people, collectively, can still wield power.

When the Arab Spring began in Tunisia at the beginning of 2011, none could have foreseen the scale on which people would to rise up against despotic rulers who had denied them democratic rights for decades. The protests, which began when an unemployed Tunisian set himself on fire after the authorities confiscated the produce he was selling, spread like a tidal wave. In a matter of weeks, Tunisia's President Ben Ali had fled from the country, the 30-year rule of President Mubarak in Egypt had ended after massive protests, and in Libya people had taken up arms to fight a bloody war that eventually led to the death of Gaddafi and the end of his regime. Protests in Yemen removed President Saleh, but threw the country into turmoil, and the regime in Bahrain only survived with the military intervention of the Saudis. Other countries in which demonstrations forced rulers to make concessions included Jordan, Oman and Morocco (although the Moroccan king had yielded nothing in the face of a massive protest in occupied Western Sahara in October 2010, the protest showed that people's quest for political freedoms cannot crushed by governments that deny them).

THE REFORM DEBATES

In all of the countries affected, protests were fuelled by economic conditions, human rights abuses, restrictions on freedoms and the perceived corruption of ruling groups, but a principal demand of the demonstrators was democracy. The Arab Spring may have failed in that democracy was not delivered (with the possible exception of Tunisia), but throughout the Arab world it demonstrated that people still have the power, and the courage, to make a stand for their rights. In many countries, and particularly in Egypt, it may appear that nothing has changed, but the Arab world cannot be the same again after the events of 2011.

An important lesson from the Arab Spring is that opposition to injustice alone is not enough to bring about reform. Hated regimes were removed but without there being sufficiently broad consensuses on the nature of what should take their place. The violent nature of the protests left little space for reasoned debate on alternatives and on the values, institutions and rules of government which would be needed to support the restoration/introduction of democracy and political freedoms.

Many countries in Europe have also seen the rise of new popular movements. In 2010 the Purple People movement was formed in Italy to demand the resignation of the then President, Berlusconi, who was seen to be abusing his considerable economic power and control of the media. Its Facebook page attracted 460,000 followers and a network of local groups was set up around the country: although Berlusconi resigned in 2011 when he lost his majority in the Chamber of Deputies, the movement had shown its ability to mobilise people in defence of democracy.

LESSONS FROM ABROAD

In Spain the 'indignados' movement developed in response to austerity measures imposed as a result of the country's economic crisis following banking crash of 2008. It organised occupations of main squares in over a hundred Spanish towns and cities (starting in Barcelona on 15 May 2011, the movement also became known as 15M). Their protests laid the ground for the development of Podemos, a radical party arguing for an alternative to austerity: according to one Podemos representative, 'Podemos's ability to stand in the European elections was very much dependent on the social power accumulated by the social movements'.

It has been in Greece, however, that the power of people to change politics has been most clearly demonstrated. With a weak and poorly managed economy, Greece was hit hard by the international banking crisis of 2008. What triggered protests that year, however, was the killing of a young student by the police. It uncapped the anger many felt about the nature of their government, and in the large demonstrations, and even rioting, which followed, the demonstrators' demands included social justice, economic reform and an end to corruption. The trade unions called a general strike in their support. Continuing protests led to the resignation of the government the following year, but not an end to the country's problems. Greece was seriously in debt and the imposition of harsh austerity measures was the price demanded by the EU, European Central Bank and the IMF for a financial bailout. Whether Greece could accept the creditors' terms, renegotiate them or dismiss them (which would have meant leaving the eurozone) dominated two elections in 2012: as the parties were unable to agree on a governing coalition after a first election, a second was held and narrowly won by parties that felt Greece had no option other than to accept the proposed bailout conditions. Implement-

THE REFORM DEBATES

ing them, however, was another matter: unemployment rose to 26% and drastic expenditure cuts and tax rises reduced many to poverty. By 2014 the economy was near the point of collapse and a further election was called for January 2015. The winner was Syriza.

When Syriza fought its first election in 2004 it got 3.3% of the votes. Eleven years later it had increased its support eleven-fold to 36.3% and therefore benefited from a bonus of 50 seats that Greece's bizarre electoral system awards to the largest party.

Syriza – the name is an acronym for 'the Coalition of the Radical Left' – had been formed in 2004, bringing together parties and protest groups to challenge what they saw as the failings of Greek politics. Until 2011 it fought elections as a coalition, and only then fused into a single party to make it possible to receive the bonus 50 seats if they came out on top. From the outset, however, it was more than a party – it was a movement. In addition to campaigning for quite radical changes in the economy, it was:

> running 'solidarity kitchens' and bazaars, working in medical social centres, protecting immigrants from attacks ..., supporting actions against the cut-off of electricity supply, providing legal help in courts to cut mortgage payments and developing new relations with trade unions.[1]

Natalie Fenton has described their priority as being building 'a sense of shared principles with practical solutions', and according to one Syriza activist:

> The idea is to change people's idea of what they can do – develop, with them, a sense of their capacity for power.

LESSONS FROM ABROAD

Syriza was therefore different in nature from the parties that had dominated Greek politics, but that did not make the economic problems it faced any easier. Syriza wanted to negotiate a new package of support, but the more powerful eurozone leaders were far from sympathetic and Syriza's victory looked like a Greek rejection of their ultimatum. The Greek economy almost collapsed and the banks almost ran out of money while the politicians played a poker game with 'Grexit' – a Greek departure from the eurozone – on the cards. Small countries cannot dictate to larger ones on which they are financially dependent, and in the end the Syriza leadership had to accept a deal that fell far short of what it had promised in its manifesto, but not before it called, and decisively won, a referendum on the stance it had taken. Hard bargaining by Syriza may have made the medicine Greece was forced to swallow just a little more palatable and some of Greece's national pride appeared to have been restored: Syriza, and the Greek people through the referendum, had demonstrated that they were not prepared to be bullied and would not meekly surrender to the dictates of Brussels.

In none of these examples from other countries did people get everything they wanted and, particularly in countries that experienced the Arab Spring, they may have ended up in a worse position than before. However, each case demonstrates that people, acting collectively, have the power to challenge unjust and undemocratic regimes, and having discovered, or re-discovered, that power it is possible that they have the capacity to use it again.

One thing that these popular movements have had in common is their use of social media. As already noted, the internet alone cannot change politics, but it can be a hugely effective mobilising tool. In Italy social media led to the formation of both the Purple

THE REFORM DEBATES

Movement and the anti-corruption Movimento 5 Stelle party that won a quarter of the votes in the 2013 election. It was Twitter that brought many young protesters on to the streets of Cairo in the early stages of the moves against Mubarak and that marshalled support for Podemos and Syriza, but Twitter also gave these movements a wider audience. While demonstrations in each country arose from particular national grievances, social media provided them with examples of what was happening elsewhere and to some extent gave the protests an international dimension: Paul Mason reports finding that some who had tweeted during the Uncut demonstrations in the City in 2011 were tweeting from Tahrir Square in Cairo only a few months later.[2]

Is it possible that we, in the UK, could see a similar popular movement demanding political reform? There is much that we need to reform although our starting point is different from the protestors who took to the streets in the Arab Spring – we do not suffer from the human rights abuses on the scale that fuelled demonstrations in the Arab world, but the democracy and rights we enjoy, although far from perfect, give us opportunities to demand change in less violent ways.

The new social movements in Europe which have opposed austerity measures have arisen in cultures and societies much closer to our own and, although the UK has not suffered to the same extent from the economic downturn of recent years, political alienation, the concentration of economic and therefore political power, and entrenched privilege are at least as bad. We may not experience any single event, like the self-immolation of a poor Tunisian or the death of a Greek student, to spark a spontaneous national outcry, but there is plenty of discontent, and indeed anger, and, if the realisation that people have collective power were to gain ground, a popular demand for a better sort of politics could become a powerful force. The European examples show what is possible when sufficient people stop being passive observers of politics and become active participants: to achieve change in Britain we do not necessarily need the same sorts of dramatic responses to injustice and unpopular leaders (and we certainly don't want martyrs), but we do need more citizens who believe that sovereignty should belong to them, who recognise that they are not powerless, and who are prepared to use all the democratic tools at their disposal to demand reform.

---

[1] Natalie Fenton, 'The Internet of Radical Politics' in J.Curran, N.Fenton and D.Freedman *Misunderstanding the Internet*, London: 2016 (forthcoming).

[2] Paul Mason, *Why It's Kicking Off Everywhere: the New Global Revolutions*, Verso, 2012

2-3 A roadmap to reform

The extent to which our political class has become aloof, and to which democracy has become corrupted by corporate interests and largely controlled by an elite 'establishment', might appear as a state of affairs over which we have little influence, but we are citizens, and we have votes, and we therefore have power. We just need to find ways in which we can use that collective power to assert our views and rights. If change were not possible, there would have been no point in writing this book and there would be none in people reading it.

We cannot of course change the world. Much as we might like to take the giants of capitalism under our control, overcome the massive disparities in wealth and income and make unearned privilege a thing of the past, none of these things will happen, at least for a long time to come. But we can take steps which will start putting politics where it belongs – in the hands of ordinary people. The reforms we want to see will require action by politicians, but politicians are unlikely to deliver what we want without us demanding it, so the initiative for change must come from below - and that means us. It is therefore time for those of us who are concerned about the state of the country and how it is run to take a stand and demand a new style of politics.

But what are our chances of success? Is a new campaign for change, with the same passion and commitment that drove the

A ROAD MAP TO REFORM

Levellers, the Chartists and suffragettes possible, and can examples from other countries inspire us with a sense of what is possible? The immediate signs might seem discouraging. The 2015 general election produced a government with little interest in democratic reform – unlike the other main parties, the Conservatives had refused to make any commitment to setting up a Constitutional Convention, and one of its first acts was to abolish the Commons' 'Political and Constitutional Reform Committee' which had recommended that the incoming government should consider a whole raft of reforms. In July 2015 when demands for reform of the Lords was back in the news (after a prominent Lord was photographed sniffing cocaine with prostitutes), the Prime Minister announced that the only change he planned to make was the addition of a whole lot more Conservative peers. When the Lords asked the Commons to rethink its plans for cutting tax credits, his response was to announce a cut in the Lords' powers. Adding such pronouncements to the general gloom and cynicism described in previous chapters, the chances of reform might appear hopeless.

However, things may be not as bad as they seem, and there may even be grounds for optimism.

Firstly, what Newton observed for physics may also apply in politics: for every action there is an equal but opposite reaction. Anger at the outcome of the 2015 election, which produced more electors than ever before with reason to belief the electoral system cheated them of the representation they deserved, and at the government's refusal to even consider matters such as the voting system, Lords reform, the case for reducing the voting age, etc., can only add to demands for change.

Secondly, the rise in support for UKIP, the SNP and the Greens shows that the Conservatives and Labour can no longer take their

THE REFORM DEBATES

political duopoly for granted. More people are turning away from the old order of the established parties and looking for something new - for them the status quo is not attractive. Even within the Labour Party, the 2015 leadership contest has demonstrated that many members want to do things differently, and although that does not necessarily mean a shift in favour of democratic reform, the desire for change offers opportunities for widening the debate.

Thirdly, the political mobilisation in Scotland around the independence referendum shows that people, given a perceived opportunity to make a difference, are prepared to use their political voices. Political apathy may just be people's reaction to situations in which they don't feel they have much power, but when politics offers them a chance to have a meaningful say on something important to them they are ready to take it. The challenge that reformers face is how to make democratic reform as relevant and exciting for everyone in the UK as the independence debate was for those in Scotland.

Fourthly, as discussed in the previous chapter, the success of the SNP has forced some constitutional issues on to the agenda. Not only does Scottish independence remain a possibility, but promises of new powers for the Scots, the consequent demands for the devolution of powers within England and a new urgency for an answer to the 'West Lothian question' mean that at least parts of our unwritten constitution will need to be written differently. The dominance of the SNP in Scotland has made the UK, in the words of Peter Hennessy, a 'constitutional building site'[1], and if we must examine the architecture of our political system, there may also be opportunities for considering its values.

Fifthly, we have the internet. Campaigners of previous generations had to rely on back-street printing presses to spread their messages, but social media sites now make it possible to contact more people more easily and more quickly, and without any significant costs. While it has been argued (in chapter 1-4) that politics cannot be conducted on the internet alone, sites such as Facebook and Twitter can be hugely effective tools in alerting people to problems and inviting them to take action. They have made the campaigns of groups such as Uncut UK possible, and if there is one thing that the international examples described in chapter 2-2 have in common it is their use of the internet to mobilise supporters.

Thus, while the obstacles to serious reform might seem formidable, the picture is not as gloomy as it might at first appear. While it would be foolish to be optimistic, it would be a mistake to ignore the opportunities in our present political circumstances, and this may be as good a time as any for reformers to push their demands for change.

A national debate

But how are we to do it? Any reforms will require action by politicians, but they are unlikely to act unless there is a clamour for change. Popular pressure is not just needed to persuade politicians that the status quo is untenable, but if our ultimate objective is to put people in control of politics then reforms should come about through citizens setting the agenda and ensuring that their elected representatives follow it. Our starting point should therefore be a national debate on what is wrong with politics and what must be done to change it. Just as people in Scotland debated the question

THE REFORM DEBATES

of independence in clubs and pubs, village halls, union branches and professional groups, we need the same sort of debate on how the country is run. Politicians and political parties, and of course the media, must have a role to play in it but, unlike the Scottish referendum, the debate should not be led by those with a vested interest in the outcome.

In its 2015 manifesto, Labour promised to 'set up a people-led Constitutional Convention to determine the future of UK's governance' while the Liberal Democrats said they would 'establish a UK Constitutional Convention, made up from representatives of the political parties, academia, civic society and members of the public, tasked with producing a full written constitution for the UK'. The idea of a constitutional convention therefore already has some political backing and would appear to offer a focus for our national debate. It might involve politicians and 'experts', but it should, as Labour proposed, be 'people-led', and that surely means that a majority of its members should be ordinary citizens. Its debates would not be dominated by party rivalries, and 'citizens with competing visions [would be] forced to reason with each other'.[2] While it would need to have a remit to define its scope, that remit should be broad enough to allow people to add to its agenda constitutional issues that they feel are important – the agenda should not be limited to what politicians are prepared to discuss.

Citizen-led conventions have already been used in other countries, including Canada, Iceland and Ireland. The first, and one of the most successful, was the Citizens' Assembly for Electoral Reform in British Columbia in 2004. A provincial government with a commitment to consider electoral reform had been elected and it

A ROAD MAP TO REFORM

kept its promise. The Assembly was formed, entirely of lay people, to choose which system would be put to the electorate as a whole in a referendum. Two people, a man and a woman, were selected at random from each of British Columbia's 79 constituencies, and a further two were selected to represent the province's indigenous communities. The selections were made in a way that ensured that all age groups were represented. As the time commitment required of members was demanding, if someone felt unable to serve then another was selected in their place. The Assembly met every other weekend for nearly a year, it had an impartial chair, and it was abled to call expert witnesses and conduct hearings in all constituencies. Around 1600 written submissions were received and studied. At the end of its deliberations, the Assembly chose STV by an overwhelming majority (not the system which even those politicians who favoured reform would have wanted).

What made the Assembly special was its complete reliance on ordinary citizens (although that was also a problem), the time it allowed for discussions (and with a budget to make this possible), and the quality of the chair whose role was to facilitate but not direct.

The process, however, was not a complete success. The referendum in 2005 was won in 77 of the 79 constituencies with a total of 57.7% in favour of STV, but the provincial government had required a majority of at least 60%. STV was not therefore adopted, but a rerun of the referendum was offered 4 years later, and then STV was defeated by a margin of about 2:1. If there was a weakness in the process, it was the complete absence of politicians in the Assembly and as a consequence there was no buy-in from the political parties which then opposed the change. Some attribute the different outcomes of the two referendums to the questions

THE REFORM DEBATES

which were asked: in the first people were asked to support the recommendations of 160 citizens, and many were keen to do, but the second asked whether people wanted STV which was less well understood and more vulnerable to opponents debating point.

There are important lessons here for any UK convention.[3] Firstly there is the time the Assembly was given to complete its work: if the British Columbians took nearly a year to discuss their voting system, no less time should be given to a convention with the task of looking at the UK constitution. Secondly there is the size: 160 may seem a large body of people, but a smaller number of people risks having the convention dominated by people who may have fixed views of the issues from the start. Thirdly, there is the need to have the participation of people from the parties, both to ensure that the convention has an understanding of the politicians' perspectives and to avoid an outcome seen as a confrontation between politicians and convention members. Fourthly, there is a need for a talented and impartial chair to ensure all voices are heard and discussions are conducted in a constructive manner. A UK citizen-led convention would be a big undertaking – probably much bigger that either Labour or the Liberal Democrats envisaged in making their manifesto commitments - but as its business would be the future of our democracy it would be foolish to take shortcuts to save time or money.

A citizens' convention would not in itself be a national debate, but it could be the centrepiece of one. It should not just be 160 or so people debating in a hall, but a whole programme of events and discussions around the country, all feeding into the convention's work. There should be opportunities for individuals to submit their ideas, consultation papers for wider debate and surveys to

A ROAD MAP TO REFORM

gauge opinion – the convention could be the thing to galvanise people into to thinking about their democracy and how they can take control of politics.

We cannot expect the proposal of such a convention to be welcomed by politicians – or at least not all of them. The starting point of a broad campaign for democratic reform may need to be a campaign for a convention and that needs people and organisations to start it. Here, however, we have a number of organisations to give a lead.

The reform lobby

Campaigning for political reform in Britain did not end with the Chartists or the suffragettes. We have many excellent organisations that have kept the flame of democratic reform burning, many of them concerned with specific issues, such as how we elect our politicians, how we defend our civil liberties and how we protect the freedom and quality of our press. Some have had successes, such as those who argued for freedom of information legislation, but most successes have only been partial. Some have been successful in winning the backing of groups of MPs, often on a cross-party basis, but where they have failed is in the difficult job of galvanising widespread popular support for their causes. Nevertheless, they are institutions which promote debates on the changes that are needed, and they provide us with organisational bases, often with expertise and sometimes with resources, to campaign for these changes.

The Electoral Reform Society, founded in 1884, can claim to be the world's oldest pro-democracy pressure group. Its initial list of supporters was impressive, and at times it almost succeeded (in

THE REFORM DEBATES

both 1918 and 1931 the Commons voted for the Alternative Vote but, as the Lords wanted STV, nothing changed). For much of its existence, however, it was a voice in the wilderness, and a fairly ineffective one at that. Since 1997, however, when the incoming Labour government appeared to put electoral reform back on the agenda, it has grown in strength and, while it still regards the promotion of the Single Transferable Vote system as a major objective, there are now more pragmatic voices within it who recognise that electoral reform is only one of the changes needed to bring about a new politics.

Charter88 was the first to demand reform over a whole range of constitutional issues (following the example of Charter77 which had published a charter calling for political change in Czechoslovakia in 1977). A letter in the 'New Statesman' in 1988, signed by 348 intellectuals and campaigners, led to an advert in 'The Observer ' with 5,000 signatories in January 1989 and the creation of an organisation to press the demands of its 10-point charter. This was perhaps the nearest to a call for popular sovereignty that Britain has seen: the pre-amble to the charter stated:

> We have had less freedom than we believed. That which we have enjoyed has been too dependent on the benevolence of our rulers. Our freedoms have remained their possession, rationed out to us as subjects rather than being our own inalienable possession as citizens. To make real the freedoms we once took for granted means for the first time to take them for ourselves. The time has come to demand political, civil and human rights in the United Kingdom. We call, therefore, for a new constitutional settlement ...

A ROAD MAP TO REFORM

The ten points of the charter included democratic reform, the protection of civil liberties, the need for freedom of information legislation, devolution of powers, and a written constitution 'anchored in the ideal of universal citizenship'.

As an organisation, Charter88 attracted around 80,000 supporters. It had been born out of concerns following the re-election of Margaret Thatcher's Conservatives in 1987, but it made little headway while the Conservatives were in government. Labour's election in 1997, seen as an opportunity, was, however, a disappointment in many respects: although some of the demands were met, Labour reneged on its promise of a referendum on the voting system, it removed most hereditary peers only to replace them with political appointees, and the idea of a written constitution which would underpin political and civil rights was simply not on Labour's agenda. In 2003, with the loss of grant support and an organisational crisis, Charter88 all but disappeared. A partnership with the New Politics Network kept it alive, and in 2007 the two organisations formally merged to form Unlock Democracy which continues to do valuable work, both through its small staff team and through a network of local activists.

Charter88 protested that our freedoms have been 'too dependent on the benevolence of our rulers' and are 'rationed out to us as subjects rather than ... as citizens', but its radicalism fell short of saying anything about the monarchy. That has been left to Republic which campaigns for an end to hereditary privilege and for an elected head of state. Although republicanism in Britain has a long history, Republic was only formed in 1983, and only became an effective campaigning force after organisational changes in 2005. Recent years have seen some big showcase events for the monarchy – the wedding of Prince William in 2011, the diamond jubilee

THE REFORM DEBATES

in 2012, and royal babies in 2013 and 2015 – but each of them has added new strength to Republic which by 2015 had a paid-up membership of nearly 5,000 and around 30,000 Facebook followers.

The Fawcett Society continues to press for more women in politics, while Operation Black Vote tries to encourage the participation of people of ethnic minorities. There are also organisations such as the Citizenship Foundation which works with young people, helping them to develop an understanding of democracy, The Democratic Society which works to encourage participation, and others, most prominently Bite the Ballot, which have done valuable work in persuading younger people to use their votes. The Campaign for Press and Broadcasting Freedom, and more recently Hacked Off, have challenged the corporations that control our media, while the Open Rights Group and others have campaigned against the misuse of digital information. Then there are thinktanks which have an interest in democracy and governance – although they may not see themselves as campaigning organisations in the normal sense of the term, many of them nevertheless exist to try to change the way the country is run.

These organisations have all done valuable work on their own particular issues and sometimes have collaborated where they have found common campaign objectives. Rarely, however, do they recognise, at least explicitly, the common interest they all have in achieving a democracy of active citizens, each with an equal political voice. Each has campaigned for a few of the changes we need to make in our politics, but without presenting their work as part of the wider campaign that is needed to make

A ROAD MAP TO REFORM

popular sovereignty real, and it is that that should be the glue which binds them together.

Their collective voice could be much more powerful than the sum of their individual voices. It does not require a coalition in the sense of a new organisation, but a group of organisations all prepared to act in their common interest.

If all members of this reform lobby were to put their weight behind a proposal for a citizens' led constitutional convention and a national debate, it would be much more difficult for the politicians to refuse their demand. It would not require organisations to abandon their own objectives, but making their concerns part of the debate would enable them to get their arguments to a much wider audience. A national debate on reforming politics would therefore offer each one of them new opportunities in their own fields.

Action by the reform lobby could therefore be the mechanism for getting a campaign under way. How it should be done would be a matter for them to decide, but a starting point might be a joint declaration calling for a convention and a national debate. It might look something like this:

> We, as organisations working in different fields but with improving the quality of our politics as a common objective, are deeply concerned at the state of our democracy. Many have lost faith in not just politicians and parties, but in politics itself. Yet politics should be the way in which citizens collectively take decisions about the sort of society they want to live in and it ultimately should belong to them.

THE REFORM DEBATES

We therefore believe that the time has come for a national debate on how we are governed. We call on the Government to establish a Constitutional Convention to produce proposals aimed at achieving a form of politics that engages all citizens and recognises that all should have an equal democratic voice.

Whilst such a Convention should include politicians and constitutional experts, it should be citizen-led. Citizens, selected at random, should form a majority of the Convention's members and, within a broad remit, they should have a role in determining its agenda. The Convention should have the powers and resources to consult widely, engaging people in all parts of the country in its discussions.

We therefore call on politicians of all parties, as people elected to represent us, to give this proposal their full support and to commit themselves to giving serious consideration to any recommendations that the Convention might make.

Starting the debate

We want government action, but we don't need to wait for it. Whatever the organisations that make up what has been termed 'the reform lobby' might do, as individuals we can start agitating for a Constitutional Convention on the lines set out above. We can act alone, or we can start campaigning with others in our constituencies and in any organisations we belong to. We are, after all, seeking reforms which would engage more citizens and give them more say on matters that concern them, and we are more likely to achieve that objective if the demands are made by citizens from the outset.

Moreover, we can all play our part in starting the national debate by thinking about, and discussing, the changes we would like to see to bring about a politics that encourages engagement and makes people aware that politics belongs to them. Here there is no silver bullet – no single reform that will produce a healthy participative democracy – but the final part of this book discusses a number of reforms that together could start the transformation of our democracy. Each chapter looks at just one aspect of our politics and political institutions, examines the problems and proposes possible solutions. It is not claimed that the proposals made are the only solutions or even the best ones, and some might be controversial, but that is why a national debate is needed. The reforms that are proposed are not just about taking better decisions, but about how decisions are taken, and together they could take us a long way towards a politics in which people really matter.

---

[1] Peter Hennessy, *The Kingdom to Come: Thoughts on the Union before and after the Scottish Independence Referendum*, Haus Publishing, 2015

[2] Robert Hazell, quoted in J Garland, *Reviving the health of our democracy*, Electoral Reform Society, 2013

[3] Jordan Kroll and Juliet Swann, *We the people: Constitutional decision making through citizen-led deliberative processes*, Electoral Reform Society, 2015, provides a useful study of constitutional conventions and the lesson to be learnt from them.

Part 3

The Debates

HOW WE ELECT OUR MPS

3-1 How we elect our MPs?

Elections are at the heart of our democracy. They determine who our representatives at Westminster will be, and consequently which party (or parties if a coalition is formed) will be in power, who will form the government and who will be Prime Minister. While democracy should involve people at all times, it is when there are elections that people have real power.

The outcome of an election, however, is decided not just by how people vote, but also by the voting system, i.e. the way votes are used to determine who wins and who loses. That different voting systems could lead to different governments with different sets of policies makes the choice of the voting system one of critical importance.

While voting systems are sets of rules and procedures for converting votes into electoral outcomes, they can also have an impact on the nature of democracy and of politics itself. They determine the extent to which elections are about finding single winners or about seeking parliaments that reflect the diversity of voters' views, and as a result they influence the nature of our political culture. They determine the extent to which people's votes are likely to influence outcomes, and consequently they have an influence on both voter turnouts and the nature of election campaigns. Changing the voting system will not be enough to produce an ideal democracy, but an ideal democracy cannot be achieved without electoral reform.

THE REFORM DEBATES

There are many different voting systems to choose from, but the **'First Past the Post'** (FPTP) system we use for electing our MPs is the simplest: in each constituency, the candidate with most votes is declared the winner. That may sound fair, but in practice it is often far from fair to candidates, to parties and, above all, to the voters. Moreover, it is not a system that is conducive to the sort of deliberative and participative democracy we want to see.

Why time should be called on FPTP

FPTP often produces unrepresentative and perverse results

In the 2015 general election, UKIP won 12.6% of the votes but just one seat. By contrast, the SNP won 56 seats with just 4.7% of the votes. Whatever view one takes of UKIP or the SNP, these results make a mockery of the idea that FPTP gives people what they voted for. The Conservatives received only 37% of the votes but they won a majority of the seats, making it possible for them to push through legislation even if it is opposed by parties that collectively received 63% of the votes. The idea that FPTP gives us representative government is clearly nonsense.

FPTP rarely produces a parliament that reflects support for the parties in terms of the votes they received. It takes no account of the winning candidates' majorities, and votes for losing candidates have no influence whatsoever on the outcome of the election. Parties with most votes generally end up with many more MPs than their share of the votes would appear to justify: this has happened in every general election other than 1951 (see below), with perhaps the most extreme example being 2005 when the results were:

HOW WE ELECT OUR MPS

	Votes	Seats
Labour	35.2%	55.1%
Conservative	32.4%	30.7%
Liberal Democrat	22.0%	9.6%
Other	10.4%	3.7%

Labour won just over a third of the votes, but it won a comfortable majority of 66 seats over all other parties. Although Labour's share of the vote was the smallest that had ever put a party into government, never since 1931 had any party won a majority of the votes.

FPTP, however, can be unpredictable. Sometimes the party with most votes may not win, as happened in 1951 when Labour received 48.8% of the votes to the Conservatives' 48.0%, but the Conservatives won more seats and therefore formed the government. Labour did, however, have its revenge in the first of the two elections of 1974 when it won in spite of the Conservatives being the winners in terms of votes.

FPTP makes it difficult for small parties to win many seats – even if they have significant numbers of votes in total, to win a seat they must get more votes than any other party in the constituency. The 4 million votes won by UKIP in 2015 did not do it much good because under FPTP there are no rewards for coming second in a constituency. The SNP was exceptionally successful in the 2015 election because, although it may have been 'small' in the context of the UK as whole, in Scotland it was dominant.

FPTP creates too many 'safe seats'

A safe seat is one where there is a party whose candidate will almost certainly win. Take, for example, Bootle where in 2015 the winning Labour candidate received 74.5% of the votes and the

THE REFORM DEBATES

candidate in second place had only 10.9%, and Beckenham where the Conservative candidate had nearly 58% of the votes while the runner-up had less than 20%. These are seats where, barring a political earthquake, the candidates of Labour and the Conservatives respectively will win, and it is right that their strong support should be rewarded. The problem with FPTP is that in most elections the great majority of seats are safe for one party or another, and in these constituencies those who do not support the dominant party are effectively disenfranchised. As the result is a foregone conclusion, electors have less incentive to vote and parties have little incentive to campaign.

It is in the marginal constituencies that the outcome of a general election is decided, and this may be only a quarter of the seats or even less. It is in these constituencies that parties will concentrate their campaigning resources. In 2010 in Luton South which, as the election approached, was seen as a three-way marginal, the parties together spent £3.07 per voter – 22 times as much as the 14p per voter they spent in safe Bootle and over 13 times as much as the 23p spent in Beckenham.[1]

Thus with FPTP, general elections are not really 'general' in the sense of involving all electors in an equal way, but elections fought just in those constituencies where it is thought that a seat might change hands. It creates a danger that when party manifestos are written, the interests of floating voters in key seats will be given much more weight than those of electors in seats that are safe.

FPTP 'wastes' votes

Whether a constituency is safe or marginal, for voters there is a risk that with FPTP their votes will be wasted. If you vote for a candidate who doesn't win, you might as well have stayed at home. Similarly, if you vote for a candidate who wins by a large majority, your vote only increases the majority of a candidate who would have won without your help. In the 2015 election, three-quarters of the votes could be regarded as having been wasted - half of the votes because they were cast for candidates who lost, and nearly a quarter just added to the majorities of winners.

A common demand of electoral reformers is that 'all votes should count'. No voting system can guarantee that all votes will 'count' in the sense of them having an equal influence on result of an election, but it is surely unacceptable that FPTP can result in so many voters finding their votes made no contribution to the election of any MP. We want a democracy which encourages participation, but we are unlikely to get one with a voting system in which so many people's votes don't matter.

Some voters will of course recognise the danger of their vote being wasted and try to overcome the problem by voting tactically, i.e. not voting for the candidate they really want, but for another candidate who has a chance of defeating a candidate they don't want to win, but there is something wrong with a system that encourages people to vote in this way.

FPTP can allow unpopular candidates to win.

If votes are spread across a number of candidates, with FPTP it is possible for a relatively unpopular candidate – or even the most unpopular candidate - to win. For example, in 2009 a BNP candidate won a seat in a local election in Hertfordshire with only 29.2% of the votes.[2] Polling at the time suggested that most voters would have preferred any other candidate over the BNP, but as the votes of the 70.8% who did not vote BNP were spread amongst other candidates, it was the BNP candidate who was elected.

THE REFORM DEBATES

FPTP distorts regional representation
As FPTP tends to give parties more than their share of seats in areas where they are strong, it produces a north-south divide. In 2015, in the North East, North West and Yorkshire and Humberside regions, Labour won 110 seats to the Conservatives' 44, yet in none of these regions did Labour come close to 50% of the votes. In the South East, South West and Eastern regions, Labour had only 11 seats to the Conservatives' 182, but only in the South East did the Conservatives narrowly pass 50% of the votes. These three regions produced 55% of the Conservatives' seats in the Commons, while 58% of Labour's seats came from the north of England and Wales. In Scotland, the SNP, although receiving only 50% of the votes, won 56 of the 59 seats. The major parties have support throughout the UK, but FPTP creates a danger of governments whose interests are focused on only parts of it.

Choosing an alternative to FPTP

FPTP is not a satisfactory way of electing our parliament, but what would we replace it with? We might want a voting system that would:
- guarantee proportional results;
- make MPs accountable to electors in defined geographic areas and not just to their parties;
- make as many votes as possible 'count' (we cannot ensure that every vote contributes to the election of a candidate, but we want most votes to do so in some way);
- allow people to vote for the candidate they really want without fear of their votes being wasted (i.e. tactical voting should not be necessary).

HOW WE ELECT OUR MPS

However, it is not possible to construct a voting system that meets all of these criteria fully, so choosing a system requires us to decide what compromises we are prepared to make.

Proportionality is not the only issue to consider in electoral reform, but it is a key one. If a voting system cannot guarantee results that are at least broadly proportional, there is a risk of it producing parliaments which do not reflect people's views, and governments whose policies most people don't want. The more proportional a system, the better the chances of minor parties getting a voice in parliament will be, and the lower the risk of a government elected by a minority being able to impose its will on the majority.

Proportionality, however, is not without its problems. To guarantee even broad proportionality, we need constituencies (sometimes called 'electoral regions') which elect more than a single MP, and the more proportional we want a system to be, the larger the constituencies we need. For example, with a proportional system in a three-seat constituency, a party with at least 25% of the votes is guaranteed at least one seat (because it would not be possible to have three other parties with more than 25%), but using four-member constituencies a party would need only 20% of the votes to be sure of winning a seat. Even broad proportionality would mean abandoning the present system in which each constituency elects only one MP and redrawing the boundaries to produce constituencies which elect several MPs. However, while making the constituencies large would improve proportionality, it would also require MPs to represent much larger areas, with the risk that it would weaken their links with the people to whom they should be accountable. A compromise must therefore be struck between proportionality and geographic representation.

THE REFORM DEBATES

Any proposal to move away from single-member constituencies is likely to be met with hostility from many MPs who argue that the present system gives them a unique link with their constituents, i.e. one that is not shared with other MPs, and a unique responsibility for representing them. However, while at present MPs can 'represent' all of their constituents in terms of attending to casework issues, no single MP can represent all of their constituents' views – they have only one vote in the Commons which they cannot split to reflect the spread of constituents' opinions. With a broadly proportional system, more than one MP will represent an area and it is more likely that people will feel that they have an MP who represents them politically. Moreover, with larger constituencies with several MPs, a constituent with a problem can choose which MP to approach – some might want a woman MP, some might prefer an older or younger person, and others may make their choice on the basis of which MP is likely to be most sympathetic to their views. The arguments for single-member constituencies therefore appear to be overstated: in most fields, politicians argue that choice and competition are good, so there does not seem to be any good reason for giving MPs a monopoly in their constituencies when it comes to representation.

Another line of argument against proportionality is that it makes coalition government more likely because it makes it more difficult for any party to win a majority of the seats in an election. The argument, however, is based on the assumption that coalitions are undesirable, but there is no evidence to suggest that coalitions are either better or worse than single-party governments. Indeed, many might regard Britain's 2010–2015 coalition as having been better than the government elected in 2015 as, in the former, the

Liberal Democrats were able to block some of the Conservatives' proposals for which there was not popular support.[3] While single-party governments with parliamentary majorities might be strong in the sense that they can implement their programmes without the need for messy negotiations with coalition partners, they may not be strong in the sense of having a strong democratic mandate from the voters. We only need to look across Europe, where coalition government is the norm, to see that coalition government does not necessarily mean bad, weak or unpopular government.

Few countries, however, use voting systems that are fully proportional as such systems could result in a proliferation of parties with significant numbers of seats, making government formation more the business of party negotiators rather than decisions of voters. Israel, where the entire country is a single electoral region and the largest party often has less than a quarter of the seats, is a case in point. There is therefore an argument for seeking a system that is only broadly proportional, i.e. one which makes it possible for popular parties to win outright majorities, even if they don't quite have a majority of the votes, but which avoids the excessive disproportionality which can arise with FPTP.

The choices on offer

There are lots of voting systems to choose from – in fact the number of possible systems is almost infinite. However, our task is not as difficult as it might seem as systems can be put into a small number of categories. These are:

- Single-member constituency systems;
- List systems;

THE REFORM DEBATES

- Mixed-member systems (AMS and TR);
- The Single Transferable Vote (STV).

Single-member constituency systems

Systems such as FPTP which only use single-member constituencies cannot guarantee even modestly proportional results. There are better single-member-constituency systems than FPTP, perhaps the best being the **Alternative Vote** (AV) which takes account of the order in which voters to rank their preferences for the candidates. AV could overcome many of the defects of FPTP – it would greatly reduce the number of wasted votes and would get rid of the need for tactical voting[4] – but it is capable of producing perverse outcomes. Moreover, because a proposal to use AV was defeated in a referendum in 2011, it is unlikely to be a starter.

List systems

We use a list system for electing our MEPs (other than in Northern Ireland where STV is used). In each region the parties present their lists of candidates, and people vote for the party they want. Parties are then awarded seats in a way that makes each party's share of the seats as near as possible to its share of the votes. If a party wins, say, three seats, then the top three candidates on its list are elected.

A major drawback of the system we use for European Parliament elections is that voters cannot choose which candidates they want - they can only vote for a party and by doing so may find their votes help elect someone they don't want. There are much better forms of list systems (called 'open lists'), used in many European countries, which get around this problem by allowing voters to support not just a party but a particular candidate on that party's list. In this case, if a party wins two seats, they will be given to the candidates with most personal support. Some countries use 'semi-open lists' in which the candidates who get a party's seats are determined partly by the support they receive and partly by their position on the list.

If a large enough region is used, list systems can be very proportional and 'open lists' meet many of our criteria, but would we want large constituencies which could weaken the ties between MPs and the people they represent?

Mixed-member systems

These systems involve elections in single-member constituencies, but to compensate for the disproportionality of such elections, additional members are elected over a wider region.

Additional Member Systems (AMS) are used to elect the Scottish Parliament and the Welsh and London Assemblies. Electors have two votes – one for a constituency candidate and the other for a party list. In the case of London, for example, there are 16 constituencies, each electing one member by FPTP, and 9 members for the whole of London who are elected from the party lists. These 'additional members' (often referred to as 'list' or 'regional' members') are awarded in such as way that the total numbers of seats won by the parties are as near to proportional as possible.

While AMS can be broadly proportional, that it produces two types of elected members has been a cause of some problems (and even tensions, although these have subsided since the system was introduced in 1999). There is also concern that while constituency members each represent electors in geographic areas, the accountability of list members, who owe their seats to their positions on

THE REFORM DEBATES

their parties' lists and who represent much larger areas, is very limited.

A variant of AMS is the **Alternative Vote Plus** (AV+). This system, recommended by the Jenkins Commission set up by Labour in 1997, uses AV rather than FPTP in electing the constituency members. Jenkins proposed that the additional members should be elected by a semi-open list, making the system a little fairer but much more complex. However, although in its 1997 manifesto Labour promised a referendum on whatever the Jenkins Commission recommended, it reneged on its commitment.

Total Representation (TR)[5] is another form of mixed-member system which has been suggested for the Commons. Although it has not yet been tried in practice, its approach to overcoming some of the worst defects in FPTP has a simplicity that leaves one wondering why it has not been thought of before.

In recent general elections, around half of the votes cast have been cast for losing candidates and these votes have no effect whatsoever on the results in terms of seats. TR tackles that absurdity by awarding additional seats to parties on the basis of the votes for their losing candidates. It does not seek to produce even moderate proportionality, but it would give smaller parties more representation and would give parties and their candidates a reason for campaigning everywhere – even in constituencies which they cannot expect to win.

Unlike AMS and AV+, with TR voters would cast only one vote, as in FPTP. All of the votes for losing candidates would then be totalled by party, and a small number of additional ('party') seats awarded proportionally to the parties on the basis of their votes for losing candidates. If a party were to win, say, 5 'party seats', then these seats would be given to the party's 5 losing candidates who received most votes. Although some electoral reformers may not favour the system because it is only very modestly proportional, it could offer a satisfactory compromise between those who want PR and those who don't.

TR would not, however, allow the transfer of votes between constituency candidates, and for some this might be considered a major defect. With AV and STV, a vote for a losing candidate is transferred to the voter's next choice, but TR would only transfer such votes to the pool used for the allocation of 'party seats'. As a result, the constituency contests of a TR election would suffer from some of the same problems as FPTP (for example, a relatively unpopular candidate could be elected). However, the potential benefits of TR make it worthy of consideration, and there are ways in which it could be developed to allow some transferability of votes in the election of constituency candidates.[6]

Single Transferable Vote (STV)

STV belongs in a class of its own. It is the preferred system of most electoral reformers as it is the one that comes closest to meeting all of our criteria. It is used for all elections in Northern Ireland except general elections, and has been used for local government in Scotland since 2007.

STV produces proportional results using multi-member constituencies in which parties can stand as many candidates as they choose. Voters, however, vote for candidates, not parties, and they do so by listing the candidates as they want in order of preference.

The first stage in an STV count is to determine the 'quota' – the number of votes a candidate needs to get elected. For example, if there are 100 votes and 3 seats to be filled, the quota is 26, because

THE REFORM DEBATES

if one candidate has 26 votes there cannot be three others with more than 26. Ballot papers are then sorted by voters' first preferences and any candidate with more than the quota is declared elected. Their votes are then reduced to the quota by transferring a proportion of each of their votes to the next preferences on the ballot papers. If that results in other candidates reaching the quota, they are declared elected and further transfers are made. If there are still seats to be filled, the candidate with fewest votes is eliminated and their votes transferred to their voters' next preferences. The process continues, transferring surplus votes from elected candidates and eliminating candidates when necessary, until the required number of candidates has been elected.

With STV there are very few wasted votes because votes cast for candidates who cannot win are transferred to others. People can therefore vote for small parties (or independent candidates) knowing that their votes will count without any need for tactical voting. STV maximises the choice given to voters – they can, for example, make their first choice a Green Party candidate, their second a Labour candidate, their third another Labour candidate and their fourth a Liberal Democrat. Parties will have more than one candidate in a constituency if they hope to win more than one seat and, as a consequence, there is at least some competition between candidates of the same party (something that candidates and parties don't always like). Where parties have more than one candidate, none can simply assume they will be elected on the basis of votes for their party alone.

Counting an election with STV, however, is much more complicated (or some would say 'sophisticated') than with other systems, although in Scotland this problem has been overcome by scanning and counting the ballot papers electronically.

A problem that is more difficult to overcome is the bias STV can produce in favour of candidates near the top of the ballot paper. Suppose there are three Conservative candidates and a voter wants to support all of them: the voter may look down the list and put a '1' against the first listed Conservative, a '2' against the second and a '3' against the third. If there are only enough Conservative votes to elect one candidate, it is the first who is most likely to be successful. The problem can be overcome by randomising the order of the candidates on the ballot papers so that no two ballots need be identical - this, however, adds to the complexity (and cost) of printing, and if a manual count were ever to be required, it would be a very difficult and long job if candidates appeared in different orders on each ballot paper.

With STV, as with list systems, there is the issue of constituency size. A constituency of 5 or 6 might be desirable from the perspective of proportionality, but giving politicians such a large area to cover risks making them more remote from those they represent. Scottish local elections use wards which elect either 3 or 4 members: while this gives a decent degree of proportionality, it reduces the choice of candidates of the same party (particularly as, in an STV election, there are reasons for parties not having as many candidates as there are seats to be won). However, while a 4-member council ward might be manageable, a 4-member Westminster constituency outside a metropolitan area would be huge.

THE REFORM DEBATES

Is reform achievable?

Electoral reform is a political process. Any decision to hold another referendum[7] on how we elect our MPs will require the support of a majority of them. Sadly, many will always favour the system by which they were elected and will be have little inclination to support a change which could threaten their positions. Governments, and in particular single-party governments, are unlikely to introduce a reform which could deprive them of their majorities (unless they are approaching elections they expect to lose). We therefore need to consider in what the political circumstances change might be possible.

The best opportunities for reform are likely to arise when an election does not produce a clear winner. When that happens, a party may need to negotiate a coalition agreement with one or more smaller parties, or a deal to sustain a minority government. The smaller parties have much to gain from electoral reform and may make the promise of reform a condition of their support.

This is what happened in 2010 when the Liberal Democrats were able to extract from the Conservatives a commitment to a referendum on AV, but that experience also illustrates the dangers – while the Conservatives agreed to hold a referendum, they did not agree to support the proposed change and instead threw their considerable political weight behind the 'no' campaign. If Labour had given firmer support to AV the referendum might have succeeded, but too many in Labour's ranks were more interested in punishing the Liberal Democrats for joining with the Conservatives in a coalition. Nevertheless, future elections may again produce opportunities for putting electoral reform back on the agenda and, with the benefit of the 2011 experience, the prospects of success may be better.[8]

However, it is unlikely that, at least in the foreseeable future, the minor parties will have sufficient strength to achieve electoral reform on their own. They will require the support, or at least the acquiescence, of one of the two major parties. It is therefore necessary to consider what type of reform might be acceptable to one of them.

It might seem that STV, in spite of its minor drawbacks, is the best system to choose. Certainly it is the system that best meets our criteria and political scientists have described it as 'the connoisseurs' choice'. However, with their opposition to multi-seat constituencies and their fear of a system which might make single-party government almost impossible, the chances of Labour or the Conservatives embracing STV are slim. STV with constituencies electing not more than two members might be just about palatable, but with such small constituencies many of the benefits of STV would be lost. It is therefore necessary to ask not which system is best, but which system is capable of winning sufficient support to make reform happen.

There may therefore be a better chance of success if the proposed change was quite modest. AMS with a relatively small number of list seats – which would increase the representation of small parties without threatening the dominance of the major parties – might be a possibility. Total Representation might be an even better alternative: it has the advantages of its delightful simplicity, making it immune to many of the preposterous criticisms that were hurled at AV, and its avoidance of the need for party lists.

Many electoral reformers will protest that a change to a limited form of AMS or STV or to TR would be too feeble. Modesty, how-

THE REFORM DEBATES

ever, may be a strength. To be successful, a proposal for reform must not just satisfy dedicated reformers – it must also be acceptable to those who are wary of full-blooded reform but who nevertheless recognise the defects of FPTP. Some have maintained that the AV referendum was lost because AV was, in the words of Nick Clegg, 'a miserable little compromise' but there is no evidence to support their argument – AV was lost because the Conservatives and too many in Labour's ranks did not want change. A compromise that at least ameliorates the distortions of FPTP, makes many more votes important and which offers smaller parties more voice in the Commons should not be regarded as miserable. Moreover, any reform would at least dismiss the idea that FPTP is the only reasonable way to conduct elections, and could alter the balance of forces in parliament in a way that would make a more radical change possible at a later date.

Whatever change is proposed, reform is likely to require winning the support of sufficient MPs for a referendum, and winning a majority in the referendum itself. There is therefore much to be done by advocates of reform, whether inside or outside parties, in keeping the issues on the agenda, challenging the MPs (who are suppose to represent us), developing the arguments and creating a climate in which change can happen. Without years of campaigning by those who wanted a better democracy it is unlikely that we would have had the 2011 referendum, and unless that campaign can be continued and intensified, we are unlikely to get another.

Local government

This chapter has been about how we elect our MPs, but the same arguments apply to how we elect local councillors in England and

Wales (councillors in Scotland and Northern Ireland are already elected by STV). Local elections in England and Wales have produced outcomes even more distorted than those of general elections and many councils can be described as one-party states: in Manchester in 2015, for example, all 96 councillors were Labour.

The case for STV for English and Welsh local elections is a strong one. Not only do many local authorities already use multi-member wards, but a ward electing three, say, councillors does not present the same geographic challenge as a constituency electing three MPs and therefore three times as large as a present constituency. Moreover, while MPs may feel personally threatened by moves to change the voting system for the Commons, any decision to change to how local councils are elected would not affect them personally (other than in their relationships with councillors on whose support they may depend) and MPs may therefore be less resistant to reform. While opposition from many councillors is to be expected, that all parties would have something to gain in some parts of England and Wales should also make a change to a more proportional system for local councils easier for the major parties to accept.

If the case for reforming how councillors in England and Wales were to be won, the Commons would be the only tier of government left using FPTP. That, surely, would provide another strong argument for changing how we elect our MPs.

---

[1] Chris Terry, *A Penny for your Vote*, Electoral Reform Society,

THE REFORM DEBATES

2   South Oxhey ward. It was not, however, a freak result: in the previous year, for example, BNP candidates won seats in Stoke on Trent with 30.3%, 31.0% and 34.6%.

3   That the Liberal Democrats were able to curb Conservative excesses, however, did little to improve Liberal Democrat fortunes: many have argued that the Liberal Democrats would have been better able to hold the Conservatives in check by refusing to join the coalition.

4   There are circumstances in which tactical voting might make sense under AV, but they are more theoretical than practical. For further information, see: Ken Ritchie and Alessandro Gardini, 'Putting Paradoxes into Perspective: the case for AV', in Dan Felsenthal and Moshe Machover, *Electoral Systems: Paradoxes, Assumptions and Procedures,*, Springer, 2012.

5   TR was originally devised by Aharon Nathan as a system which could increase the accountability of Israeli politicians and give Israel a government with the strength to negotiate peace with its neighbours, but its potential for improving Britain's democracy soon became apparent. It has also been considered by politicians in Italy. For further information on TR, see A Nathan and I Skrabalo, *Total Representation: a New Electoral System for Modern Times*, 2009, and K Ritchie, *Fixing our Broken Democracy: the Case for 'Total Representation'*, 2012, both published through Amazon.

6   For example, TR could be modified by allowing voters to express a second preference.

7   While there is no constitutional need for a referendum to change the voting system, the 2011 referendum has set a precedent which it would be dangerous to ignore. In January 2016, however, the Liberal Democrat leader, Tim Farron, argued that if a proposal for reform appeared in the manifestos of all parties, other than the Conservatives, then in the event of the Conservatives not winning power, there would be a sufficient mandate for change without a referendum.

8   For an analysis of why the 2011 referendum was lost, see Lewis Baston and Ken Ritchie, *Don't Take No For An Answer: The 2011 Referendum and the Future of Electoral Reform,* Biteback Publishing, 2011.

3-2 Cleaning up politics

Alexandra Runswick and Ken Ritchie

The way that money and financial power can corrupt both politics and politicians has been described in chapter 1-4. It may be regrettable, but it is also understandable that large corporations and wealthy individuals will want to influence politics to their advantage. If politics is to belong to people, we therefore need to put safeguards in place to remove the corrosive effects of money on our democracy.

This chapter looks at three areas in which there is a need for action:
- The extent to which corporations can exert undue influence on policy must be held in check;
- We must ensure that our politicians work for us and not for other paymasters; and
- We must prevent the independence of our political parties from being compromised, or even bought or sold, in return for political donations.

Controlling the lobbyists[1]

There is nothing intrinsically wrong with lobbying – that people, companies and organisations make their cases to politicians and government is a perfectly acceptable part of democracy. It is also important that politicians listen to those with expertise and experi-

THE REFORM DEBATES

ence in the business world, as well as to the many voluntary organisations that want the ear of government on issues such as human rights, international development and protecting the environment and, of course, democracy.

The influence of companies, however, is not always benign. What is not acceptable is the extent to which companies can use their considerable resources and expertise to gain access to politicians and influence government in ways that would be impossible for ordinary citizens, and the extent to which our politicians are complicit in allowing them this access and influence. Rarely is lobbying about improving policy-making: it is more often about creating opportunities to make money, opposing regulations that might restrict commercial activities, seeking a tax regime that protects profits and directors' income, etc.

There has always been lobbying, but what is relatively new is the growth of lobbying as a business. The firms that offer lobbying services to major companies are now worth around £2 billion and employ about 4,000 lobbyists (although the number involved in lobbying is probably much greater[2]) – a lot of people for influencing 650 MPs - and that companies are prepared to pay their huge fees demonstrates that they can be effective in getting the policy changes their clients want.

'We all know how it works' said David Cameron of lobbying. But do we? All too often effective lobbying is carried out in the shadows, even by front organisations, and, as one lobbyist noted, 'The influence of lobbyists increases when it goes largely unnoticed by the public'. As well as helping their clients gain access to politicians and even ministers, lobbyists can prepare and present their clients' cases using whatever language, arguments and half truths are most likely to convince their audiences. They can conduct 'research' and 'consultations' designed to gather 'evidence' to support their arguments but without any requirement of objectivity, and they can orchestrate media work to present their clients and their intentions in the best possible light. Such lobbying is not designed to make politics better or serve the public interest, and too often it is about subverting democracy.

There are of course lobbyists who act with integrity, but there are others who have developed the black arts of their profession. Tamasin Cave and Andy Rowell[3] report that lobbyists have doctored Wikipedia pages on arms manufacturers, financial firms and others and have created 'phoney blogs' in hope to pushing the posts of critics further down Google rankings; they have monitored and, in extreme cases, even infiltrated opposition groups with the intention of gaining intelligence; and they have funded spurious front organisations to support their arguments. Not only do their own ethics leave much to be desired, but neither are they fussy about the ethics of their clients - many a despotic regime has used their services to improve their public image and neutralise their critics.

Services that lobbyists offer include what they euphemistically call 'public relations' or 'public affairs'. These might sound like good things, but they are generally about persuading us – and of course our politicians – through partial, misleading and downright false messages about their clients and their work. The following examples illustrate their approach.

- When the High Speed 2 rail project was running into flack, lobbyists Westbourne Communications were tasked with redefining it from something to help a few commuters to a project that supposedly benefited the many by creating jobs. The reframing 'pitted wealthy people in the Chilterns ... against the economic benefits to the north'. The strategy was 'posh people standing in the way of working-class people getting jobs,' said Westbourne's James Bethell. 'Their lawns or our jobs,' shouted the ad campaign.'

- When people associated with the Taxpayers Alliance were asked to lead the 'No' campaign in the 2011 referendum on the voting system, they quickly made the debate about the costs of reform rather than the pros and cons of electoral systems. He led with the claims that switching to AV would deny troops badly needed equipment and sick babies incubators. The claims were entirely bogus, but the tactic worked.

In the first example, Westbourne sidestepped the controversy over whether HS2 would indeed produce benefits for the north and instead went for a populist argument that was likely to deter objectors. It may have been a clever bit of marketing, but its aim was to avoid a reasoned debate on the project.

The second example, however, is more sinister: it is an example of what has been called the 'dead cat' strategy. Boris Johnson describes it thus:

> The facts are overwhelmingly against you, and the more people focus on the reality the worse it is for you and your case. Your best bet in these circumstances is to perform a manoeuvre that a great campaigner describes as 'throwing a dead cat on the table, mate'...

The key point, says my Australian friend, is that everyone will shout "Jeez, mate, there's a dead cat on the table!"; in other words they will be talking about the dead cat, the thing you want them to talk about, and they will not be talking about the issue that has been causing you so much grief.

It is probably that Johnson's Australian friend was Lynton Crosby who has masterminded most of the Conservatives' recent election campaigns. His position with the Conservatives was controversial as, just weeks before his appointment as Tory election strategist was announced, Crosby lobbied a government minister against the introduction of plain packaging. The conflicting interests did not seem to worry David Cameron, however, and Crosby was awarded a knighthood in 2016.

The campaign against plain cigarette packaging is one that has seen lobbyist using all their skills. Newsagents have been funded by the tobacco industry to argue against the proposal, and the campaign had the support of the 'Common Sense Alliance', a body that sounds worthy enough, but which is funded by British American Tobacco. Similarly, Philip Morris International paid a former police officer to front a campaign linking plain packaging with tobacco smuggling. It is also known that BAT and Imperial Tobacco have funded the free-market think tank, the Institute of Economic Affairs, which the BBC has invited to talk on the issue without any mention of its financial links to tobacco.

Think tanks are useful to lobbyists in other ways too. When Patricia Hewitt, together with fellow former cabinet members Geoff Hoon and Stephen Byers, was secretly filmed by undercover reporters supposedly seeking lobbying advice, the former Health Minister suggested that: 'the think tank and the seminar route I think is a very good one and will remain a good one'. She advised finding a think tank with the right ministerial connections (Policy Exchange and Demos were recommended) which might run a seminar through which the client would get access to the minister.[4]

Some think tanks will provide companies with a lobbying package just as any public affairs company would: a media-friendly report, a Westminster event, ear-time with politicians.

Relationships with politicians and civil servants are of course essential for lobbyists. This is not to say that access always equates to influence but research on lobbying in the US suggests that knowing a senior politician can be worth £113,000 a year to a lobbyist.[5] Companies have also set up networking events to meet senior civil servants. The Guardian revealed that a company called the Chemistry Club ran invitation-only, £1,800-a-head networking events to allow senior corporate figures to meet ministers, MPs and civil servants that were billed as 'speed dating for executives'.[6]

Many of those engaged in lobbying are political insiders – people who have worked in politics, who know how the system works and who have the contacts to arrange the all-important access to ministers. As the Alliance for Lobbying Transparency puts it, 'You can only cook up deals once you are in the kitchen (the rest of us, incidentally, only ever see front of house)'.

Some politicians set themselves up as lobbyists once they leave office, using not just the understanding of parliament that they have gained and relationships they built while in office but also the parliamentary passes they still hold and their full access to the Palace of Westminster. A 2011 investigation by the Bureau of Investigative Journalists found a wide range of former MPs working for public affairs companies or with consultancies they have created themselves.

Alternatively former ministers can just go to work for the companies they used to regulate. There is a perception, at least, that decisions taken in government could be influenced by the reward of future employment. The concern is by no means new but the scale of such appointments is shocking. As of January 2016 over 25 former ministers in the Coalition government had taken jobs in the industries they regulated.

That the people we elect to represent us so often end up using the experience they have so gained to represent corporate interests has got to be a matter of concern: although there are some limitations on what former ministers can do for a period after leaving the cabinet, there is surely a case for tighter restrictions that apply to all politicians and their advisors.

Lobbying companies also foster relationships with the political establishment by employing friends or former staff members of relevant ministers. 'Holyrood Exposed', published by Spinwatch, Unlock Democracy and the Electoral Reform Society Scotland, outlined the links between former SNP staff and key lobbying agencies in Edinburgh.[7] Kevin Pringle, who until summer 2015 was the SNP's chief spin doctor, and Luke Skipper, their chief of staff in Westminster until June 2015, both joined lobbying firms.

None of this is to suggest that lobbyists are necessarily bad people. Honest lobbying is legitimate and may even lead to better decision-making. The problem, however, is that while politicians should be trying to represent their constituents, lobbyists are there to represent their clients and rarely will their interests coincide.

Early in 2010 election, David Cameron described lobbying as 'the next big scandal waiting to happen' and 'an issue that exposes

THE REFORM DEBATES

the far-too-cosy relationship between politics, government, business and money', and when it came to the 2010 elections, all major parties called for a statutory register of lobbyists in their manifestos. A bill was subsequently introduced in 2013 and the register became operational in 2015.

The register looks like progress, but is only progress on paper. All 'consultant lobbyists' are required to register and name their clients. However, although David Cameron claimed he wanted to 'shine the light of transparency' on lobbying, in the view of some the register provides only a small torch. Not only are consultant lobbyists not required to state who they are lobbying, on what issues they are lobbying and how much money they are spending on it, but in-house company lobbyists are not even required to register. Research conducted by the Association of Professional Political Consultants found that register would capture about 1% of lobbying interactions with ministers[8], and The Alliance for Lobbying Transparency went as far as to describe the register as 'a fake'.[9]

For real transparency, a much more comprehensive register is needed – one that focuses on the lobbying activity, showing us, for example, how much money each sector (oil or tobacco for example) spends on influencing. If the register is to be really effective it should include

- all lobbyists (in house as well as agency)
- who is being lobbied
- what policies they are lobbying on
- names of the lobbyists and whether they have held public office in the last 5 years
- how much they are spending on lobbying

Such a register would not bring inappropriate lobbying to an end but bringing lobbying out into the open is a crucial step towards controlling it: we need to know who are pulling the strings if we are to hold our elected politicians to account.

Who do they work for?

It's bad enough that our politicians, when they leave office, sell their experience to lobbyists and companies seeking government contracts, but there are others who sell their services even when they are supposed to be in parliament representing us. Research in 2014 found that 281 MPs registered earnings additional to their parliamentary salaries, and of 180 of these could be classed as having at least a second job.[10] There were 26 who earned more from directorships, paid employment or shareholdings than from their work as MPs.

MPs do not need to earn money to supplement their salaries. In the past 25 years their salaries have soared from 42% above the average income to nearly three times the average. They have salaries that most of us envy. Yet for some, it is not enough: Conservative MP and former minister, Malcolm Rifkind, on being caught offering his services for £5,000 a day, maintained that it was 'quite unrealistic' to expect an MP to exist on a parliamentary salary,[11] and Michael Heseltine argued in a BBC Newsnight interview that an MP's salary was 'not designed to be the total income of all MPs'.

In 2014, Mark Simmonds quit as the Africa minister in the Foreign Office because of the 'intolerable' pressure of needing to live on around £120,000 in salary and expenses.[12] After he left parliament in 2015, the committee which vets the job applications of

THE REFORM DEBATES

former ministers allowed him to take ten new jobs – three of them with companies he met while a minister.[13]

Some, however, attempt to justify their extra earnings on the grounds that work outside parliament gives them real world experience that enhances their effectiveness as MPs, and others argue that outside incomes make them less reliant on their MPs' salaries and therefore more independent of party whips. There is no evidence, however, to support either contention.

The danger with MPs having second incomes is that those who pay the piper may from time to time call the tunes. Companies employ MPs as directors or consultants because they are MPs – people who know the minds of governments and who have access to decision-makers. An MP on a company board provides not just a source of information but can effectively be an in-house lobbyist. Rather than making judgements about how to vote based on constituents' views and the needs of the country, there is a risk that MP-directors will also be guided by those who pay them, or at least will be perceived as having been so guided. For example, few will believe that Conservative, Tim Yeo, was not unduly influenced by the wishes of the energy companies of which he was a director when he chaired the Energy and Climate Change Select Committee.

A Guardian investigation[14] found six Conservative MPs, as well as over 60 peers, to be directors or have controlling interests in companies linked to tax havens. Thus, while there is public outrage over tax avoidance and while the government claims it wants to take action to end such practices, we have legislators who are engaged in it and benefiting from it.

CLEANING UP POLITICS

There are others whose second jobs do not so directly raise conflicts of political interests. The Conservative, Paul Beresford, for example is a dentist. However, there is still a risk that situations will arise when he needs to decide whether a patient's toothache or work for a constituent takes priority.

As we elect MPs to work for us, to work full-time for us, and to work exclusively in our interests, there is at least a good case for ban on second incomes, and, according to a YouGov poll in 2015, that is what voters want by a margin of about two to one.

Nevertheless, a survey by Unlock Democracy found that one in five of the new MPs elected in 2015 had second jobs, slightly increasing the overall percentage in the Commons. Although the SNP appeared to try to set an example by banning its MPs from being company directors or holding second jobs, in February 2016 it was alleged that one in four of its MPs had second incomes.[15] In its 2015 manifesto, Labour committed itself to going further by banning all MPs from holding paid directorships or consultancies. This policy, if it were ever implemented, would go a long way towards removing one of the holds that money has over politics.

Whether there should be a blanket ban on MPs having any additional earnings is, perhaps, less clear. When MPs agree to provide services such as writing articles, appearing in media programmes or speaking at conferences, there is an argument that they are effectively working overtime and it might be churlish to argue that they should not be rewarded in the same way as others. However, when the rewards are large and regular, there is a danger that financial attractions may tempt MPs to put more effort into seeking earning opportunities than into their constituency responsibilities. Diane Abbott's constituents may be pleased to see her on television from time to time, but some may raise eyebrows

THE REFORM DEBATES

at her being paid nearly £130,000 p.a. for her appearances on BBC's 'This Week' programme, and, until George Galloway's defeat in the 2015 election, voters in Bradford West had cause for concern over his £150,000 p.a. income from regular programmes on Iranian Press TV and the Beirut-based Al-Mayadeen TV.[16]

Labour's suggestion that MPs' outside earnings should be capped at 10 – 15% of their salaries might be a sensible compromise between allowing MPs compensation for occasional additional work they undertake and preventing outside work from impinging on parliamentary duties.

However, whatever the level of earnings, if MPs decide to take paid second jobs, it should be because it helps them become more effective MPs, rather than because being MPs help them do their second jobs more effectively.

The pitfalls of party funding

Not only is there a danger of money influencing the behaviour of some of our MPs, but it can also influence our parties.

Parties are large organisations. They need funds not just for elections but for maintaining their staff, offices and activities between elections. Labour and the Conservatives have turnovers of the order to £35 – 40 million, so they need to be fundraising organisations as well as campaigning ones. Membership subscriptions form a relatively small part of their incomes – most money comes from donations from wealthy individuals and companies, or, in the case of Labour, trade unions. Problems can arise, however, as major donors often want something in return for their contributions.

CLEANING UP POLITICS

Stuart Wheeler, who made his fortune in the betting business, donated £5 million to the Conservatives' 2001 election campaign. He was at least honest when, in 2010, he told the Committee on Standards in Public Life that 'a party is going to take more notice of somebody who might give them lots of money than somebody who won't'.[17] Most donors are a little more subtle, but it would be naive to believe that their motives in giving are always altruistic.

Perhaps the Conservatives would have opposed EU attempts to limit City bonuses even without donors, but that City firms contributing more than half of the party's income in 2010 must raise eyebrows, and it has been suggested that Chancellor, George Osborne, gave priority to cutting the top rate of tax because 'among those that give significant amounts to the party, it's a big issue'.[18] In 2014, the Bureau of Investigative Journalism estimated that attendees at a Conservative fundraising dinner were collectively worth at least £11 billion (an event at which the more you paid, the closer you got to the Prime Minister), and when hedge funds were exempt from tax duty in 2013, Labour research found that half of the richest hedge fund managers were Conservative donors.[19]

Labour has also had its scandals. When in 1997 it announced that Formula 1 racing would be exempt from a ban on tobacco advertising at sports events, it emerged that Formula 1 boss, Bernie Ecclestone, had donated £1 million to the party: it provoked outrage and the money was returned, but the reputation of the new Labour government had been tarnished.[20]

Tony Blair's fundraiser, Lord Levy was arrested and questioned by police in 2006 over allegations that he had offered peerages for large donations, although he was not charged (he may have seemed an odd choice as the Prime Minister's Middle East Envoy, but he had raised over £100 million for Labour). In

THE REFORM DEBATES

2012 the Conservatives' Treasurer, millionaire businessman Peter Cruddas, had similar difficulties: he resigned following allegations that he had offered access to the Prime Minister in exchange for donations of £250,000. Lord Strasburger of the Liberal Democrats was a casualty when he was filmed offering a bogus donor advice on how to get around the Electoral Commission's rules on the registration of donations.

Parties have been talking about how to regulate party funding for more than a decade, but nothing has been resolved. Discussions have focused on two approaches:

1. A cap on donations so that no donor has, or appears to have, undue influence over party policy; and
2. A reduction in the limits on election expenses so that parties do not have the same fundraising needs.

The main obstacle in debates over a donations cap has been how to treat the money Labour receives from the trade unions. If unions are regarded as 'major donors', then Labour is more dependent on large donations than the Conservatives. Treating unions in the same way as companies and millionaires would of course suit the Conservatives – cut off the unions' support and Labour would crumble – but it makes little sense. While large companies are controlled by their boards which must make profits for their shareholders, unions are, at least in theory, democratic organisations of working people. However, the questionable democratic credentials of some unions is a weakness in Labour's position: although Labour was created to give workers a political voice, too often union leaders, without consultation with their members, have used, or threatened to use, their power as donors to make demands of Labour leaders. Ed Miliband, when Labour leader, attempted to defuse the issue by changing the way unions affiliate to the party: instead of unions affiliating through a block donation and claiming voting rights based on the size of the donation, affiliation fees are now only accepted on behalf of union members who pay the political levy. It should have opened the way to any cap being applied to individual union members rather than to a union's total support, but the reform was not enough to unblock the discussions with other parties.

Following the 2015 election, the Conservative government introduced a new Trade Unions Bill which was still being debated in parliament in early 2016. The bill seeks to make it much more difficult for unions to call strikes by requiring a 50% turnout before strike ballots are recognised. For public sectors workers it goes further by requiring the support of at least 40% of those eligible to vote before a strike can take place. However, the bill is not just an attack on the unions but on Labour. At present union members can opt out of paying the political levy (which provides funds for political campaigning, including the support unions give to Labour), but if the bill is passed, members will need to opt in. Labour has estimated that the change could deprive it of around £8 million each year, and the government cannot be unaware of the consequences. The bill is not therefore just about union power, but an attempt by a governing party to cut the income of its principal opponent outside any wider, cross-party agreement on political funding.

If a cap were ever agreed, a decision would be needed on the maximum size of donation permitted. The Electoral Commission (in 2004) recommended £10,000, but a review in 2007 by Hayden Phillips commissioned by the then Prime Minister, went for

THE REFORM DEBATES

£50,000. When it came to the 2010 general election, all the major parties referred to the need for party-funding reform in their manifestos and the new government asked the Committee for Standards in Public Life to look at the issues again. The Committee recommended £10,000, noting that the cap:

> Should not be set so high that it fails to convince people that the concern about big money in politics has been properly addressed ... It also needs to be seen to be reasonably fair between the parties, and not set at a level which manifestly favours one of them because of the economic circumstances of their supporters.[21]

This latter point is an important one. If we want a democracy in which everyone has an equal political voice, we should not allow those who can afford £50,000 – nearly twice the national average income - to make such donations in support of their political objectives. Some may argue that £10,000 is also a lot of money, but it seems a much fairer balance between the right to donate and the quest for political equality.

Limits on election spending are important if we do not want election results to be determined largely by money. However, although at the time of the 2015 election, parties contesting all seats in Britain were allowed to spend nearly £19 million on their campaigns, no party came even near to the limit: the Conservatives spent £15.6 million and Labour only £12.1 million. Although the Committee on Standards in Public Life had recommended a reduction in the limit of 15%, in 2015 it would have made no difference. Unless there were a very drastic cut in the spending limits, which might be detrimental to parties' abilities to communicate with elec-

CLEANING UP POLITICS

tors, any reduction in limits is unlikely to reduce the dangers of parties being improperly influenced by major donors.

These figures refer to what parties spent, and were allowed to spend, centrally. There are also limits, however, on what candidates can spend in their constituencies. In December 2014, in spite of the ongoing debate on the case for reducing limits and against the advice of the Electoral Commission, the government increased these limits by 23%. Critics alleged opportunism, noting that the Conservatives had amassed a considerable war chest which they hoped to use in target seats. Whether or not the critics were right, as the Electoral Commission was created to distance decisions about the conduct of elections from MPs, ignoring the Commission and acting in a way that might have advantaged the governing party was surely an abuse of power. By the time of the election, the limits were typically around £35-37,000 in the 'long' campaign (roughly three and a half months before the dissolution of parliament) and £13–15,000 in the following 'short' campaign (the limits depend on the size and nature of constituency[22]), although few candidates spent anything near to these limits.

If donations to parties were capped at £10,000, they would suffer significant losses in income. In the period 2001-2010, their average losses would have been £12.7 million for the Conservatives, £14.7 million for Labour (£7.3 million if union affiliations were not capped) and £1.6 million for the Liberal Democrats.[23] It raises the question whether, if a cap were introduced, they should be at least part compensated by public funding.

Parties play an important role in our political system and an effective democracy needs effective parties. There are therefore grounds for giving them the resources they need to do their jobs properly. The principle of public funding for parties has already

THE REFORM DEBATES

been accepted – Policy Development Grants, totalling £2 million, are awarded to the parties to assist them formulating policies and preparing manifestos, and opposition parties receive 'Short' money to support their work in the Commons and 'Cranborne' money in the Lords and there is a similar system in the Scottish Parliament. For major elections, parties are given free television time for election broadcasts and the costs of mailing a leaflet to all electors.

Short money (named after Edward Short, the minister Harold Wilson's government who introduced it) was introduced more than 40 years ago to help opposition parties in their parliamentary work and its principle has had cross-party support. The anger at the government's announcement, in November 2015, that the amount would be cut by 19% was not therefore surprising. The Conservatives claimed their aim was to reduce the cost of government, but attempting to save money by taking funding away from their opponents was a hugely controversial move. Moreover, as the saving will be less than £2 million each year, the move appears to be more political than economic (and, as Hannah White has pointed out, the saving may be much less the costs of the new peers the government has appointed[24]). As with the rules for political donations, arrangements for the public funding of political parties should not lie in the hands of a single party: if possible there should be a cross-party consensus, or failing that oversight by an independent commission.

It is commonly assumed that public funding for parties would be opposed by electors who generally take a dim view of parties. Research by the Electoral Reform Society, however, suggests that is not necessarily the case: a poll they commissioned in 2014 found that 41% agreed that 'a politically-funded political system would be fairer than the one we currently have' and only 18% disagreed.[25] Moreover, while the public funding of parties in the UK amounts to only £0.36 per voter p.a., the average for EU is £3.25.[26]

In recent years there has been much debate over how a scheme of public funding might operate. Some have suggested an amount per voter in general elections (ranging from 50p to £3) and lesser amounts for votes in European Parliaments and devolved assembly elections. One objection to such a scheme, however, is that, as our present voting system encourages tactical voting, the party we vote for may not be the party we want to support. Others have proposed tax relief on small donations, but then there is the problem that not everyone pays tax. An alternative option that avoids these difficulties is for membership subscriptions and even small donations (up to, say £100) to be matched by state funding.

Whatever system might be used, the public cost might seem large – even 50p per vote in a general election would mean around £15 million – but it is not large when compared with the total costs of our democracy. And if it resulted in a politics free from the influence of big money, then it would be money well spent.

Nearly a century ago, H G Wells began his essay on proportional representation by remarking that:

> British political life resists cleansing with all the vigour of a dirty little boy.[27]

If we are to achieve a democracy which treats us all, rich or poor, as equals, then we must start cleaning up politics now, and with vigour. The measures discussed in this chapter – getting lobbying under tight control, ensuring that our politicians work for us and

THE REFORM DEBATES

only for us, and taking big money out of party funding – are not alternatives, but are all things that must be done to produce a cleaner politics.

---

[1] The authors are grateful to Tamasin Cave for her help in the writing of this section.

[2] There are around 4000 registered with the Association of Professional Political Consultants, but this does not include staff of all companies and organisations which lobby. In 2007 research by Philip Parvin estimated that 14,000 might be engaged in lobbying (*Friend or Foe: Lobbying in British Democracy*, Hansard Society, 2007)

[3] Tamasin Cave and Andy Rowell, *A Quiet Word: Lobbying, Crony Capitalism and Broken Politics in Britain*, Vintage (Penguin), 2015. Several examples in this chapter have been taken from this excellent book.

[4] Channel 4, *Dispatches* programme, 'Politicians for Hire', broadcast on 22 March 2010, quoted on http://www.powerbase.info/index.php/Patricia_Hewitt

[5] Jordi Blanes i Vidal, Mirko Draca and Christian Fons-Rosen, *Revolving Door Lobbyists*, CEP Discussion Paper No 993, Centre for Economic Performance (LSE), 2010

[6] Leo Hickman and James Ball in The Guardian, 25 January 2012.

[7] Tamasin Cave, *Holyrood Exposed*, Spinwatch, Unlock Democracy and Electoral Reform Society Scotland,.2015

[8] http://www.appc.org.uk/ti-report-lobbying-appc-view/

[9] http://www.lobbyingtransparency.org/westminster/

[10] Research by the Telegraph, reported in http://www.parliament.uk/business/publications/research/key-issues-parliament-2015/parliament-politics/mp-second-jobs/

[11] Channel 4 *Dispatches*, and Telegraph, 21 February 2015

[12] The Telegraph, 11 August 2014

[13] Tribune, 20 December 2015, and

[14] Guardian, 20 September 2012.

[15] Scottish Daily Mail, 1 February 2016

[16] Reported by Tom Moseley, BBC, 15 February 2015 (www.bbc.co.uk/news/uk-politics-31619780).

[17] Reported by Aditya Chakrabortty in The Guardian, 8 July 2013. Wheeler subsequently changed his allegiance and became Treasurer of UKIP.

[18] ibid

[19] *Political party funding: controversies and reform since 1997*, House of Commons Library (SN/PC/7152), 2015

[20] BBC News, *How the Ecclestone affair unfolded*, 22 September, 2000

[21] Committee on Standards in Public Life, *Political party finance: Ending the big donor culture*, 2011

[22] The limits are calculated as a fixed amount plus 6p per elector in 'borough constituencies' and 9p in 'county constituencies', recognising the additional costs of campaigning in semi-rural areas.

[23] Committee on Standards in Public Life, op.cit.

[24] Hannah White, *Short Money: cutting the cost of politics?*, Institute for Government blog, 27 November 2015

[25] Jess Garland, *Deal or No Deal*, Electoral Reform Society, 2014.

[26] Committee on Standards in Public Life, op.cit.

[27] H G Wells, Proportional Representation, in *The Fourth Year*, Chatto and Windus, 1918

3-3 Holding our politicians to account: reporting and recall

We elect our politicians to work for us, but what happens if we are not satisfied with the way they are doing their jobs? MPs are our agents at Westminster but what if, after being elected, they break the promises they made in their election campaigns, do not appear to be making the efforts they should to represent their constituents, behave badly, or even unlawfully? Democracy should not just be about elections, but about us being properly represented in parliament at all times, so we need ways in which we can ensure that our MPs (and of course our local councillors) are listening to us and working effectively on our behalf at all times.

Edmond Burke, the eighteenth century MP and political philosopher wrote that:

> It ought to be the happiness and glory of a representative to live in the strictest union, the closest correspondence, and the most unreserved communication with his constituents. Their wishes ought to have great weight with him; their opinion high respect; their business unremitted attention. It is his duty to sacrifice his repose, his pleasures, his satisfactions, to theirs; and above all, ever, and in all cases, to prefer their interest to his own.

Unfortunately it would be difficult to find many present-day politicians who show this sort of respect for those they represent. Although there are many good people in the Commons with a deep commitment to serving their constituents, there are too many who, once they have joined the exclusive club that is Westminster, pursue their own agendas (some worthy, some not), seek to advance their own careers, develop their financial interests and pay scant regard to what their constituents want. While it would be unreasonable to expect MPs to make the level of self-sacrifice suggested by Burke, we should at least be able to satisfy ourselves that they are doing what we sent them to parliament to do, and be able to take action if they are not.

Reporting to, and listening to, constituents

MPs do not have a formal job description but, if they did, it would probably include the following major headings:

- Acting as national legislators, taking account of the views of constituents and the manifestos on which they were elected;
- Holding the government to account, ensuring that it acts rationally, economically and in the national interest;
- Assisting constituents who raise problems which they have not been able to resolve through other channels.

How do we know if our politicians are effectively performing these tasks? Nowadays it is possible for constituents to access MPs' attendance records, to see how they voted on different issues, to see how often they contributed to debates and questioned ministers, but very few constituents are going to take the time to search for all this information. It is more difficult to find out whether MPs have been consulting constituents on their views, responding to

THE REFORM DEBATES

their letters and emails in a timely way, and efficiently dealing with casework issues. If we are to hold our MPs to account, we need to know what they have been doing.

There would appear to be a case, as some have suggested, for requiring MPs to report back to their constituents, perhaps every year. Having MPs themselves report on their performance would be like asking students to write their school reports, but a formal report produced by parliamentary staff on the statistics of an MP's activities – attendance in the House, voting record, contributions to debates and questions, and of course their expenses, in each case making comparisons with the averages for all members – perhaps accompanied by a commentary by the MPs themselves, would at least give constituents a basis for making assessments. Most staff in executive positions need to tell their managers what they've been doing, so it does not seem unreasonable to ask MPs to do likewise.

Some have suggested that MPs should also be required to report back in person at constituency meetings in which electors can question them on the work they have done and on the positions they have taken on policy issues. This would give constituents an opportunity not just to challenge MPs on the policies they have supported or opposed, but to have more dialogue with MPs in which constituents can express their concerns and MPs explain their actions. While the logistics of such meetings would require careful thought (for example on who would convene the meetings, and who would chair them to allow critics and opponents as well as supporters a fair hearing), the approach may go a long way in not just improving accountability but in building more trust and understanding in politics and in politicians as a class.

HOLDING OUR POLITICIANS TO ACCOUNT

Another option, proposed by electors in a Fabian Society organised discussion,[1] is a 'governing body' set up in each constituency after each election. This body might be formed in the same way as a jury: it would receive monthly reports from the MP and have the authority to decide whether the MP was fulfilling his commitments. Clearly there would need to be rules to ensure that MPs did not face governing bodies dominated by their opponents, but the proposal merits consideration.

Dialogue between MPs and constituents should not, however, just be based on what MPs have done – it should also be about what MPs plan to do. We want MPs to take account of constituents' views when speaking and voting in the Commons, but how do they know constituents' views if they don't ask? Should MPs not be required to advise constituents of important issues that are to be debated, inviting them to submit ideas and comments for MPs to consider beforehand? It would not of course be possible for MPs to consult on every debate, but when controversial matters are on the agenda, or matters of particular relevance to a constituency, it is difficult to see how MPs can take account of constituents' views when they have done nothing to ascertain them. Many MPs have websites which tell constituents what they have done, but few if any use their websites to ask what people think they should do.

Whatever an MP does, there will of course be some who are supportive and others who are dissatisfied. An MP cannot support the views of all constituents – on some issues there may be almost as many views as there are electors. Most reasonable people accept this, providing they are satisfied that their MP is at least listening to them and has been acting reasonably and in good faith. Burke,

THE REFORM DEBATES

having written in such passionate terms about how he perceived his relationship with his constituents (see above), went on to say:

> Your representative owes you, not his industry only, but his judgment; and he betrays instead of serving you if he sacrifices it to your opinion.

Burke was right. In a representative democracy such as ours, MPs are not delegates who simply carry out the instructions of their constituents but people who will weigh up the facts and the arguments and then, taking account of constituents' views, make their judgements on issues. It is unlikely that anyone will ever have an MP with whom they agree on everything, but what is important is that we can have a reasonable degree of trust in their judgement. However, judgements are made on the basis of values and MPs are elected as much on the values they profess as the specific promises they make, and we have a right to be critical if MPs appear to betray the values which they claimed would guide them in their work.

Recall

What should happen if constituents have legitimate concerns over the judgements or conduct of their MPs? Proposals for reports on MPs' work and for report-back meetings should give constituents some opportunity for expressing dissatisfaction and demanding that MPs change their behaviour or rethink their ideas, but constituents cannot dictate to their representatives. At present the most they can do is express their disapproval by voting for someone else when the next election comes (although with our voting system most MPs, provided they are not rejected by their own parties, are able to upset large numbers of voters with impunity). If, however, the level of concern over an MP's actions is acute, should people be required to wait until the next election, which may be several years away, or should they have other remedies?

In recent years there has been much discussion about the need for 'recall' procedures. The argument is that if a sufficient number of constituents are dissatisfied with their MP to the extent that they prepared to sign a petition calling for the recall of an MP, there should be a fresh election in the constituency. The MP in question may then be allowed to stand again for re-election, but if voters felt that there was someone better able to represent the constituency, they would be free to choose a new MP.

On the face of it, recall sounds very sensible. We want a form of politics in which people are 'sovereign', i.e. it is the views and wishes of citizens that should count most, and if they have grounds for wanting to change their representative, why should they not be able to do so? However, while the case for allowing constituents to recall their MPs is a strong one, in practice the circumstances in which recall is possible and the procedures to be used need careful consideration.

In a sense, constituents are, collectively, their MP's employer. All well-run companies have procedures for dealing with staff with whom they are dissatisfied. Employers can summarily dismiss a staff member for gross misconduct (although with appeal procedures for staff who feel unjustly treated), while for lesser transgressions the employer may impose sanctions giving the staff member an opportunity to change their ways. Employers can also dismiss staff for poor performance, but here good practice demands that there should be clarity over what is expected of the employee and a series of warnings before dismissal, together with

THE REFORM DEBATES

measures to help and encourage the staff member to reach the standards required. Then there is employment legislation, as well as employment tribunals, to ensure that staff have been treated fairly and that they have not been victimised for reasons unrelated to the complaints against them.

Although constituent-MP relationships and company-employee relations may not be strictly comparable, the analogy suggests that while a power of recall might be necessary, it should be the final remedy and only one to be used when other measures, such as the report-back procedures referred to above, have proved fruitless. There is undoubtedly a need for procedures for removing MPs who are guilty of serious wrong-doing or who have singularly failed to represent their constituents, but there is a danger that a focus on recall diverts attention from broader issues of accountability (after all, even good MPs need to be held to account).

The demand for a right to recall MPs was intensified by the expenses crisis of 2009. Many MPs were found guilty of submitting fraudulent or frivolous expense claims – some were prosecuted and many were required to repay claims they had made, but there was nothing that constituents could do to remove MPs who had acted improperly, or worse. In the run up to the 2010 general election, all three major parties included a right to recall in their manifestos, but they all restricted the trigger for a recall action to serious misconduct rather than to wider grounds for recall which many wanted to see.

After much wrangling between the coalition partners, a recall bill was eventually tabled in 2014. It proposed a recall mechanism when either an MP receives a jail sentence of a year of less (it was already the case that MPs lose their seats when jailed for more than a year) or when the Commons suspends an MP for at least 21 days. If these conditions for a recall are met, the bill allows constituents to demand a recall petition, and if more than 10% of electors support the petition then the seat is declared vacant and a by-election held (in which the former MP could again stand as a candidate).

Few would argue that constituents should not be allowed to recall MPs who are jailed, but proponents of recall savaged what they saw as the bill's weaknesses – the restriction of recall to cases where an MP is guilty of serious misconduct, and that decisions on whether a recall can be triggered is ultimately in the hands of MPs themselves.

This latter point is indeed a weakness. Before the Commons votes on the suspension of an MP, it receives a recommendation from the parliament's Committee on Standards. Although this body now has lay members, it is dominated by MPs – 10 out of the 13 members. Thus it is effectively MPs who pass judgement on their colleagues. Can we really expect MPs to be entirely objective when the MP in question might be someone of their own party, whose vote may be needed to provide a government majority, or who may have given support to a Committee member in Commons debates? No-one is selected for a jury if they have any personal or professional relationship with the accused, but the Committee on Standards is largely composed of people who are either political allies or opponents. If an MP has broken the law or the rules of parliament, constituents may not be the people best placed to weigh up the seriousness of the transgression, but neither are MPs. Surely we need a Committee on Standards which is, or is largely, composed of people who are not politicians themselves: perhaps a Committee consisting entirely of lay people, or

THE REFORM DEBATES

with only a small minority of politicians to help provide an understanding of the background to any case.

However, even if the Committee on Standards were independent of MPs, under the procedures introduced by the bill, the Committee's recommendation would still need to be approved by all MPs in the Commons. There is surely a case for arguing that if an independent committee were to decide that a recall should be allowed, MPs should have no further say in the matter and it should then be up to the MP's constituents to decide whether they want to demand the MP's recall.

There was much opposition to the bill, including from many at Westminster. A Conservative MP, Zac Goldsmith, led the opposition in the Commons, arguing that the bill would not empower voters in any meaningful sense and that it fell 'scandalously short of voter expectations'. Although the amendment he proposed was defeated, it received the support of 166 MPs.

Many opponents of the bill wanted to see 'full recall' – the right of constituents, and constituents alone, to demand a recall vote for whatever reasons they might have for wanting to replace their MP. Even if MPs are not guilty of serious wrongdoing in the narrow terms of the bill, if people have lost confidence in their MPs because of how they have voted or because of the constituency service they have given, should constituents not be able to call for a recall action? Only full recall, they argue, would put power back into the hands of the people.

Full recall, however, has its dangers. MPs, as we have noted, are not delegates, but representatives who are required to use their judgement in considering the arguments and facts presented in debates, and, of course, what they know about constituents' views.

HOLDING OUR POLITICIANS TO ACCOUNT

There will always be constituents who disagree with their MPs (and with our present voting system the number who disagree will often be a majority) and allowing recall actions simply because some don't agree with their MPs would introduce the risk of politically motivated recalls: an MP elected by a very slender majority might expect challenges from political opponents, particularly at times when the MP's party is doing badly in opinion polls, and a MP who challenges vested interests might find these interests conspiring to remove him or her. When only around a third of MPs were elected with a majority of the votes in their constituencies, the ability of constituents to challenge them at any time and on any issue would make many of them vulnerable to recall actions, and of course in constituencies where no party is clearly dominant there is no guarantee that any replacement MP would fare any better. Here we have an issue that requires serious debate: on the one hand, MPs should be accountable to their constituents and removable by them if constituents feel they would be better represented by someone else, but on the other an unfettered right to challenge MPs at any time may undermine the ability of MPs to get on with the job of representing us.

We also need to consider how recall would operate if we were to move to a more proportional voting system (or apply it to elections for tiers of government which use such systems). With a proportional system, MPs would be elected who represent minority views and full recall could give the majority an opportunity to deny a minority its representation.

A way forwards may be not full recall, but a recall system that recognises there are particular situations in which recall for reasons beyond 'serious wrongdoing' may be permissible. These could include:

THE REFORM DEBATES

- If an MP switches party. In general elections most people do not vote just for the MP but for the party the MP represents. They expect that by voting for the MP they are voting for the policies of the MP's party and in hope that that party will become the party of government. If they find they have voted for an MP who changes sides and consequently supports a different set of policies, it seems only fair that electors should have an opportunity to make a new choice.
- If an MP regularly fails to support the policies on which they stood in seeking election. Again, having voted for a party and not just for an individual, it is only reasonable to allow electors to replace the MP with someone who will do what they said they would do. The right of MPs to rebel must of course be respected but rebellion to the point of sustained opposition to their party might be grounds for recall. (Should Liberal Democrat MPs be subject to recall because they reneged on their 2010 promise not to increase tuition fees? Foolish though the promise might have been, circumstances in which promises made in good faith cannot be delivered probably do not merit recall, but again it is a matter for debate.)
- If an MP appears to be excessively engaged in lobbying unrelated to constituency interests of party policy. It is of course legitimate that MPs lobby for causes which are not part of their party's policies – it would be wrong, for example, to penalise an MP who spends time working for animal welfare – but those MPs who have been found to lobby for commercial interests, often with company directorships and consultancy contracts, should be subject to recall.

- If an MP does not appear to have attended to their duties. If an MP's attendance in the Commons is a cause for concern, or if the MP has made very little contribution to Commons debates, then there is an argument that the MP has not fulfilled the requirements of the job and constituents should have a right to recall them.

Representative democracy is likely to work better when there is a relationship of trust and respect between people and their politicians. If our MPs are regularly telling us what they are doing and why, and if they are providing opportunities for us to give them our views, our representation will be more meaningful. Our politicians must be accountable to us, but that accountability is best achieved through constructive engagement between MPs and their constituents. That is why the measures for feedback and consultation proposed in the first part of this chapter are important. Regrettably there may be occasions when trust breaks down and respect is lost, but even then the big stick of recall should only be used when other forms of remedial action have proved ineffective, and only in situations in which there is a clear failure by politicians to do the job they were elected to do.

---

[1] E Wallis and A Skrzypek-Claassens, *Back to Earth: Reconnecting people and politics*, Fabian Society, 2014.

3-4 Reforming the House of Lords

Damien Welfare

Reform of the House of Lords will not go away, despite most observers assuming it to be off the political agenda after the Conservative general election victory in 2015. Yet the future of the House of Lords comes back into issue every time there is a controversy involving the House.

In particular, every time there is a new round of appointments, there is controversy over the numbers. In late August 2015, the protests were lent colour by the scandal the previous month over the private behaviour of Lord Sewel, the former Deputy Speaker. This time, however, Conservative-supporting newspapers attacked the partisan nature of the list; of which the ruling party took 26 places out of 45, and which included serving and former political staff of the government, former MPs who had left the Commons after the expenses scandal, and significant donors to the Tory party. Writing in the Daily Mail, Quentin Letts said of the House: 'Today it looks like the Upper Chamber of a decayed, decadent Ruritania. The sooner it is abandoned, the better'.[1]

The reputation of the second chamber was damaged by both events. A second chamber with weakened credibility is not healthy for parliament. The second chamber is now playing a part in fuelling public cynicism with politics.

Yet a reformed second chamber could play a positive role in relation to many contemporary political issues. These include: the continuing uncertainty over devolution (especially in Scotland); English Votes for English Laws ('EVEL'); the devolution of greater powers and decision-making to English cities and regions; and, our possible relationship with Europe (if we remain members) after the referendum; as well as combating public alienation from politics and its perceived undemocratic nature.

This chapter will attempt to set out: why the Lords should be reformed; what a new House would be expected to do; and, how an issue which is often seen as a roadblock to reform – the need to preserve the primacy of the House of Commons – can be addressed. Finally, it will look at the possible composition of a new House.

Why should the Lords be reformed?

There are six main reasons why we should pursue Lords reform.

(i) Size of the House

The first is the sheer size and unmanageability of the present chamber. After the appointments in 2015, its size was expected to reach well over 800; larger than the House of Commons (currently 650; proposed to be reduced to 600), and vastly exceeding the size of the US Senate (100), the German Bundesrat (69), the Australian Senate (76), or the Canadian Senate (105) (the only other appointed second chamber in a Western democracy). Peers complain constantly about the lack of space and facilities, and the sheer difficulty of tabling questions or speaking in debates.

THE REFORM DEBATES

It is obvious that so many members are not necessary, and it follows that they cannot all be effective. This in turn calls further into question the legitimacy of the House.

(ii) Barrier to wider reform

Because it is so familiar, we tend to overlook the extent to which the Lords is an anachronism, and a continuing symbol of the country's unequal and undemocratic past. Its membership is disproportionately wealthy, based in London or the South East of England, and unrepresentative of the country as a whole. Its flummery and ermine robes (although the latter are only used on state occasions) hark back centuries, and define its popular image. Yet the present-day House matters because it performs an important series of functions, and exercises some real power.

It should concern us that the SNP refuse to make nominations to it; and that all living former Prime Ministers (Major, Blair and Brown) have declined to serve in it; as did Churchill and Heath. It should be a matter of debate in a democracy that, although it meets in public, the public has almost no part in its affairs. It should matter to us that, since its members are either appointed, or (uniquely in a democracy) members of an hereditary aristocracy, it is wholly distinct from the rest of the political system, because the public are not allowed to choose who should sit in it. If some part of a mature democracy is not to be elected, there should be some reason of overwhelming importance for this to remain the case; and the case for this state of affairs to continue should be subject to regular review.

Yet there is no such reason. The case for the Lords in its present form is pragmatic ('It is the best we can expect'), or historical ('It has always been like that'); but never principled ('It is better than other systems'). The nearest apologists come to a principle is when they argue that an elected second chamber would unbalance the two Houses of Parliament, within the UK's unwritten constitution. It is said, with an apologetic smile, that no-one would have designed it this way, but that somehow a British genius for evolutionary institutions has produced an unplanned model that works; and, that tampering with it would destroy a key check and balance in the system. It is a convenient myth. Even adopting a written constitution – highly desirable as it would be as an eventual outcome – would not be necessary to the reform of the second chamber.

(iii) Functions not performed effectively

It is often claimed that the House of Lords is doing a good job. The real position is mixed at best. While the House does much good work, overall it does not perform its functions as effectively as it should; mainly because of its lack of democratic legitimacy. It is difficult to prove a negative; indeed, there can be no definitive proof, since the same legislation or decision cannot be run twice through differently composed second chambers to compare how each performs. The evidence, however, is there in its structure.

First there is the simple fact that all other second chambers in advanced democracies, bar one (Canada) are wholly or largely elected. (Even the Canadian chamber is much smaller than the UK's, and has no hereditary members). If the others all start from a position of some democratic legitimacy in relation to the government chamber, and if this is thought to be necessary, the first question is why the UK should be different. On what basis is its second chamber believed to be effective, when it lacks the legitimacy of others?

THE REFORM DEBATES

Second there is the question of the powers of the Lords. An important function of a second chamber is to apply restraint to the main House on contentious issues. Second chambers vary in the extent of their powers to do this. The House of Lords has more substantial powers than most: it can delay bills, effectively for a year; vote down statutory instruments;[2] and even still exercise some financial powers. Yet these powers are rarely used, because the House knows that it has only limited legitimacy, and does not wish to call its actions into question.

Instead, it has evolved a range of lesser practices; using some of its powers in a very limited way, mainly on amendments to bills. It tends to choose small or medium-scale issues, or a partial aspect of a larger issue, on which to take a limited stand. Usually, if the government has been defeated on a bill, it will override the House summarily in the Commons, if necessary on the grounds that the Lords are unelected; whereupon the Lords normally concede. The Lords will usually only seek to resist further where it both has a very strong case, and it believes that public opinion is with it. Even then, it will usually put forward a lesser proposal than it originally passed. Only very rarely will it persist with its resistance to the point of a government concession; and generally, in such cases, some other factor (e.g. lack of Parliamentary time) will have proved decisive.

While it is important that the primary chamber should be able to prevail, it is significant that a process of debate and discussion between the Houses is seen as irregular, rather than one of normal give and take between two chambers, as in other systems. A government defeat in the Lords on a contentious issue is seen as a challenge to the government's authority. There is, moreover, no

REFORMING THE HOUSE OF LORDS

procedure to negotiate (e.g. in a committee of both Houses). Instead, the constant concern of the House not to over-use its powers in itself distorts how it approaches the issues in hand. What may appear to be a working system is in fact an accidental process, whose scope is defined more by expediency than rules, and which addresses legislative scrutiny through the distorting prism of whether or how it will affect the relationship between the two Houses. On more significant issues, in particular, the impact on the relationship –rather than the intrinsic rights or wrongs of the government's measure - becomes the defining question.

This undercuts the effectiveness of legislative scrutiny. The work of the Lords, whether in the revision of legislation, or in scrutinising the Executive, can generally be overridden by government, or politely ignored. Ministers and civil servants know that scrutiny in the Lords (while often more detailed than in the Commons) will be conducted away from the public gaze, in an unaccountable body lacking political legitimacy. Giving democratic legitimacy to the second chamber would lend its legislative and executive scrutiny greater weight within Westminster and Whitehall; resulting in better laws and decisions, and greater public understanding and acceptance of them. The weakness of the Lords also means that the UK, despite having a second chamber with extensive formal powers, actually has little in the way of an effective brake on extreme measures.

It might be argued that the votes on tax credits on 26th October 2015, which led the government to change its policy, show the effectiveness of the House. In fact, the votes underlined how rarely the veto power has been used (only the fifth occasion since 1968); and led to proposals to remove it. The debate at the time, and

THE REFORM DEBATES

since, has been more about the constitutional propriety of the House's actions than the issue itself.

(iv) *Rights of electors*

It is axiomatic that the members of the House of Lords represent no-one (despite attempts in the New Labour years to argue that peers from ethnic minorities, for example, or women peers, represented their respective communities; as though this were somehow determinative of their views). At the most basic level of democratic principle, reform would give voters the core democratic right to choose who scrutinises government and its legislation on their behalf. The denial of that right, without an overwhelming reason for it, underlines the extent to which we have lost sight of a fundamental principle: that power in a representative democracy should be exercised through persons elected by those whom they represent, who are accountable to the electorate. The stark fact is that voters in the UK have fewer democratic rights, in relation to their national parliament, than in almost all other democratic countries. None of the pragmatic arguments for an appointed House address this basic objection.

Electing the second chamber would not only give it democratic legitimacy, and make it accountable. It would also open it up to the electorate. Most of the present business of the House arises from interest groups who lobby the respective frontbenches, or individual peers. While lobbyists are active in the Commons too, many of the issues raised by MPs come from the experiences or concerns of their constituents. In the Lords, the issues rarely arise from individual electors, because peers have no constituents. The majority of them, moreover, are insufficiently in the public eye to

REFORMING THE HOUSE OF LORDS

be accessible to voters. Reform would open the second half of Westminster to the electorate.

(v) Voice for the nations and regions

The idea, which has grown recently, that an elected second chamber could be a voice for the nations and regions of the UK, is a new and stimulating development.

At a basic level (and one that should hardly need to be stated) electing the second chamber would ensure that all parts of the UK were equally represented in it. London and the South East predominate in the present House. Whether individual peers happen to come from Wales, Northern Ireland, the West Midlands, or the Highlands of Scotland, is wholly adventitious. Yet any parliamentary chamber should represent the different parts of a country, on at least a broadly equal basis.

More importantly, an elected second chamber could be given a major new function, at a critical time for the devolution settlements in Scotland, Wales and Northern Ireland; and when the English question, and devolution to city regions, are being driven by the Conservative government. An elected House of the Nations and Regions would enable the nations and regions of the country to be represented in a new way. In Scotland (if it remains in the Union), this could help to refashion the relationship. In Wales and Northern Ireland, the concerns of those countries – often remote from our general political debate – would be brought more directly into it. The second chamber could play a significant role in addressing emerging English nationalism, and give strengthened cities and city regions a national profile.

Some indications of how this could be done are outlined below.

(vi) A popular reform

The final reason for reform is that it is popular with the public; in itself, an indication that it should be taken seriously by politicians; and that ignoring it for short-term political advantage may contribute in some degree to political disaffection. A Survation poll for the Daily Mirror in July 2015, for example, found that just 12% supported the status quo. A similar poll in December 2013 found almost the same level of support for the present system of appointments (11.2%), while 76% wanted members to be elected to the second chamber for a fixed term. In the latter poll, furthermore, only 27% of voters believed that the House 'does a good job of representing Britain today'; while 54% did not. While few voters would place Lords reform at the top of their desired programme for government, there is plenty of evidence that voters see it as an 'of course' measure.

What should a reformed House do?

Most of the present functions of the Lords should continue to be roles of a democratically reformed chamber. It should still revise legislation, scrutinise government, and conduct select committee inquiries into long-term or non-partisan issues; all undertaken with a new democratic legitimacy. It should also continue to act as a constitutional 'longstop', with power to veto a bill to extend the life of a parliament.

It should add a wholly new function, as outlined above, of debating and focusing attention on issues affecting the nations and regions of the UK. Its present function, of scrutinising European legislation should (if the UK votes to remain a member) be significantly upgraded, to address what is currently an under-filled need in our present political arrangements.

House of the Nations and Regions

Second chambers in federal countries such as the United States and Germany have a core function of representing the interests of the states of the federation in national questions. The UK is not a federal country, although the devolution structures now applying to Scotland, and to a lesser extent in Northern Ireland and Wales, arguably already give it a quasi-federal character in those areas.

An elected second chamber, acting as a House of the Nations and Regions, could play a very important role. Unlike the House of Commons, which sustains the government of the day, it could play a representative role without the UK government (and thus the question of the government's view) being central to its debates. It could constitute a forum for the raising of common concerns across the UK; or specific concerns particular to a nation or region. Such a forum could enable economic prospects, levels and standards of public provision, and cultural issues, to be raised at one remove from the daily business of the UK government, and separately from the devolved institutions or any regional or local government bodies. The House could even, if desired, have a role in considering devolved as well as reserved matters.

As an example, the second chamber could have a function of considering the state of each nation, region or city region on an annual basis, perhaps developing through twelve-monthly reports and debates on each; comparing and assessing their economic performance, infrastructure, state of public services, and levels of individual well-being, in order to inform and enlarge debate at Westminster, and in the nations and regions as a whole. As a further example, national or regional select committees could scrutinise the likely impact of UK legislation (on non-devolved matters, or raising England-only issues) on the nations or regions.

If elected by proportional representation (for example, under STV or an open list system), the new House would be well-placed to reflect broad national and regional perspectives, and their diversity; reflecting party differences, but also going beyond them. The creation of a forum in which to debate national, regional and city regions' concerns across the country as a whole, in the context of the varied devolution arrangements in place, could provide a new way in which to focus those concerns, and to develop shared understandings between different areas; helping to bring the Union together, while respecting differences within it.

Leading EU scrutiny

The present House of Lords does undertake significant EU scrutiny, with a main EU Select Committee and six sub-committees examining policy and draft legislation covering Energy and Environment; External Affairs; Financial Affairs; Home Affairs; Internal Market; and, Justice. (The Commons also has a European Scrutiny Committee, examining the legal or political importance of EU draft legislation). Despite this scrutiny, however, most members of the public are not well-informed about European legislation or policy, or our relationship with the EU. Much EU business passes unacknowledged in political debate and press coverage in the UK; or (if controversial) becomes prominent only at a late stage of policy-making.

If the UK votes to stay in the EU, a more public and accountable process of scrutiny of European policies and proposals could form a key role for a more democratic second chamber, raising the level of political, media and public awareness. A more structured process of scrutiny of legislation could see a select committee of the second chamber holding hearings and reporting as a necessary stage of parliament's consideration of EU measures; perhaps before Ministers were able to seek a mandate from the Commons before a decision in the Council of Ministers. Such a role - again undertaken at one remove from the day-to-day business of government - would provide a regular source of information about the domestic implications of EU measures, and draw the significance of European policy to the attention of the UK electorate at an earlier stage. It would also assist MEPs to reach voters more easily, through providing more information, and helping to counter-act a sense of remoteness in this country from EU decision-making.

How can the primacy of the House of Commons be preserved?

The concern often voiced about Lords reform is that strengthening the second chamber, and specifically making it elected, would have the effect of weakening the primacy of the House of Commons. In particular, there is a fear that the second chamber could, if under different political control from the government of the day in the Commons, seek to block Commons bills, or to try to insist on major amendments, causing a legislative logjam. These concerns can be answered. Before doing so, we need to rehearse what the present relationship rests upon.

The primacy of the House of Commons rests on a mixture of legislation and conventions. Although the right of the Commons to secure key bills blocked by the Lords, after about a one year delay,

THE REFORM DEBATES

under the Parliament Acts is often referred to, this is only one aspect of primacy.

The first feature is that, under convention, the government of the day is chosen and maintained in office by the House of Commons, and remains in office provided it retains that confidence. The Prime Minister and the majority of Ministers sit as MPs. The Commons controls finance, partly by claiming 'financial privilege' (its right to take sole decisions on finance), and partly through restrictions on the Lords' powers over Money Bills (under the Parliament Acts). By a recent convention, a decision to go to war is dependent on a vote by the House of Commons alone (not of the Lords).

The restrictions on legislative powers in the Parliament Acts give the Commons control over bills first introduced in that House, after about a one year delay, and subject to the Commons re-passing the same measure, so that it can override the Lords after the delay.

The 'Salisbury Convention' ensures (in its modern form) that the government of the day gets its manifesto bills through the Lords without wrecking amendments (while allowing the Lords to pass amendments which do not change the manifesto intention). The "reasonable time" convention, which is often overlooked, ensures that the Lords consider and return government bills in a reasonable amount of time.

Also important in relation to exchanges between the Houses at the end of bills is the custom and practice (known as 'ping pong', and not strictly a convention) that allows amendments to be continue to be exchanged without losing a bill, unless both Houses vote twice for an amendment which has been rejected by the other,

REFORMING THE HOUSE OF LORDS

and neither offers an alternative (known as 'double insistence'). In practice, this gives a government with a Commons majority considerable scope to withstand objections from the Lords. It also allows the Lords plenty of scope to avoid a clash with the Commons.

With the amendments suggested below, these rules should continue in a reformed structure.

The main weakness of the Coalition Bill on Lords reform in 2012 (the 'Clegg bill') was that it did not address what the powers of the new House should be (apart from stating that that they would not be affected by the reform; and also belatedly clarifying that the Parliament Acts would continue to apply). The bill failed to show how the existing balance with the Commons, or some variant of it, would be carried forward under reform. A mechanism to do so, however, was prefigured in the report of the Joint Committee of both Houses on the draft Bill, chaired by the Labour peer, Lord Richard.[3] The report called this approach a "Concordat" between the two Houses. Labour's commitment to a reformed House of Lords in its 2015 Manifesto, based on its National Policy Forum report to the Party Conference in 2014, was similarly based on this concept.

A Concordat of both Houses

The objective would be for the existing Houses to agree on what the relationship should be under the reformed structure; and for this to become part of the reform package. If done by agreement, it would be expressed in joint (or identical) resolutions of the two Houses. (If the Lords did not agree, the relationship could be set out in the reform legislation; itself a powerful incentive to voluntary agreement).

THE REFORM DEBATES

The use of joint resolutions to form constitutional rules on the powers of the two Houses enjoys a very longstanding precedent. In 1704, both Houses passed resolutions limiting the scope of 'Parliamentary privilege' (ie matters on which the actions of parliament may not be called into question in any court). The resolutions said that neither House was to create any new privilege that was not already justified under arliament's existing laws or customs. This effectively established the boundaries of privilege, and prevented it from expanding. The resolutions remain in effect to this day, and form a convention of the constitution. In practice, neither House could now end or alter the convention without the agreement of the other.

Resolutions in the same area have been used more recently as well. In 2014, the Houses passed identical resolutions on the issue, in relation to Parliamentary privilege, of whether they should be bound by legislation that creates individual rights which could impinge on Parliamentary activities (and effectively clarified part of the boundary of privilege).[4]

The core proposal in this chapter is that the same mechanism could be used to secure Commons primacy as part of Lords reform. Identical resolutions of the two Houses (or short resolutions referring to a common statement) could describe in factual terms their respective status, roles, functions, and powers; state the main elements of the present conventions and practices; and, specify that, with certain changes, these would apply to both Houses after reform of the second chamber.

Thus the resolutions would: confirm the present conventions as to the role of the Commons in choosing and maintaining the government, and that the PM and senior ministers sit as MPs; confirm the maintenance of the Commons' privilege over finance, and note that the existing statutory restrictions on the Lords' powers over money bills would continue (although the second chamber might be allowed, as now, to discuss financial issues or public spending, but with no power to make decisions); note the continuation in statute of the Commons' right to insist on a bill after the one-year delay (which could also be extended to bills introduced in the second chamber); and, confirm that the Salisbury convention, and the conventions on decisions to go to war, and on reasonable time, would continue. The Salisbury convention should continue as an important statement of the primacy of the Commons, and of the decisions made by the electorate in a general election. The resolutions should also create a new joint committee of both Houses (the 'conciliation committee') to handle disagreements over amendments (see below). The same committee, or another, could review the relationship from time to time and propose any necessary changes to the operation of the Concordat.

In this way, a clear framework would be set out within which the new House would be expected to operate, which could only be changed by agreement between both Houses. It would represent a national decision that the Commons was to remain the primary chamber, chosen at a general election, which determined the government of the day, and which should ultimately prevail in a dispute. (In fact, it would set the conventions of this kind onto a stronger basis than at present, by making them express and explicit). The second chamber would have an expressly secondary role. The reform legislation, introduced after the process of considering the resolutions, would then give effect to them so far as necessary in statute (eg by re-applying the Parliament Acts). A feature which might appeal to parliamentarians opposed to a written constitu-

THE REFORM DEBATES

tion is that, while strengthening the conventions, the resolutions would not be subject to judicial interpretation.

Two aspects of the relationship were not covered in the outline above: the rules for 'ping pong', and the powers of the second chamber in relation to statutory instruments. Both should be changed, but these would be the only amendments necessary to produce a workable balance with the Commons.

On ping-pong, the conciliation committee could be brought into operation automatically at the point where 'double insistence' was reached (to avoid losing the bill); or, after a certain number of exchanges (e.g. four rounds of voting in each House), or a given period (e.g. one month). The committee could make recommendations to MPs (with written reasons), with the final decision on the outcome resting with the House of Commons. Once the bill had been amended to reflect this, it could be passed. In this way, the primacy of the Commons would be given practical effect.

In relation to statutory instruments, the House has sought to use its power of veto only rarely. When it does so, the argument invariably becomes one of whether it is proper for it to do so, more than the issue in hand. Indeed, the government now proposes to remove the veto in favour of a power effectively to ask the Commons to consider the statutory instrument again. Since the House has only been likely to attempt to exercise its veto on a major issue, it has had no effective power over SIs on less important matters (beyond passing a resolution expressing objections, which has no effect). The veto has thus been too drastic a power for use other than exceptionally. Rather than introducing a mere power to require the Commons to vote again, the veto should be replaced in a reformed House by a delaying power of three months; which could be used from time to time to ask the government to reconsider the matter during that period, while allowing it ultimately to prevail, without mounting a constitutional challenge. (There should also be a process enabling the Commons to vote again before the end of three months, in cases of genuine emergency).

How should a reformed House be composed?

A new House should be significantly smaller than the Commons. The Clegg bill originally proposed a membership of 300 (although increased to 450 in the light of a recommendation from the Joint Committee). A size of 300 would reduce cost, and be nearer to second chambers in other countries. France and Italy have larger second chambers of 321 and 326 respectively.

The new House should be wholly (100%) or largely (80%) directly elected by proportional representation (i.e. by the Single Transferable Vote, or by an open list system), with elections on the same date as either a general election or the European elections. The unit of representation should be the devolved nations, or English regions, as in European elections; or constituencies sufficiently large to represent (and be expressed as) recognisable sections of those nations or regions, including city region areas. As well as giving the new chamber the character of a 'House of the Nations and Regions', this would allow a sufficient size of constituencies to achieve a significantly proportional result and a proper spread of representation.

Indirect election from devolved assemblies, or city regions may be suggested, but it would not give the new House the legitimacy of direct election which it would need to carry sufficient weight with the Executive. Apart from the lack of such bodies at regional level in England, this system would also raise a continuing prob-

THE REFORM DEBATES

lem, that the members sent to the second chamber would have no mandate from the electorate on national issues; and no suitable forum to which to be accountable on such issues, since they would be outside the competence of their assembly, region or city region body. (In Scotland, if MSPs were sent to Westminster, the position would be further complicated, since they have a mandate on devolved matters, whereas the Second Chamber would be considering UK and reserved matters, either alone or in addition to devolved matters. Similar problems would arise in Wales and Northern Ireland). City regions in England, moreover, will themselves be indirectly elected bodies, made up of councillors from the different local authorities involved; and membership of the second chamber would thus amount to two levels of indirect election.

Those elected to the second chamber should be able to stand again, to preserve their accountability. If the term were 10 years, the House could be elected in halves, reducing the scope for major oscillations of political balance, and preserving a greater degree of continuity in the House. Another option could be elections in thirds, for a term of 15 years, although this length of term, proposed in the Clegg bill, might be seen as excessive. (It is obviously not conducive to accountability; as well as potentially limiting the pool of those willing, or young enough, to undertake it). An advantage of staggered elections would be the greater differentiation of the term and mandate of members of the second chamber from those of MPs. Otherwise, a term of five years. as in the Commons, would be the simplest arrangement. Ministers should be drawn from the elected members of the governing party or parties.

Whether to move to a wholly elected second chamber, dispensing with crossbenchers, is debatable. The disadvantage of appointed members is that they undermine to a degree the democratic nature of the second chamber. The advantages are that the new House would retain the benefit of independent expertise (although many crossbenchers do not fit this description), thus further differentiating the memberships of the two Houses; and also underlining the secondary nature of a chamber that was not wholly elected. In arithmetical terms, retaining crossbenchers would also make it more difficult for one party to command a majority; a longstanding objective in relation to the second chamber that has received cross-party support. The question of whether, in that situation, to retain a small number of bishops should perhaps be left for future negotiation. If an appointed element were to remain, however, terms should be limited to a single elected term (eg 5 or 10 years); and only demonstrably non-political experts in professional, scientific, artistic, or charitable fields, or others with expertise or experience in public life should be eligible. Former MPs should be excluded.

Conclusion

As we move as a society into an age with increasing expectations of choice, individual rights, and democratic entitlements, the UK both needs and deserves a second chamber that reflects these assumptions. The House of Lords reflects the patriarchal structure of a former age. The time is right to move belatedly towards full democracy at Westminster, and to pioneer a new type of second chamber which meets the needs of the UK in the twenty-first century.

THE REFORM DEBATES

[1] Daily Mail, 28th August 2015

[2] Until the veto is removed by the Conservative government, as recommended by the Strathclyde Review (December 2015), following the vote on tax credits in October 2015.

[3] Joint Committee on the Draft House of Lords Reform Bill, Report, Session 2010-12. HL Paper 284-1; HC 1313-1. It supported a Concordat agreed with the reformed House, rather than the existing one.

[4] Official report (HL), 20th March 2014, col 345; Official Report (HC), 8th May 2014, col 357

3-5 Politics and the media

Professor Chris Frost

If democracy is to work, if government of the people for the people is to have real meaning then it is crucial that citizens are well informed, are able to question those in authority and debate the important issues of the day in order to help them to choose a government and cashier them if they fail to carry out their wishes.

Democratic systems vary around the world, as do voting systems, but without a mechanism allowing voters to be informed about what the government is doing, and a process for discussing their plans, there is no true government of the people. The right to free expression and opinion allows for discussion and consultation before decisions are made. It enables citizens to suggest ideas, start petitions and, when the decisions are finally made, it allows for criticism both of the final plans and their implementation. The right to be informed ensures that governments and others keep us informed of what they are doing in our name.

There are plenty of countries around the world that do not have democracy and in all of them free speech is either limited or non-existent. After all, what's the point of allowing free speech if no notice is to be taken by the leadership of the views put? It merely sows discontent and potential rebellion.

Freedom of opinion and the right to free expression are vital because they allow for every citizen to have an equal right to say

THE REFORM DEBATES

how they would like their environment and community to be run. By coming together to discuss ideas and then elect leaders who will implement those favoured by a majority society is able to find a path that is agreeable or at least acceptable to most of its members whilst giving those who disagree the opportunity to put and argue for their minority view. This is important for two reasons: first, each person has an equal right to put their viewpoint. No one person's view should be given more significance merely because they are richer, more influential or by fortune of birth. Secondly, as John Stuart Mill identified, '...if any opinion is compelled to silence, that opinion may, for aught we can certainly know, be true... and though the silenced opinion may be in error, it may, and very commonly does, contain a portion of the truth'.[1] Failure to debate and discuss may mean missing the right path. More importantly perhaps as Mill goes on to say, if things are not regularly challenged they become simply dogma: 'the meaning of the doctrine itself will be in danger of being lost, or enfeebled and deprived of its vital effect on the character and conduct: the dogma becoming a mere formal profession.' We often do things a certain way simply because we've always done them that way, not because that is the best way to do them and challenging debate is the best way to move forwards. Discussion and debate are crucial to building a society that has the goodwill of the majority of its members and remains forward looking and fully able to take advantage of its opportunities whilst remaining able to debate and maintain the standards on which its humanity depends.

Media freedom is an extension of personal free expression. If we all have the right to free expression in our day to day lives then of course we have the right to free expression through the media

POLITICS AND THE MEDIA

whether that is publication in a newspaper, a TV or radio broadcast or the newest technology of the internet and social media. Not only are we entitled to express our ideas and opinions through the media, but we also have the right to be informed. This right to be informed implies a duty on behalf of government but also on the media to ensure that information is passed on to the public. This duty for the press means that alongside its right to make money as a business selling information and entertainment it has an obligation to keep the public informed about matters of public interest, concern and debate. It is this obligation to inform that sits alongside the media's right to free expression and right to make money through the legitimate business of selling information that underpins many difficulties of the regulation of the media.

Changing technology over the past twenty years means that every citizen now has the opportunity, cheaply and as a matter of course, to act as a publisher, broadcasting their views into the public sphere for all to read or view if they wish. Social media allows us all to tweet, blog and Facebook to groups of people large or small about anything we wish. Of course we can't oblige them to take any notice but it doesn't take long for the average activist on social media to get several hundred followers and some attract many more. However, few of these micro-publishers are intent on doing anything more than expressing their opinions or involving themselves in debates about local issues. There are now a number of community systems that allow people in discrete geographic areas to discuss issues of purely local concern: a new supermarket, changes in local parking regulations and a new road layout have been recent debates in my own area. There is no expectation from anyone that anything people write on these sites is anything other than their opinion. Whilst the laws of defamation and other limits

THE REFORM DEBATES

apply there is no expectation that these micro-publishers should behave responsibly, checking their accuracy or distinguishing fact from comment, nor does there need to be. Hardly any micropublishers are publishing for gain, they are merely seeking the advantages of scale previously the sole province of the mass media in order to develop their personal right to free expression. Lord Justice Leveson addressed some of these issues in his Inquiry into the Culture, Practices and Ethics of the press when he was challenged by mainstream media who claimed that widespread publication on the internet made his inquiry into journalism ethics irrelevant. He told them:

> …the internet does not claim to operate by any particular ethical standards, still less high ones. Some have called it a 'wild west' but I would prefer to use the term 'ethical vacuum'. This is not to say for one moment that everything on the internet is therefore unethical. That would be a gross mischaracterisation of the work of very many bloggers and websites which should rightly and fairly be characterised as valuable and professional. The point I am making is a more modest one, namely that the internet does not claim to operate by express ethical standards, so that bloggers and others may, if they choose, act with impunity.[2]

This is an important distinction between the mainstream media publishing for financial gain and the micro-publisher who puts out matters of direct interest to themselves as and when the mood takes them.

Whilst a reading of many British tabloids might suggest otherwise, there is not an editor of a newspaper, magazine or broadcast programme in the UK who would admit to publishing material they know to be inaccurate, false or misleading. All would claim to be acting in the public interest, providing their readers or viewers with accurate, up-to-the-minute information to help the make sense of their lives, communities and futures. Paul Dacre, Managing Editor of Mail newspapers told the Leveson Inquiry that one of his core functions was to '...ensure that our journalists understand and comply with the highest professional standards.'[3] However, for a variety of reasons including reducing staff, limited time and resources false stories do get into newspapers and often take on a life of their own, being accepted as fact regardless of the evidence; what Nick Davies describes as *Flat Earth News* in his excellent book of the same name[4] and Christopher Booker and David North describe as Media Scares.[5]

A media free and responsible?

A free media, able to take up all the advantages of the personal right to free expression along with the obligation to pass on accurate information implied by the right to be informed, needs to be independent, beholden to no person or special interest group and certainly not at the beck and call of any government or authority. Paul Dacre told the Leveson Inquiry:

> ...I would argue that Britain's commercially viable free press, because it's in hock to nobody, is the only real free media in this country. Over-regulate that press, and you put democracy itself in peril.[6]

He is right of course, if somewhat disingenuous. What he fails to identify is that the very nature of a commercially viable press is it that immediately risks putting itself in hock to several groups: advertisers, proprietors and shareholders. It is here that we start to

THE REFORM DEBATES

see the problems facing a free media in the UK. Ownership puts its own pressures on a media that is commercially based. James Cameron, writing about the death of the *News Chronicle* as far back as the 1960s said:

> Here is the most insoluble problem of what we fulsomely call the free press: how is it possible to equate the commercial success that is indispensable to a liberated paper with the business interests that will always encroach upon that liberation?[7]

Ownership of media generally falls into three categories. First there is commercial ownership where the publication or broadcaster is owned by an individual or company. This allows money to be made, usually through purchase, subscription or advertising. All depend on high readership or viewing figures from an appropriate market segment. This dependence leads editors to choose stories for their attractiveness to the market rather than their significance and also tempts them to behave less responsibly as they pursue sensational stories produced at the lowest cost possible. Complex investigations of government policy for instance tend to attract low audience numbers and, whilst those audiences are more likely to be people with higher disposable incomes and therefore be more attractive to advertisers, there are so few of them that the high cost of production tends to limit them to the quality newspapers that specialise in providing that type of readership. More entertaining, gossip and celebrity-based stories are much cheaper to produce, often provided free by the celebrity's press agent, and yet despite their ease of production, they attract large audiences. They do little to add to the public-sphere debate about issue, events and policies (although they may have something to

POLITICS AND THE MEDIA

say about the moral and cultural standards of society) yet are popular with the public. Of course popularity is an important measure, free expression does not depend on the worthiness of what is being discussed in the public sphere. We are all equally entitled to discuss and debate whatever interests us, but it would be wrong to suggest that commercialism does not influence the mass media's decisions about what to publish. The same is true of the mass media's choices even when reporting issues, events or policy discussions because the choice of stories and the line taken through those stories by a commercial publisher is likely to be heavily influenced by the dominant political ideology; capitalism in the case of the UK. The majority of the news media in the UK is politically central or right wing because that is the system in which it operates. There are also the private whims of the proprietor of course. Wealthy press barons who have easy access to politicians and world leaders are unlikely to seriously oppose a status quo they have helped build and they often ensure their newspapers take a similar view.

The second category of ownership is public service. This largely concerns broadcasting in the UK with the BBC as the major player. The BBC, the world's biggest news organisation, is funded from the licence fee, a near-universal annual payment made by UK households. It is set up under a Royal Charter that gives it independence from the government although the government does get to appoint, through an appointments panel, the trustees who run the BBC. The Royal Charter, agreed by the Privy Council sets up the conditions under which the BBC works and this means pressure can be brought to bear from the government. At the time of writing the present Royal Charter is shortly due to be renewed and the government has made it clear that it will seek significant

THE REFORM DEBATES

changes that will place some limitations on the way the BBC operates in the future. Public Service Broadcasting in the UK is likely to see significant change over the next few years.

The third method of ownership is community or crowd-funding or cooperatives. This type of ownership is so far limited to small-scale, community internet or printed newspapers. Often it is a mix of cooperative ownership with additional funding from the local community. With a number of 'owners', all with a small stake in the operation, there is little direct influence but such publications are still commercial and need to make money through subscription or advertising with the problems that these bring. This is a relatively new idea but with savage reductions in traditional editorial staffs, particularly in provincial newspapers, and a number of newspapers closing, it is a method of keeping local news alive that is gaining ground.

Whatever system of ownership drives a particular publisher or broadcaster there are elements about its ownership and control that will influence how it presents the news. Another influence that is guarded against very strongly in the west is government control. Governments can limit what can be broadcast or published in a number of ways starting with censorship, running through licensing to more subtle controls such as limiting access to information. Censorship is rare in western liberal democracies, but many have limitations on what can be broadcast or published, usually in the areas of harm and offence. Hate speech, discrimination, content that is considered damaging to children and matters of cruelty, violence, religion, sex and nudity that are considered offensive or even harmful are often areas limited by law, with obscenity and blasphemy laws introduced to make offensive items illegal.

Licensing of publications, broadcasters or journalists is less rare, even in the west. Many Western countries, partly at least because there are still a limited number of channels even with digital broadcasting, still license channels for broadcast, often with a requirement that the broadcaster is a fit and proper person and with the power to remove their license (franchise in the UK) if they breach content regulations. Some countries, Italy is one, license their journalists in the same way that doctors and some other professionals are registered in the UK. That is not widespread in the west with most countries taking the view that this would be counter productive and that journalism should be 'the exercise by occupation of the right to free expression available to all citizens'[8] Of course in some non-democratic countries, government control is even more draconian involving prison or even torture and death for journalists or editors who step out of line. The International Federation of Journalists reported that 120 journalists were killed as targets in 2014 with a further 15 accidental deaths.

Of course in any democracy, the people, through parliament, can decide that there should be limits on what can be published or broadcast. There need to be protections of people's private rights; freedom of expression is not absolute. I shouldn't be allowed to tell lies about you, make up stories or reveal every minute detail of your private life just because I have free expression and could make money by so doing. Most countries, if not all, have laws of defamation to protect people's reputation. Privacy is often protected to a greater or lesser degree and in the UK the right to a fair trial and to be presumed innocent until proven guilty are also strongly protected by law. There have also been attempts in the

THE REFORM DEBATES

UK to introduce laws demanding accurate reporting and granting a right or reply but these have all failed in favour of having a regulatory system that takes responsible reporting out of the legislative framework leaving it in the hands of a regulatory body.

Because of the historical development of broadcasting in the UK, its regulator, Ofcom, is a statutory body enshrined in the Office of Communications Act 2002 and the Communications Act 2003. Ofcom is obliged to ensure that programmes deal fairly with participants and do not unduly intrude on privacy. It can also take complaints about accuracy and harm and offence. Broadcasters that breach the broadcasting code can be fined or even have their license suspended or removed.

Publishers in the UK on the other hand have fought tooth and nail to keep a system of self regulation. This allows them to set up a regulator and draw up its constitution, rules and code of practice. A self-regulatory body ensures there can be no government interference as the regulator answers only to those who set it up and pay for it. However, its weakness is that it is bound to play to the lowest common denominator. It can only work well if all publications adhere largely to its code and follow its rules. If those rules become too tough for some publishers to accept, they will leave which means the industry is no longer regulated, even if some publications remain in membership. Newspapers are not like other products where the consumer might choose to buy from a trade-body protected supplier as that might give them some redress should things go wrong. Trade bodies exist in a number of fields to give some guarantees of quality and protection for the consumer. However, despite a call for a 'kitemark' for newspapers adhering to the code, it is unlikely that would affect consumers.

Consequently the publishers' regulator tends to do the minimum possible.

This is the clear story of press regulation in the UK since the first General Council of the Press that was set up in 1953. Criticised regularly from that date it finally made some changes, including a name change to the Press Council in the sixties. A further change of name and direction to the Press Complaints Commission was made in 1990 but despite getting praise from publishers for years, it was quickly scrapped during the Leveson Inquiry, with many witnesses exposing its failings, and then replaced with the Independent Press Standards Organisation in 2014, another body beholden to the publishers who had decided that Leveson's recommendations were a step too far. Leveson had recommended self regulation but with an additional, statutory body that had the sole job of verifying that any new regulator matched agreed criteria. The publishers claimed this was tantamount to statutory regulation, despite the fact that the verifier would not have had the power to instruct newspapers not to publish or even deal with complaints. Consequently IPSO will not be applying for recognition by the Recognition Panel set up by parliament to verify compliance of any regulator with a royal charter.

Duties of the media

The media, whether commercial public service or other, has a number of obligations if it is to claim the right to free expression and the right to inform on which it is based. Whilst any news provision is bound to be partisan in favour of the editor's understanding of the publication's readership, an editor can hardly claim the right to inform (as opposed to the duty) if that informing is so selective as to be misleading. A publication needs

THE REFORM DEBATES

to inform the public responsibly about matters that are significant to them if it is to claim it is acting in the public interest.

How the UK media matches up

The UK news-based media should be central to a healthy democracy providing citizens with the information they need to make their decision about political policy and their voting intentions but does the UK media match up? Broadcast media, particularly public service broadcasters, provide a good alerting system through several news bulletins a day. They also carry a number of programmes examining politics, although these are mainly outside prime time viewing and listening on Sunday morning or late evening. Associated websites also carry a good range of support material such as interviews and analysis.

Newspapers are more mixed in their ability to provide a range of quality information, analysis, opinion and comment. A growing concentration of ownership has had its effect on the news carried. One of the purposes of the 1947-49 Royal Commission on the Press was to examine concentration of ownership. At the time it did not find a serious problem, but since then, only 60 years ago, the number of newspapers has fallen dramatically and the number of owners has reduced to a handful. Approximately 90% of newspapers in the UK are owned by ten companies with five of those owning the biggest share of these. This means that in most towns, the newspapers are owned by one company. Indeed, after years of wheeling and dealing, some of the companies own all the newspapers in large swathes of the country offering no competition at all. This does not encourage the provision of a prime service in an industry that is suffering dramatic losses in its traditional revenue streams as advertising moves to the internet for such staples as cars, classified ads, property for sale and situations vacant. Revenues for local and regional newspapers have plummeted.

National newspapers have not been so badly hit by reductions in advertising revenue but their reliance on purchase revenue has been hit with falling sales directly affecting profits. Reducing profits has led to cuts in staffing which of course risks reducing the newspaper's ability to provide news people want to read. This has tempted many newspapers to become even more gossip oriented. It is much cheaper to print celebrity gossip provided by a PR agency for free than to pay for a reporter to sit in a courtroom, or political arena never mind sending them halfway around the world to cover a disaster that could be picked up from an agency or local stringer. Researchers at Cardiff University identified for Nick Davies that 70% of the home stories in the most prestigious national newspapers came directly or indirectly from newsagencies, usually the Press Association.[9] This means that most of the newspapers were carrying very similar stories, many of them driven by press releases sent to the Press Association and all of them driven by public events or information that were open and available to all – news that someone somewhere was keen for others to know about and very far from Lord Northcliffe's definition of news: 'News is something someone wants to suppress. Everything else is advertising.'

So if ownership is a problem and a serious influence on media freedom, how does the industry face up to regulation, ensuring codes of professional conduct are upheld?

THE REFORM DEBATES

Regulating for a responsible press

One of the slightly surprising elements of the Leveson inquiry was that whilst editors expressed their shock at the phone hacking scandal and were quick to announce the closure of the PCC, they still told Leveson that they wanted and needed regulation – on their terms - but regulation none-the-less.

Similarly, whilst there are a number of broadcasters who complain about the regulation of the statutory body, Ofcom, there are far fewer who would significantly reduce its powers and hardly any who would scrap it. Broadcasters are the most tightly controlled sector of the news-gathering industry. Ofcom is obliged by the Communications Act to draw up a broadcasting code that requires fair treatment and accuracy and sets standards for harm and offence. Ofcom polices this code and regularly reprimands and even fines broadcasters who fail to measure up and so compliance is taken seriously. Even so Ofcom levies fines totalling several millions of pounds every year although these are mainly about advertising infractions. Programme complaints normally concern entertainment programmes with complaints about bad language at a time when children may be viewing or listening the typical complaint.

Most newspapers and magazines are members of the new press regulator the IPSO. It says on its website that:

> IPSO is here to serve the public by holding publications to account for their actions. We will strive to protect individual rights, and by upholding high standards of professional conduct, will help maintain freedom of expression for the press.

POLITICS AND THE MEDIA

The editors' code of practice that IPSO polices obliges publications to report accurately and to distinguish comment from fact. It also protects individual rights such as the right to privacy, the right not to be harassed or discriminated against and the right of children to be protected from intrusion. The key question then is whether IPSO has sufficient power and goodwill to do what it claims to do.

IPSO has been running for a little over a year at the time of writing but has already considered 260 complaints, 58 of which it upheld. Its predecessor, the PCC, operated in a different way conciliating many complaints but it adjudicated 1,224 complaints over its 25 year history, an average of 49 a year of which it upheld an average of 21.[10] Interestingly one of the most vocal supporters of the IPSO and the PCC and strongest detractor of the Leveson Inquiry was DMG Media Editor in Chief, Paul Dacre, who is chair of the editors' code of practice committee. Despite this, his *Daily Mail* and *Mail on Sunday* newspapers racked up far and away the most number of complaints dealt with by the PCC and are busily repeating this with the IPSO. Only the Sun newspaper came close to the Daily Mail's total of 803 complaints considered by the PCC with 495 (the *Mail on Sunday* had 252). Most other nationals were in the 145-184 range whilst regional and local newspapers rarely reached double figures with many never troubling the PCC or IPSO.

It is doubtful that IPSO will fare better than its predecessor. Whilst it is a tougher organisation, able to investigate and monitor the industry and even fine reckless newspapers, it is simply not sufficiently independent to survive a major press scandal nor has it shown itself willing enough to take the leadership required to improve standards.

THE REFORM DEBATES

A free press is vital to democracy, but an unethical and irresponsible media is not a free press, merely one that is in hock to a different range of pressures to those facing the media in non-democratic countries. Gaining a truly free and independent media that provides information that people need and entertainment that they want that is gathered and published ethically and responsibly is a difficult political ball to juggle but its mastery is essential for democracy.

---

[1] John Stuart Mill, *On Liberty and Other Essays*. Oxford University Press, Oxford 1991

[2] Lord Justice Leveson, *An Inquiry Into The Culture, Practices And Ethics Of The Press: Report*, The Stationary Office, London. 2012 (p736)

[3] Ibid.

[4] Nick Davies, *Flat Earth News*, Chatto & Windus, London, 2008.

[5] Christopher Booker and Richard North, *Scared to Death: From BSE to Global Warming: Why Scares Are Costing Us The Earth*, Continuum: London, 2007.

[6] Leveson, op cit.

[7] Davies, op cit.

[8] Geoffrey Robertson, *People against the Press*. Quartet, London, 1983

[9] Nick Davies, op cit (p. 74)

[10] Chris Frost, *Journalism Ethics and Regulation* (4th edition) Routledge, London 2008) 335-339)

3-6 Broadcasting reform in an age of digital communications[1].

Professor Tom O'Malley

The British Broadcasting Company was founded in 1922. It was a private company the members of which were brought together by the government of the day to solve the problem of how to establish radio broadcasting to the UK. By 1926 the government turned it into a public corporation funded by a licence fee payable by owners of radio sets. The legal instrument under which it operated, and has operated since, was a Royal Charter.[2]

Almost a century since the foundation of public broadcasting in the UK, it is possible to note two important and recurrent factors shaping its development. The first is rapid technological change, from radio in the 1920s to mobile computing today. The second is the central role governments have played in shaping the form and purposes of broadcasting. Successive governments have provided the framework within which, BBC radio and television, Independent Television, commercial radio, and latterly satellite, digital and computer based communications operate.

This chapter focuses on the issues raised by the policy frameworks within which broadcasting and latterly digital communications have developed. It discusses the nature, strengths and shortcomings of these policies. The chapter opens by providing some historical context and then notes the dramatic shift in government policy towards communications that took place in the

THE REFORM DEBATES

1980s. It then raises a series of issues relating to the ways in which broadcasting is regulated. It argues that, since the broadcasting and mass communications industries are of central importance to the political and cultural health of our democracy, they should be much more accountable to the public than they are presently. It also argues that there should be a robust legislative framework in place to promote diverse content, which is made available to the whole population, across a range of platforms.[3]

Some History

The UK does not operate a system of pre-publication censorship for newspapers, books and magazines. It does, however, have many laws and regulations which frame the environment within which printed material can be produced legally. These include laws relating to official secrets, race relations, equal opportunities, criminal justice, terrorism and contempt of court. There has also been a strong tradition in the UK arguing that, on matters of standards such as accuracy and privacy, the press should be regulated by statute.[4]

These laws and regulations evolved because governments and members of the public were aware of the power the press exercised on public opinion. So, when radio broadcasting became a possibility in the first two decades of the twentieth century it is not surprising that governments, believing it could, like the press, have important economic and social consequences, established a tradition of regulating the new medium. In particular, the view that the press was far too commercial and partisan shaped the idea that the BBC should not rely on commercial funding and should be required to treat matters of public controversy in a balanced and impartial manner.

From 1926 broadcasting was regulated by a Royal Charter, which created a Board of Governors, laid down the BBC's responsibilities and established the power of the government to intervene to ban content if it felt it necessary.[5] This power still exists. The 1954 Television Act established a system of regionally based advertising funded television, overseen by an Independent Television Authority, with a strict separation imposed between advertisements and content and obligations to be impartial on matters of public controversy. Both the Board of Governors and the ITA were peopled by appointees of the government who, up to the 1990s, were meant to represent broadly a variety of geographical and social constituencies. A similar model was established for commercial radio when it was set up in the 1970s.

The result was the development of a diverse and creative form of broadcasting, with public service at its centre, producing content that was very popular and often of a high quality. Yet there were voices critical of the system. The Left argued that broadcasting was run in an elitist fashion, paid insufficient attention to the range of social and political views in society, and its coverage of key issues such as Ireland and industrial relations was biased in favour of the government and employers.[6] The Right argued that state regulation, in the form of the Royal Charter and broadcasting legislation, which laid down the requirement that broadcasting should be a public service, inhibited the market, fostered censorship, promoted economic inefficiency, was biased towards the Left and, some argued, contributed to a decline in moral standards.[7]

THE REFORM DEBATES

Direction of policy post 1986

The election of a Conservative government in 1979, committed to cutting back the welfare state and promoting market forces, changed the framework within which broadcasting and, eventually, digital communications operated. Following the publication of the report of the *Committee on the Financing of the BBC* in 1986[8], which advocated organising communications, not as public services, but as markets, where programmes could be bought and sold like newspapers, successive governments, Tory, Labour and Coalition, have promoted the expansion of under-regulated commercial satellite, cable and digital broadcasting, removed many of the public service obligations governing Independent Television, and encouraged the growth of contracting out BBC and ITV production to independent producers. Defenders of this shift away from organising broadcasting first and foremost around the principles of public service, have argued that it has improved services and enhanced consumer choice; detractors that it has undermined the link between public service and mass communications, limited the range of content and views available to the public, is moving dangerously close to the commercially dominated system operating in the USA, and has allowed policy making to become the preserve of media corporations and right of centre politicians and think tanks.[9]

In addition, in the last twenty years access to the top posts in the media, and broadcasting in particular, has become increasingly the preserve of people from the upper-middle classes; privately educated and graduates of elite universities, who by dint of their socialisation are far removed from the experiences of most people in the UK. The Boards of the BBC Trust and of the commercial media regulator, Ofcom, are populated by people of similar social background, who often come from the worlds of finance and commerce and do not properly reflect the breadth of people who make up our society.[10] On the latter point the defence is that the people at the top should be commercially experienced and able to hold their own in the upper echelons of politics. Though this may be true, it should not be at the expense of ensuring communications are run by organisations which are as socially representative as possible.[11]

Finally, in spite of the drift towards the market in broadcasting, governments remain keen to exercise control, indirectly and directly, over the ways in which broadcasters cover controversial issues, such as the 2003 Iraq war[12] and have in place a raft of laws designed to constrain the communication of information considered supportive of 'terrorism', itself a highly contested category. For example the Terrorism Act 2006 criminalises the "encouragement of terrorism" something which includes making statements that glorify terrorist acts.[13]

Policy Making

The extent to which the making of broadcasting and latterly communications policy has been an open process has been a subject of intense controversy. Prior to the 1980s, governments set up regular inquiries or specially convened commissions, such as the Pilkington Committee in the 1960s and the Annan Committee in the 1970s. These ran for a number of years and gathered a great deal of evidence from a wide variety of groups and individuals. They were criticised as being cumbersome, too dominated by influential individuals and too wedded to the status quo. Nonetheless they

THE REFORM DEBATES

allowed for a long period of often controversial and high profile debate about the future of broadcasting policy.[14]

Since then governments have preferred short consultations, increasingly using the internet, conducted either by the relevant ministry or, more often than not, by the commercial media regulator Ofcom. This has speeded up decision making and produced outcomes which have re-regulated the industry away from public service and towards the market. The downside has been that policy making is now the preserve of those organisations, usually powerful media corporations and right of centre pressure groups, who can mobilise the resources over a short period of time to respond fully to complicated issues and who have the ear of sympathetic politicians in all parties. This has effectively closed down large areas of public debate about policy.[15]

There need to be major changes in the way policy is debated and made. Each parliament or devolved assembly in the UK should establish a standing Communications Committee. It should be composed of elected representatives, academics, media trade unionists and members of civil society. Their remit would be to scrutinise communications policy and fund independent research from academics and civil society organisations to feed into that process. The Committees' findings would then input into policy making. In other words, policy making should be opened up to civil society.

All meetings between ministers and civil servants with any person or body of people on an issue relating to communications policy, in any context, have to be fully minuted and placed online within one week. All elected representatives must fully register all their interests in relation to the media industries. No politician or civil servant should be allowed to engage in any financially rewarded lobbying activity for any media interest on retirement from their posts. All consultations should be given sufficient time to involve the widest possible number of people. Once decisions are made, ministers should publish the reasons why they have taken them and the reasons why they have rejected major counter propositions.

The major objection to proposals such as these is that they may increase the time taken to make important policy decisions. That is likely to be true in many cases. The fact that communications policy impacts on the daily lives of all people in the UK, and that its shape and nature should therefore be a matter of intense political debate is, however, reason enough to put quality of decision making above speed.

Devolution of Powers

The devolved parliament and assemblies do not have powers over communications policy, largely because Westminster has traditionally retained ultimate control over technological infrastructure, financing and regulation of content. While some elements of the status quo may need to remain in place, there seems no good reason why significant power over communications policy should not now be devolved. The nature of this devolution should be subject to internal debate in the nations of the UK, and between them and the parliament at Westminster. This might include, increased control over BBC policy and funding; powers to regulate commercial TV, satellite and radio; powers to oversee relevant internet initiatives; and the resources and power to fund future public service media content across all platforms.

THE REFORM DEBATES

Production

The BBC should continue to be the cornerstone of public service broadcasting and should no longer have to put any of its production out to tender to independent producers. It might want to contract out some production, but it should also build up continuity of training, experience and creativity within the organisation.

Commercial broadcasters should be given tax incentives, and where appropriate regulatory incentives, to invest in public service programming. Finally, a levy on major media corporations, such as Sky, Facebook, Google and Microsoft, would release funds for a Public Service Media Board to fund community and public service media across all platforms. The Board should be constructed so as to be as representative and accountable as possible.

Public ownership of the communications infrastructure

British Telecom needs to be brought back into public ownership. This would allow its profits and expertise to be utilised to invest in innovative communications infrastructure and provide an accountable way of rolling out access to new developments for both private and public concerns. This is tied up with arguments about the role of the state in industry and there will be those who out of principle or financial interest oppose such a move. Nonetheless governments need to be able to plan decades ahead in this area and need the resources to hand in order to implement their decisions. Communications infrastructure is too important to be left to the vagaries of the market. Pragmatism dictates such a move.

Governance

The governance of broadcasting has, and is likely to remain, an issue that generates a great deal of debate. While it is vital that appropriate expertise is drawn on to support governing bodies, there is no good reason why these bodies should be dominated by people from very narrow social backgrounds and occupations.

The BBC Trust and the Ofcom Board, or their successors should be elected, not appointed. This could be done using an electoral college with places allotted for organisations from civil society, the industry and the trade unions. The civil society organisations would rotate across time, to allow for a broad field of representation. This college would be subject to revision of membership at three year intervals, and charged with both organising elections for members of these boards amongst its constituencies and with the scrutiny of candidates prior to election.

These boards should stand apart from the organisations they oversee, and no former or prospective member should be allowed to engage in any lobbying for financial gain on matters of communications policy. The BBC Trust and the Ofcom Board, or their successors, should be charged with the obligation to promote public service communications, first and foremost, and to represent the diversity of opinion and cultures in society in their output, as well being transparent in their decision making. The notion of impartiality, which currently operates within the system, should be expanded to ensure that a wider range of views are consistently aired. The BBC should be established by statute and continue to be publicly funded. The current system using the Royal Charter places too much power in the hands of the government of the day

THE REFORM DEBATES

and undermines Parliamentary scrutiny. The license fee should continue until a more satisfactory method is found that can replace it and make collection more effective, possibly one based on a household levy. Provisions should be made out of the public purse to cover the cost of providing the licence fee, or its successor, for pensioners and people on low income.

Ownership rules

A goal of communications policy should be media pluralism. In theory competition legislation prevents market abuse. In reality it does not prevent the growth of over mighty media concerns with far reaching political influence, as was clearly evidenced in the revelations about the connections between politicians and media corporations presented to the Leveson inquiry into press standards from 2011 onwards[16].

There needs to be a radical rethink of the rules governing ownership and acquisitions in the media. Among the key issues are those relating to the need to impose a proper test to ensure that any mergers are in the public interest, and that proper limits are applied to just how big any one company can become in a given market. There needs to be 'a system of clear ownership thresholds, established in law, and applied both within and across key sectors ... These should act as triggers for intervention rather than definitive market caps'.[17] In this context it has been argued that any 'party with a significant share of 15 per cent in one media market should be subject to a public interest test' [18] The BBC and all public service communications bodies should be exempt from these provisions. There should be public intervention to support new ventures and to encourage diversity of media ownership.

Censorship

There is a long tradition of government censorship and manipulation on issues such as the General Strike (1926), the coverage of the Irish question in the 1970s, the 1984-5 coal dispute, the pressures on broadcasters relating to their coverage of the Israeli-Palestinian conflict and the Iraq war. There is also disturbing evidence of the covert links between broadcasters and the security services.[19]

There should be a thorough review of all the mechanisms used by governments and commercial organisations to restrain proper independent reporting. The methods, circumstances and devices which govern censorship and manipulation should be laid bare for public debate. From this it should be possible to establish new, transparent protocols and monitoring mechanisms, to ensure that the wider public interest is protected where matters of government policy come into conflict with the communicators' obligation to represent properly the complexities of public, social and cultural issues.

Conclusion

The combined share of the main five PSB channels accounted In spite of the proliferation of new forms of content and delivery systems, public service television remains the lynch pin of UK broadcasting. As Ofcom pointed out, in 2014:

> for over half (51.2%) of all viewing in 2014, up by 0.1 percentage point on the previous year. Taking the main five PSBs and their portfolio channels together, the combined family share was 71.9% in 2014. The share of viewing to all 'other' digital channels remained stable at 28.1% in 2014.[20]

THE REFORM DEBATES

Broadcasting as it is, and is likely to develop, will remain of central importance to the health of our democracy. We therefore need a proper and wide ranging debate about how to reform broadcasting so that it, in its various forms, can play its part in representing us, properly, to ourselves and to the wider world. That means major structural reform to open up channels of diverse communication and to make all organisations involved in broadcasting accountable to the public they are there to serve. The proposals in this chapter are meant both to encourage, and be a contribution to that debate.

---

[1] Broadcasting is now integrated into a digitally based communications industry. Broadcast programmes are now also transmitted via the internet and as such the term broadcasting, relevant up to the late 1990s now seems increasingly inappropriate as way of describing the object under discussion. This chapter uses both broadcasting and communications, interchangeably to denote the same subject matter, given that what was once broadcasting policy is now subsumed within communications policy.

[2] A. Briggs, *The History of Broadcasting in the United Kingdom. Volume 1*. Oxford: Oxford University Press, 1961. For a one volume survey of broadcasting history in the twentieth century see A. Crissell, *An Introductory History of Broadcasting*. London: Routledge, 2002, 2nd Ed.

[3] The arguments in this chapter are, necessarily, compressed. Anyone interested in pursuing these issues can find detail in: T. O'Malley, *Closedown? The BBC and Government Broadcasting Policy 1979-1992*. London: Pluto, 1994; D. Freedman, *Television Policies of the Labour Party 1951-2001*. London: Frank Cass, 2003; D.Freedman, *The Politics of Media Policy*. Cambridge, Polity, 2008; T.O'Malley and J. Jones eds, The *Peacock Committee and UK Broadcasting Policy*. London: Pal-

grave Macmillan, 2009; J.Curran and J.Seaton, *Power Without Responsibility* London: Routledge, 2010, 7th ed. Broadcasting reform is an issue pursued by the Campaign For Press and Broadcasting Freedom for which see www.cpbf.org.uk.

[4] T.O'Malley and C.Soley, *Regulating the Press*. London: Pluto, 2000; T. O'Malley, 'The Regulation of the Press' in M.Conboy and J.Steel, eds, *The Routledge Companion to British Media History*, Abingdon: Routledge, 2014:228-238

[5] Briggs, *History of Broadcasting... Vol.1.*

[6] Glasgow University Media Group, *Bad News*. London: Routledge & Kegan Paul, 1976; C. Heller, *Broadcasting and Accountability* London, BFI, 1978; D. Miller, *Don't Mention The War. Northern Ireland, Propaganda and the Media*. London: Pluto, 1994; Freedman, *Television Policies.*

[7] O'Malley and Jones, *Peacock Committee*; T. O'Malley 'The Response to Television in the UK 1947–77: A Study in the Media and Social Fear,' in S. Nicholas and T.O'Malley, eds, *Moral Panics, Social Fears, and the Media: Historical Perspectives*. London: Routledge, 2013: 104-125

[8] HMSO, *Report of the Committee on Financing the BBC*. London: HMSO, 1986, Cmnd. 9824.

[9] T O'Malley, *Closedown?*; Curran and Seaton, *Power*; O'Malley and Jones, *Peacock Committee*; Freedman, *Politics*. The problems with the media in the USA are outlined in J. Nichols and R. McChesney, *It's the Media Stupid*, New York, Seven Stories Press, 2000 and V. Packard, *America's Battle for Media Democracy. The Triumph of Corporate Libertarianism and the Future of Media Reform*. New York: Cambridge University Press, 2015.

[10] Details of the members of the BBC Trust and Ofcom Board can be found at: http://www.bbc.co.uk/bbctrust/who_we_are/trustees and http://www.ofcom.org.uk/about/how-ofcom-is-run/ofcom-board/members/ respectively; both accessed on 25 September 2015.

[11] Sutton Trust, *The Educational Background of Leading Journalists*. London: Sutton Trust, 2006; O. Jones, *The Establishment and How they get Away with It*. London: Penguin, 2015: 85-123.

[12] For an interesting account of the media and the run up to the invasion of Iraq see, D. Miller, ed, *Tell me Lies. Propaganda and Media Distortion in the Attack on Iraq*. London, Pluto, 2004.

THE REFORM DEBATES

[13] Liberty, 'Speech Offences', London: Liberty, 2010 available at https://www.liberty-human-rights.org.uk/human-rights/free-speech-and-protest/speech-offences accessed 25 September 2015.

[14] Freedman, *Television Policies*; O'Malley, 'The Response'.

[15] Freedman, *Politics*.

[16] See, *Leveson Inquiry: Culture, Practice and Ethics of the Press*, at:: http://webarchive.nationalarchives.gov.uk/20140122145147/http://www.levesoninquiry.org.uk/evidence/ accessed on 25 September 2015.

[17] Media Reform Coalition, *Media Pluralism*. London: MRC, 2015, at: http://www.mediareform.org.uk/resources/media-pluralism accessed on 25 September 2015.

[18] CPBF, *Submission on Media Pluralism to Ofcom* London: CPBF, 2011, at http://www.cpbf.org.uk/body.php?subject=media%20ownership&doctype=policies&id=2605 accessed 25 September 2015.

[19] Curran and Seaton, *Power*; Miller, *Don't Mention,* and *Tell me Lies*; G. Philo and M. Berry, *Bad News From Israel*. London, Pluto, 2004; G. Williams, ed, *Settling Scores. The Media, the Police and the Miners' Strike* London, CPBF, 2014; S. Milne, *The Enemy Within. The Secret War Against the Miners* London, Verso, 2014, 4th Ed.

[20] Ofcom, *The Communications Market, 2015*. London, Ofcom: 185, available at: http://stakeholders.ofcom.org.uk/binaries/research/cmr/cmr15/UK_2.pdf accessed 25 September 2015.

3-7 The dog that needs to bark: the case for regionalism

Introduction

Our political system is one of the most centralised in Europe. Most of the decisions that affect us are taken at Westminster, and although we have a system of local government, too often our local councils can do little more than implement the policies handed down to them from the centre. The resources they have, and what they are allowed to do with them, are largely determined by central government departments.

The 'Westminster bubble' is not just geographically remote from most parts of the country – it is also politically remote. The grand Victorian civic buildings in many of our cities and towns demonstrate that local government was once important and powerful but, although governments of left and right have talked about local democracy and 'localism', the ability of local politicians to respond to local concerns is now extremely limited.

Scotland, Wales and Northern Ireland, however, have to some extent broken free from the reins of Westminster. The creation of the Scottish Parliament and the Assemblies in Wales, Northern Ireland and Greater London have given these parts of the UK some freedom to do things differently, but the powers devolved to them

THE REFORM DEBATES

have put the spotlight on the regions of England. As a country, England is not homogeneous: not only do people in the North tend to vote differently (see chapter 3-1) but they live in an area that has suffered disproportionately from economic stagnation and lower living standards, yet they do not have the opportunity to vote for regional policies better suited to their circumstances and aspirations.

The 1997-2001 Labour government gave some thought to devolution to English regions in which there was a demand for it, and in response campaigns developed, particularly in northern England (the North East, the North West and Yorkshire and Humberside) and the South West. What was on offer, however, was limited and, when it was rejected in a referendum in the North East in 2004, the policy was abandoned.

When more powers were offered to Scotland at the time of the independence referendum of 2014, there were new demands for devolution to the English regions, and in 2015 the Conservative government introduced its own ideas for a 'northern powerhouse'. However, although this might lead to additional investment in the north, which would of course be good, the proposals are top-down and essentially about management and bureaucracy and not about democracy.

In this chapter, Professor Paul Salveson argues that the north of England now needs a new movement for regional democracy, but what he advocates for the north is of course also needed in other parts of England where citizens need more say on the policies that affect them.

Northern Regionalism – has its time come?

Professor Paul Salveson

The Scots historian Chris Harvie once called English regionalism 'the dog that never barked'. Well, perhaps it has at last. The establishment of Yorkshire First (YF) and The North East Party (NEP), both of which contested the 2015 General Election and gained small but respectable votes, suggest that the pup is starting to make its bark heard. With our present voting system, new parties face huge obstacles, but the support these parties received is probably just the tip of an iceberg of discontent at the lack of a regional political voice.

The movement is being driven by developments in Scotland (not just the independence referendum but what has happened since) as well as a growing awareness of the widening economic gap between the North and London/South-East. The outrage in March 2016 over proposals to move the National Media Museum's photo archive to London has, perhaps unexpectedly, become a touchstone for the North's sense of injustice. People in the North, as no doubt in other parts of the country, are starting to think that they need a voice of their own, though how that would be structured and articulated needs a much more extensive debate. It's time for the establishment of 'citizens' conventions' which take the conversation out of the hands of a small political elite and involve a much wider cross-section.

It's very early days for both the new regionalist parties and their development has been a fascinating process already. Both parties have their roots amongst 'centre-left' political activists, mostly but not exclusively Labour or Lib-Dem. Neither YF nor NEP is very happy with the traditional 'left-right' political labels

THE REFORM DEBATES

and in this they echo the approach of the immensely popular Podemos ('We Can!') movement in Spain. 'Left' and 'right' political tags mask an equally important distinction between 'centralist' and 'de-centralist' thinking. Hilton Dawson, leader of the North-East Party, describes his party as 'progressive democrats' and that is a good description for starters.

My own approach, coming from a 'decentralist left' background, is to look at ways in which a socially progressive agenda can be built that mobilises strong regional identities with policies which put social justice and equality to the fore. It isn't a million miles away from the SNP which emphasises social and economic democracy. Neither YF nor the NEP want independence but the 'devo-max' approach of substantial devolution which can usher in radical, progressive policies is something they have in common with the SNP.

The starting point should be building the case for directly-elected regional government. Yorkshire, with its five million or so inhabitants (about the same as Scotland), is the right size for effective regional government. Some things should be delivered on a pan-Northern basis (e.g. rail) but others are best left to the UK level, such as defence, foreign affairs and ensuring a balanced redistributive fiscal system. A single Northern Parliament may be too big, but there is a good argument for pan-Northern fora involving the three (or more) Northern regions on issues like transport, economic development and health. For example, we already have a 'Transport for the North' whose governance is provided by no less than 29 local authorities. It seems eminently sensible that bodies such as TfN should be accountable to a handful of elected regional bodies, not to an unmanageable crowd of

THE CASE FOR REGIONALISM

local councils whose focus will inevitably be on their own backyards. Not on the strategic needs of a super-region of 15 million people.

Crucially, radical regionalism should push for strong, well-resourced local government. At the moment, politicians in the established parties are confusing *local* and *regional* devolution. The two are separate but complementary. Local government should be the basic unit of government upon which everything else is built – regional, national and international. Currently, our local government structure is a mess and we don't have *regional* government, at least in England. The way forward is a debate which involves local, regional and national interests, through citizens' conventions. The Hannah Mitchell Foundation and Unlock Democracy have been calling for a 'Northern Citizens' Convention' which could feed in to a national constitutional convention. But we need 'citizens' conventions' in every community.

To an extent, the experience of the Scottish Constitutional Convention offers a model from the 1980s and 1990s, when civic groups, the business community, trades unions, faith groups and most political parties came together to discuss the best form of Scottish devolution. My only caveat would be that the discussion needs to go beyond 'the great and the good' and get out to every community, neighbourhood, college and workplace. The more recent experience of the Scottish referendum on independence, during which huge meetings were held in some of the most socially-excluded housing schemes in the country, with large-scale participation of young people, is a much more exciting model.

There will be different views (e.g. an English parliament? Combined authorities?) and these need to be argued through, sensibly. Currently, we are not being offered a say at all, having

THE REFORM DEBATES

combined authorities imposed on us by the local (mostly Labour) political establishment and elected mayors imposed by George Osborne and the national political elite (mostly Tory). It's worth pointing out that when a 'citizen's panel' was organised in South Yorkshire by a group of academics (supported by YouGov), a large majority of the participants, having examined every conceivable model for devolution, opted for a directly-elected regional assembly for Yorkshire.

It is remarkable that the 'combined authority' model is being accepted almost without demur. Major areas of public policy are being transferred to what are at best indirectly-elected bodies, controlled by politicians who were elected with a very local mandate to sort out neighbourhood problems like getting the bins emptied and clearing up dog mess from the pavements. Elected mayors is a step in the right direction, but even the London model, of an elected mayor overseen by a fairly toothless elected assembly, is denied to the rest of the country.

The case for directly elected regional assemblies is powerful but relatively unheard in mainstream political debate. The Corbyn-led Labour Party has shown little interest in the democratic aspect of devolution, and the formerly enthusiastic Liberal Democrats have retreated into silence. Of all the main parties, only the Greens have shown serious interest in extending democratic control to the regions.

Elected regions offer an opportunity to develop new forms of democracy which involve much wider sections of the community than are currently involved in politics. They should be elected by voting systems which ensure proportionality but also address issues around women's under-representation in political

THE CASE FOR REGIONALISM

institutions. How can we find ways of involving young people, people from varied ethnic backgrounds? There are positive models out there and a new English regionalism is an exciting opportunity to look at new forms of political engagement.

What should regional assemblies do? They must have with real powers to deliver the sort of things that the German lander (and Scottish and Welsh devolved governments) already do. Radical devolution is only a means to an end and devolutionaries need to make their case based on a progressive social and economic agenda which includes a new approach to transport, energy, health, education, housing and – above all – sustainable development. Much can be learnt from the Welsh experience, where 'promoting sustainable development' is a fundamental principle of the Welsh Government.

Whatever the outcome of the European referendum, the EU concept of a 'Europe of the regions' in which nation states are of lesser importance offers a useful model, and most regionalists are pro-European and pro-social justice in their outlook. Within the European debate is the issue of immigration: even some supposedly progressive politicians are being swept along by the anti-immigrant tide. I would argue that immigrants are not the problem facing the UK economy. The problems we're facing, of a sluggish and hugely unbalanced economy are being caused by national Government policies.

The outcome of the European referendum will have major implications for the future of the UK. In the short-term, if most Scots vote to stay in, the pressure for a Scottish referendum on independence will be overwhelming and the chances are that Scotland could vote to leave the UK. But what if a substantial majority of people in the North also vote to stay in Europe? Their voices won't be heard. An increasingly marginalized North – in both political and economic senses, could pave the way for a much more aggressive regionalism based on a very real sense of grievance. An alliance between an independent Scotland and possibly Wales with the North starts to become a possible scenario.

My hope is that Scotland stays within the UK and champions a very different settlement between the nations and regions of the British Isles which fundamentally re-balances our polity.

There must be radical hope. A new 'Northern' politics which embraces Yorkshire, the North-east and the North-West with an egalitarian vision underpinned by a strong emphasis on social justice and inclusion should be forged, through an inclusive and innovative process of grassroots debate.

I'm convinced that an alternative to the reactionary Anglocentric politics of UKIP is not only desirable but eminently achievable.

My own feeling is that the existing northern regionalist parties – mainly Yorkshire First and the North East party, but also the smaller Northern party – should federate and agree a common 'Northern Platform' which is pro-European, pro-social justice and for extending democracy not only to regions but to neighbourhoods and communities. It must promote a specifically Northern approach to sustainable development and embrace gender equality and social diversity in everything it says and does.

A new North is possible: will English regionalism be the 'Podemos' moment for England?

3-8 No Short Cuts To Democracy: the problem with referendums

Lewis Baston

Publics, across the world, seem ever more disengaged and contemptuous towards their political elites and even the process of representative democracy. One tempting route is to cut out the middle man – direct democracy, from the vote of the electorate to a policy outcome without the unpleasant business of politicians mediating the process. In this chapter, I argue that far from being an unnecessary middle step, the process of forming party programmes and priorities and applying the rule of law is actually the essential bit of democracy as opposed to majoritarian dictatorship. Representative democracy is in a poor state of repair, to be sure, but replacing it with something worse is the wrong answer. Referendums can be and often are bad for minorities, federal systems, constitutional politics, fair and rational policymaking and a public discourse that accepts complexity. There are some legitimate uses for the mechanism, in establishing the basic ground rules (what constitutes an independent state, what are the fundamental constitutional principles) and sometimes in rescuing representative democracy from itself when it becomes insular or corrupt, but it is strong medicine for limited use, not a panacea for all political ills.

THE REFORM DEBATES

Referendums are antithetical to minority rights

The evolution of constitutional democracy is in part a story of learning to live with the restraints on majority rule. The referendum is a dangerous device when used to decide questions of minority rights. If one has the concept that there are basic human rights that apply to all members of the community, there are some questions that even large majorities should not be able to determine if they involve undermining – directly or indirectly – those basic rights.

The referendum is a direct instrument by which majorities can impose their will on minorities and even in sophisticated and broadly liberal democracies has been recently used to do this, as with California's Proposition 8 on same sex marriage in 2008 and the Swiss vote on minarets in 2009. The minarets vote was not really about architecture, of course, it was about 'monstration' – the politics of showing something, saying something, even if it is incoherent and not about the immediate issue on the ballot. Passing an idiotic, illiberal and anti-federalist policy into the constitution of a country is a high price to pay for an emotional spasm.

Without a framework of constitutional law – or with constitutional amendment by referendum – there is not much that can be done to reverse the impact of a referendum. Even if it is deplored by politicians and large sections of society, and passed on a low turnout, opponents will be wary of trying to cancel it by having another referendum, because results are uncertain and a second defeat would merely further entrench the law they wish to abolish.

Even with a strong system of legal principles and judicial review, a referendum result inconsistent with constitutional principles can still have effect. Proposition 8 was eventually struck down, but it was in effect from November 2008 to June 2013, a lengthy period for people affected who wanted to get married and for the gay community as a whole to endure being unequally treated by majority decision of their fellow citizens.

It can take a number of years during which those rights have been denied, and the often expensive and draining efforts of individual plaintiffs to achieve. Even worse, the UK lacks a truly entrenched system of human rights law in which the judicial system can – eventually – undo the damage done by referendums, and indeed legislation, that impinges on minority rights. British political discourse is also more primitive when it concerns the rule of law and constitutional principles than it can be in the US; a government would face heavy opposition for 'defying the will of the people' in trying to reverse or amend an oppressive referendum decision.

Referendums can be centralising

Even in Switzerland, with an electorate long familiar with referendums, federalism and a party system that is geared towards broad consensus, referendums can go badly wrong. In November 2009 a national vote (57.5 per cent of a 53 per cent turnout) banned the construction of minarets across Switzerland. There were a grand total of 4 in the country and 2 more planned.

The areas where minarets might conceivably have been erected and there were more than a handful of Muslims tended to vote in favour of allowing minarets – Geneva quite strongly so, with narrower majorities in many of the other urban centres of Switzerland like the city of Basel, Lausanne and Bern. The canton that was most enthusiastic about the ban was Appenzell-Innerrhoden, where

THE REFORM DEBATES

there are hardly any Muslims and whose strong direct-democratic history involves repeated rejections of women's suffrage until it was imposed by the federal courts in 1991. The democratic justification for the people of Appenzell to dictate planning law in Geneva seems flimsy, but majoritarian referendums like the minarets vote are inconsistent with federalism and a liberal society.

Referendums are a bad mix with checks and balances

If the referendum were an entirely healthy political device, Venezuela would be a political model. There were three major national votes between 2004 and 2009, the first triggered by the opponents of Hugo Chavez who were trying to overthrow him by recall (admittedly a more wholesome method than the attempted coup in 2002) and the second two called by Chavez to overcome constitutional obstacles to the exercise of power such as term limits. Chavez was in a long line of populist, demagogic leaders who had fought referendums pitting majority support against the restraining effect of constitutional rules; Napoleon's referendums of 1802 and 1804 are among the most noted examples. His nephew Louis Napoleon pulled a similar stunt in 1851, ratifying his coup d'etat with the electorate in a referendum shortly afterwards. Charles De Gaulle played a more benign but still unconstitutional version in 1962 to introduce direct presidential elections, using his personal prestige to achieve an even more presidential republic than the public had approved in 1958.

Referendums are therefore a tempting mechanism for a popular leader to impose his (or her) will on other institutions. They are prone to a totalising argument that it is either the leader or chaos, using status quo bias to cement the regime in power, and that the will of the people should not be impeded by such fripperies as constitutions and judges.

Referendums produce bad public policy (even if voters are rational)

Issue-by-issue, it is perfectly possible for referendums to produce concurrent majorities for things that are incompatible with each other. The most familiar pattern for the problem of inconsistent majority wishes is the eternal dilemma of taxing and spending. The assumption that the individual voter is engaged in a rational choice (rather than an act of expression or a piece of wishful thinking) is often flawed but social choice theorists have long shown that it is quite possible for rational voters to produce inconsistent or cyclical patterns of preference when cumulated to become an entire electorate. Imagine three propositions on the ballot at the same time, when the government has a windfall of £10bn – say from an auction of mobile phone licenses.

- Prop A is in favour of distributing £5bn of the windfall as one-off tax cuts.
- Prop B is in favour of spending £5bn on new roads.
- Prop C is in favour of spending £5bn on new railways.

For simplicity, the electorate is divided into three equal-sized groups of voters, all of them with consistent preferences that do not defy arithmetic or public accounting standards. Group 1 likes tax cuts and roads, but thinks the railway investment is a wasteful white elephant. They vote Yes on A, Yes on B, No on C. Group 2 thinks that transport investment is highly productive and more important than a one-off tax cut. They vote No on A, Yes on B, Yes

THE REFORM DEBATES

on C. Group 3 likes public transport but feel that roads are destructive and that some of the windfall should be shared with taxpayers. They vote Yes on A, No on B, Yes on C. All of these groups have consistent, well-formed proposals that use up the £10bn but no more.

The problem is that each Proposition will win with a 2:1 majority. Collectively, the result is that the electorate has committed the government to disbursing £15bn from a £10bn fund.

Referendums do not offer an escape from the problems of social choice between multiple options.

Straddling the boundary between bad public policy, a mobilised interest group and the tyranny of the majority was the Proposition 13 vote in California in 1978, whose baleful influence undermined the state's budget for thirty years. It was a case of an electoral majority choosing to shift the property tax burden away from themselves as established homeowners and transfer it to businesses, new homeowners and the state's finances.

Political parties perform several unglamorous but vital roles in the political system. The relevant one here, short-circuited by 'direct democracy', is to impose consistency and a broad set of values that will decide the choices and priorities that are made. Parties that make impossible and inconsistent promises in their manifestos are exposed to scrutiny and hopefully held accountable for it. Piecemeal referendums destroy the consistency and practicality of policy, and the accountability mechanism when referendums produce failed or unfair policies. 'The language of priorities is the religion of socialism,' said Nye Bevan. By reordering priorities in an essentially selfish way, referendums are therefore, in Bevan's terms, a species of blasphemy.

Referendums are easily manipulated

In any system of referendums, timing and turnout can be manipulated to influence the outcome. An off-year referendum on a particular policy issue (as opposed to an existential issue) is likely to produce a low turnout. This fact is known by proponents of causes that attract enthusiastic support from a minority but for which the opposing majority is less excited by the issue and less likely to turn out. A passionate minority can mobilise in an off-year low turnout referendum and outnumber the disengaged majority. Because it is so difficult to override referendum results, 51 per cent of a 30 per cent turnout can be translated into a near impassable blockage to changes desired – albeit not passionately – by the remaining 85 per cent of the electorate.

The other timing issue is also well-established. People use referendums, particularly mid-term, to have a poke against governments that have become unpopular or to raise a finger to the 'political elite' – voting against the government's preferred option regardless of what the actual issue on the ballot might be. Referendum campaigns are rarely exercises in deliberative democracy, particularly from a cold start on an issue with which the electorate is not familiar. If they are about dull technical issues, as they often are, the campaign discussion will drift further away from what is actually on the ballot and towards symbolism or the projection of exaggerated or even unrelated hopes and fears. There is very rarely any kind of deliberative process.

Controlling the agenda is the most powerful way of winning political campaigns, and a referendum is much the most easily controlled agenda. The choice of issue on which a referendum is called is a product of the way the political system is structured, either in legal constitutional terms or in the day to day management of politics. Even among broadly constitutional issues, the principle is applied inconsistently in the UK. Devolution to Scotland, Wales and Northern Ireland gets a referendum; within England, London got one, elected mayors used to get one but don't any more, 'devolved' units in the city won't, and local government structural changes tend not to. Referendums tend to be discouraged when the balance of interests is likely to favour redistribution – it may be interesting to imagine what a referendum on the optimal highest rate of income tax might look like.

Wording the question is another area in which the referendum can be a manipulative technique. On issues in which public preferences are weak and knowledge of the issue is sketchy, question wording can have a strong effect. Electoral reform is a notorious example, in which if one wants a positive outcome one should ask whether the electoral system should ensure that the proportion of seats in parliament are more or less in line with the votes cast by the people, and to get a negative outcome one should ask if we should get rid of our long-established system in which everyone has an MP and there is usually single party government. Having a biased referendum on the least attractive version of a proposed change can be a very effective way of keeping the demand for change off the agenda.

The UK at least has a relatively sensible system of establishing national referendum questions, set up by law in Political Parties, Elections and Referendums Act (PPERA) 2000 and overseen by the Electoral Commission. Although obviously not divorced from the political context, a good faith effort is made through research and consultation to produce a fair question and governments accepted the results of the work of the Commission in the 2014 Scottish referendum and 2016 European referendum. However, if one side of the referendum fails to engage with the process (as the Yes side did in 2011 on electoral reform), a subtly loaded question can still result. Without the PPERA framework (or other independent or judicial oversight to question-setting), question wording can be ludicrously biased. In 2004 for instance Tewkesbury borough council organised a local referendum on a Gloucestershire county council policy, with ballot papers circulated asking:

> Should Alderman Knight - a special school that caters for children with moderate learning difficulties and a wide range of other needs - be closed?

It is perhaps surprising that 304 people voted 'Yes' to this leading question (28,683 voted No).

The principal bias in referendums is towards the status quo. The irony is that people wanting change are usually the ones who campaign to have a referendum, and the people wanting no change are the ones who win. This applies particularly to higher-turnout referendums that run concurrently with first-order elections, in which a large number of voters will have a referendum ballot without having been remotely interested in the cause. The usual reaction to favour the status quo in these cases, particularly if the case for change is complicated (and politicians tend to legislate the obvious cases for change themselves), is understandable. The change proposition generally needs to have a double-digit lead in the polls shortly before the end of the campaign in order to win.

THE REFORM DEBATES

The principal exceptions to the status quo rule in British, as distinct from Northern Irish, history were the Scottish and Welsh referendums in the honeymoon period of the Blair government in 1997 and the London government referendum in 1998. The Scottish case was really just the ratification of a settled decision that the Scottish electorate had made some years previously, while the Welsh referendum, however narrow, was more of a genuine decision point.

Referendums don't resolve the basic question

Referendums are sometimes imagined to settle political issues for a generation, if not longer, or for all time… But of themselves, they settle nothing, even when they are about the big existential issues. Scottish Nationalists have not given up their aspirations to independence as a result of the vote to stay in the UK in September 2014, and the two-to-one referendum vote for the UK to stay in Europe in 1975 did not stop people who wanted to leave from believing in and arguing their cause, and withdrawal to become the policy of the official Opposition before 1983.

A little known fact is that the referendum that had the most overwhelming, lopsided result in UK electoral history solved precisely nothing. On 8 March 1973 there was a referendum in Northern Ireland on whether the province should stay in the UK or join the Republic of Ireland. The vote was in favour of the UK with the support of 57.5 per cent of the whole electorate – and 98.9 per cent of those voting (it was boycotted by the nationalist community). Suffice to say that disputes over the constitutional status of Northern Ireland did not disappear from that day forward.

NO SHORT CUTS TO DEMOCRACY

Uses for referendums

Ultimately, there are some issues for which the referendum is probably necessary. When the fundamental basis of the political system is in question, as with the decision on Scottish independence in 2014, it seems reasonable to give the final decision to the people on whose sovereignty any democratic system rests, and that as in Scotland the electorate will take an active interest and make their decisions on the basis of some thought and discussion. Even so, changes made at this basic level without a referendum can be legitimate and accepted (such as the separation of the Czech and Slovak Republics in 1993) and those ratified by referendum can still be legally illegitimate (such as the adherence of Crimea to Russia in 2014). At a slightly less fundamental level, the introduction of a new constitution is a suitable matter for a referendum because it gives a stamp of legitimacy to new arrangements and deters political actors from flouting the rules thereby established. It can also be a reasonable device to make constitutional amendment difficult but achievable.

In some political environments where the system has been made unaccountable and the representative nature of the legislature has been deliberately subverted through gerrymandering or other manipulation, referendums may be a necessary evil. Florida's hopelessly gerrymandered electoral districts were never going to be sorted out by their beneficiaries, so the referendum upholding a fair districting law in 2010 was essential – as were the courts in imposing non-gerrymandered districts after the legislature tried not to follow the principles of the new law.

Different individuals may take different views about whether a political system has reached the requisite of dysfunction to necessi-

THE REFORM DEBATES

tate unblocking by methods with dubious liberal democratic credentials such as referendums or term limits, but a limited use of direct democracy to clean up a corrupted representative democracy (rather than replace it) seems a valid use of the mechanism.

However, this justification can spill over into arguments legitimising the Napoleonic plebiscite and allowing populist leaders to overrule constitutional checks and balances. It can also open the door to the 'recall' of elected officials, a device that could be tailor-made for well-funded interest groups to harass people who take decisions they dislike and intimidate people who are thinking about taking decisions they dislike. Recall should be entirely unnecessary in a political system that has a robust system to police standards of conduct and in which electoral accountability works to any degree.

Conclusion

A democratic parliament is embedded in a network of other institutions – constitution, law, opposition parties, tradition and convention. The limitations of its legitimate role are defined by the system and the population's scepticism about institutions. Referendums are less dangerous in political systems in which there is a written constitution that establishes principles such as federalism, human rights, judicial review, checks and balances and can override simple majorities, but they still erode those features.

Representative democracy, of course, sometimes does stupid and reprehensible things without the help of a referendum. But there are important differences. If it goes wrong, there is someone to blame – the party that insisted on passing the relevant legislation. Blaming the electorate, even if it is essentially their fault, is rarely a successful reform strategy. It is easier for the electorate, and the politicians, to learn from mistakes if they are not baked in by an event purporting to be an expression of the popular will. The barriers to judicial review will also tend to be lower for legislation than they are for a referendum result.

The difference is that the referendum, at root, purports to be an expression of the general will. Its popular legitimacy trumps the niceties, rules and interdependencies of pluralist democracy. It is a 'direct' short cut that steers around the messy but important bits. Margaret Thatcher and Clement Attlee both said that referendums were devices of 'dictators and demagogues' and on this they were largely right.

3-9 Political parties that serve democracy

If there is one thing people distrust more than politicians, it is political parties. Individual politicians may be viewed with suspicion, but a whole cabal of them is often seen as something far more sinister. However, there is not a single major democracy in which people of similar political views do not band together to use their collective political weight to advance their common goals. In 1942 Elmer Schattschneider, a distinguished American political scientist, observed that 'political parties created democracy and modern democracy is unthinkable save in terms of the parties',[1] and the situation is no different today. As Conrad Russell put it, 'Political parties are like death – you might not want either of them, but both are inevitable'.

Parties nevertheless have important functions. Not only are they support groups for the leaders and their teams that compete for the right to govern the country but, as Lewis Baston has put it:

> They have been the main providers, or at least agencies, of political ideas, both at the level of broad ideological visions and also detailed policies. They train and provide candidates for public office. They are brand names, which enable electors to come to rapid, perhaps rough, conclusions about what values and ideas underlie people putting themselves forward for office. They are a means for people who wish to see their ideas put into practice, or who just wish to get involved in community activities. They are channels of

communication for political ideas, upwards from members to representatives to leaders, and from leaders to public as well.[2]

If parties are to fulfil these roles effectively, they need to change their ways and connect better with the people and communities they claim to represent. This chapter looks at what parties need to do, or do differently, to make them real and attractive contributors to a democracy that engages people and ensures that their views and concerns are heard.

Why people don't like parties

In spite of their importance to democracy, parties are among the country's most distrusted institutions. The parties cannot just dismiss this uncomfortable fact as a manifestation of people's general distaste for politics because the parties themselves are largely responsible for our political culture and many of the things that people don't like about politics. While competition, and indeed conflict, is part of the essence of politics, people don't like the acrimony that characterises much of our political debate. They see parties as vehicles for those who want power, both at local level and nationally, rather than as social movements for change. Distrust of politicians leads to distrust of the parties that support them in office.

At Westminster they see parties at war with each other, with MPs behaving like semi-intoxicated fans of rival teams at a football match, senselessly jeering and behaving in a way that would not even be tolerated even in public school debating societies (where too many of them learnt their craft). They see party election campaigns that appear to be more about denigrating opponents'

THE REFORM DEBATES

policies (and often opponents as people) than presenting alternative visions for society. They see parties determined to find things to disagree about and bad-tempered exchanges instead of seeing parties engaged in constructive debates.

Within parties, the main news stories are not about comradely debate but about power struggles, factional infighting, clashes of personalities and egos, backbiting and even accusations of treachery. Much of the history of the Labour party has been about divisive feuds, many of them bitter, such as between Bennites and supporters of Healey for the deputy leadership in the 1980s, between the Blairites and Brownites, and more recently between the Corbynistas and the rest. The civil wars of other parties have been equally unedifying.

What parties need most is a change in their cultures. If they are to attract more respect and trust, they need to make themselves more attractive. They must become places where people with shared values will want to come together to discuss their ideas, respecting alternative points of view and those who hold them. Parties are unlikely to win trust if their members appear to distrust each other. It is not enough for parties to have good policies - good practices, and even good manners, are also needed. Party policy should be a matter for debate, not battle, and while party factions may form to promote particular views, there should be no place for intolerant factionalism.

It will, however, need a determined effort to change patterns of thought and behaviour that have been around for generations and until there is recognition that a new party culture is needed, for the sake of politics as well as the parties themselves, there is unlikely to be progress. Internal debates should be conducted openly and constructively with opportunities for differing views to be heard and considered. Parties' politicians need to lead by example: it does not mean that they should not criticise each other, or even suggest that their parties might do better under alternative leadership, but criticisms should be reasoned and respectfully expressed. Parties must value debate: they must stop pretending that they have solutions to all the problems that arise, and that they are always correct and their opponents generally wrong. There must be recognition that political decisions are generally matters of judgement and that people with similar values and objectives may reach different conclusions: disagreeing with the party line should not automatically be seen as a sign of disloyalty.

Party members also need to understand the need for open and constructive debate in which different views can be respectfully heard and considered. They also need to know the standards of conduct expected of them and parties must be prepared to admonish those who overstep what their parties regard as permissible. Of course there must be a place for dissent, but it should be expressed in a context of common values and party solidarity.

Following Labour's bruising row towards the end of 2015 over whether to bomb targets in Syria, the case for a code of conduct was raised. While a code might not completely reform the behaviour of all politicians or members, it could send a strong signal about language and behaviour that are unacceptable. There is surely a case for all parties adopting such a code.

Parties and their members

Parties are membership organisations. All who become members do so to express support for their party in a way that goes beyond just voting. They are willing to identify with their parties and, be-

THE REFORM DEBATES

lieving that the success of their party will be good for the country and/or themselves, are prepared to put their money where their mouths, or at least their thoughts, are by contributing a subscription.

For parties, members are important. They provide the people who will support local campaigns, they contribute funds, they form the pool from which candidates are selected, and while their role in policy-making may be limited, they help to keep politicians in touch with those they represent. Although the participation of most members goes no further than signing a direct debit form, those who get actively involved are hugely important to democracy. They distribute millions of leaflets at every election, they hold street stalls, they canvas for support on the doorsteps and on the day of an election they 'knock-up' supporters to remind them to vote. It is the work of these volunteers that keeps politics alive at local level. The national media may now be the main source of information for most electors, but researchers reckon that a good local campaign a few percentage points to a party's vote: that might not seem much, but in many constituencies it can be the difference between defeat and victory.

Nowadays only around 1% of the electorate belong to any party. In the past, however, it was very different. Around the middle of the last century, the Conservatives had about 3 million members – about 20 times as many as they now have. Labour had about 1 million, but only 180,000 at the time of the 2015 election. In the post-war years, Labour was more clearly the party that represented the working class while the Conservatives stood for middle-class interest and most electors knew on which party was for them, but with changes in society (see chapter 1-4) party loyalties have been weakened: while in 1964, 44% of people strongly identified with a party (and a further 38% identified fairly strongly), by 2001 this had dropped to only 11%. Needing to win the middle ground of politics, the major parties had moved away from offering radically different visions or ideologies (ideology was explicitly rejected by Blair's 'New Labour') and instead appeared to compete by offering packages of promises in a bidding war for people's votes.

Labour under Jeremy Corbyn's leadership may, however, have started to reject this trend. His campaign for the party leadership injected a new excitement into left politics, attracting many new members wanting to give him their votes, and his victory brought many more. Labour's membership rose from 180,000 to around 400,000. Some other parties, too, have recently seen big increases in their memberships: with the Scottish independence referendum and the SNP successes in the 2015 general election, the SNP's membership has mushroomed to over 100,000, and with more people turning away from the two major parties, the numbers of members of both UKIP and the Greens have increased significantly. Whether or not these increases are just transient responses to events, only time will tell. However, they do show that many people are still prepared to join parties, but only when parties appear to be taking a stand for things that are important to them.

Party policy and party democracy

Many join parties because they want to participate in politics – they want to contribute their ideas and feel they have a part in shaping party policies. The huge surge in numbers joining Labour in 2015 has been a result of people not just wanting to have a voice in the selection of Labour's leader but wanting to move the party

THE REFORM DEBATES

in a particular direction. However, the extent to which ordinary members can influence policy is limited, as is often the extent to which party hierarchies are inclined to allow them influence.

Local meetings provide opportunities for members to discuss issues and submit their ideas to their party leaders, but without any assurance that their parties will take much notice of them. Although motions passed at party conferences carry much more weight, the conferences of the major parties are now tightly managed and opportunities for debates instigated by members are more limited. Although in the past Labour conference agendas were full of motions from constituency parties and trade unions, it did not mean that Labour was then more democratic – what was discussed and decided was often in the hands of union power brokers and others who were able to work the system - but many now complain that conferences have become primarily showcases for party spokespeople, designed more for media coverage and with delegates often reduced to being the audience rather than participants. Only the minor parties now have conferences which offer their members a significant role in shaping their parties' policies.

As parties are membership organisations, it might seem reasonable to assume that it is the members who should make policy. However, it is not quite as simple as that. The business of government is complex and even when party members have a clear policy preference, its political leaders must to take account economic constraints, legal issues, international obligations, etc. as well as what is politically achievable. They also need to recognise that they need political power if they are to have a chance of putting their policies into practice – they therefore need to heed to views of the wider electorate as well as their own members, and often opinion polls and focus groups will influence them as much as their supporters. It does not mean that politicians ignore their members, but they must negotiate what they think is the best course of action that reflects party values and members' aspirations.

Even when party leaders have agreed a position, there is no guarantee that all the party's MPs will support it. Politicians may have been selected by members, but they are elected by constituents. They do not hold office as delegates of their parties and all politicians must decide themselves how they will use their votes. There is still of course accountability in that an MP who persistently disregards party policy is likely to face problems when it comes to reselection.

There is thus much potential for tension between what party members want and the positions taken by their politicians. The Labour Party has perhaps suffered more than others from the conflicts that can arise. The Campaign for Labour Party Democracy (CLPD) began in 1973 and over the following years fought a relentless campaign to give members more power over politicians. David and Maurice Kogan[3] have described how:

> A party, stabilised by established procedures and a tradition of deference, was suddenly forced to change its ways. A new style of small group politics ... came to dominate the Labour Party.

That, however, was a problem. What power had been transferred was not to the membership but 'small group politics' on the far left of the party. CLPD's concept of democracy did not extend to one-member-one-vote (that had to wait until John Smith's leadership) and the divisive nature of its campaign no doubt contributed to

THE REFORM DEBATES

the split in Labour in 1981 and the party's worst electoral defeat for decades in 1983. A former shadow minister reported that when Neil Kinnock became leader in 1983:

> The party was a shambles ... What we inherited was a situation in which the party had gone off in one direction and the parliamentary party had gone off in a totally different direction.[4]

Reforms that followed in some respects made the party more democratic, and electable, but by the time Tony Blair became Prime Minister Labour was in many ways more centralised than ever.

Jeremy Corbyn, on becoming leader in 2015, promised members more involvement in policy-making, particularly through online consultations. The first consultation, on whether to support the bombing of ISIS in Syria, however, was a demonstration of what a consultation should not be. It was held only after leading MPs had taken their positions on the issue and appeared to be more of an attempt at putting pressure on MPs not prepared to follow the leader's line. Only 60% of those who responded were party members and less than 18% of responses were read before the result was declared. Reports of the recruitment of thousands of people by a Corbyn-supporting pressure group just to 'vote' added to the disquiet over the exercise.

Nevertheless, online consultation with members was a welcome innovation. For the future, however, protocols are needed to cover the conduct of consultations, their purpose and the circumstances in which they are appropriate. Consultations should inform policy-making within parties, but should not be a substitute for it.

There have also been demands for more democracy in the Conservative Party,[5] and there have been many tensions between groups of members and the leadership over issues such as EU membership and gay marriage, but Conservative members have in general been a little more deferential to their leaders. The referendum on EU membership in June 2016, however, is likely test party unity and loyalty to the limits.

The role of members in policy-making in local government, however, may be a slightly different matter. Members may feel remote from national politics, but local meetings often involve local councillors who need to take positions on matters before their councils. The issues may sometimes appear mundane – planning matters, rubbish on the streets and bin collections, support for voluntary groups and protests over service cuts – but they are ones that impact on local members and on which they can sometimes make a difference. Tip O'Neill, the former Speaker of the US House, may have exaggerated when he claimed 'All politics is local', but he had a point.

Candidate selection

It is in selecting candidates that members have their most direct influence on their parties. In making their choices they no doubt consider the extent to which potential candidates have the personal qualities that would make them effective representatives, but more important are their views. Would a candidate be to the left or the right of their party, have they strong views on the environment, where do they stand on EU membership or the need for Trident are all questions which might lead a member to support one person rather than another, and selecting a candidate can change a party's centre of gravity, albeit slightly, on such issues.

All party members can put themselves forwards as potential candidates and all parties try to follow equal opportunity policies which treat all aspiring candidates in the same way. On the face of it, this is all fair and satisfactory, but the reality is different.

Too often there have been concerns about insiders – those favoured by the party hierarchy – having an advantage over others, about irregularities in selection processes, and about the 'parachuting' of candidates backed by national parties with little local consultation when selections must be made at short notice. In Labour there have also been concerns that some unions having used their members and muscle to give union-backed candidates advantages over others. Nevertheless, although any abuses of the selection procedures are deplorable, it is reasonable to assume that most selection contests are conducted fairly.

A broader problem is that parties' selection procedures do not produce candidates, and hence MPs, who represent the make-up of society. In the 2015 general election, only a quarter of the candidates were women, although this resulted in the election of 191 women MPs – 29% of the Commons (this was a record high – until 1987 the number of women had never risen above 5%). In England less than a third of councillors are women and in the rest of the UK it is only around a quarter. Women's representation is stronger in the devolved assemblies, but not by much – in 2015, only 35% of the Scottish Parliament (a drop from nearly 40% in 2003), 40% of the Welsh Assembly and 32% of the London Assembly are women, while in the Northern Ireland Assembly it is a woeful 19%.

POLITICAL PARTIES THAT SERVE DEMOCRACY

The 2015 election also saw a large increase in the number of black and ethnic minority MPs – from 27 to 41 – but well over twice that number would be needed if their representation were to reflect the size of the BME communities in the country. Disabled people remain hopelessly unrepresented.

Does this matter? Some argue that it is the job MPs do that is important and not their gender or the colour of their skin. But in the twenty-first century an all-male or an all-white parliament would simply not be acceptable, and if all parts of society are to feel that parliament represents them, we need a parliament that looks like society in its social composition.

Although politics is not as male-dominated as it once was (for example, following the independence referendum, the leaders of the three main parties in Scotland were all women), movement towards gender equality has been painfully slow, particularly at Westminster where the rate at which incumbent men retire allows only modest improvements in women's representation at each election. Too often men have been the ones who attend party meetings while women stay at home or find more productive things to do: as a consequence it is too often men who dominate both candidate shortlists and those making the selections. The lack of adequate progress has resulted in a group of women launching a new Women's Equality Party in 2015, but with our present voting system it will have difficulty in winning seats.

The figures for women's representation would be very much worse if it were not for the Labour's use of women-only shortlists for some seats, including many key marginals. Of Labour MPs, 43% are women: the SNP is not far behind on 37%, but the Conservatives have only 21% and the Liberal Democrats no longer have any women in the Commons. Women-only shortlists have,

THE REFORM DEBATES

however, been controversial. Many don't like their choice of candidate being restricted in this way, and on occasions there have been concerns that the party might have used the procedure to prevent a strong local male candidate, unwanted by the party hierarchy, from standing. Nevertheless, it appears to be the only approach that has made a significant difference to the number of women in parliament, as well as on local councils.

All major parties have quota systems to ensure there are women and BME candidates on shortlists, but these measures have had only limited effect. Until parties have more women and others from unrepresented groups playing more prominent roles in their affairs, we are unlikely to have a parliament that reflects the diversity of our society. Achieving that change will require changes in the way many local parties conduct their affairs – a greater commitment to equality issues, a less macho political culture, and more encouragement and help (possibly including financial help with the costs of seeking selection) to women and members of minority groups could all make a difference.

Another factor here is the voting system. With systems of proportional representation, several candidates must be selected in each electoral area and it is then in the interests of parties to ensure that their team appeals to as many voters as possible. A group of candidates that includes women, and BME candidates where there is a significant BME community, is likely to be more attractive to many voters than a group of white men. In countries which use some form of PR, women's representation is generally much higher than in countries which do not.[6]

Primaries have been much discussed in recent years and the Conservatives have used them on a number of occasions. These have been 'open' primaries in which all electors are allowed to vote in the selection of the party's candidate. For a party, there is the advantage that a candidate who does well in a primary is more likely to do well in the actual election, and there is an argument that in safe seats, where selection almost guarantees election, the involvement of a wider selectorate is good for democracy. Primaries, however, also have their downside. Firstly there are the costs to the candidates of reaching out to the entire electorate, giving a huge advantage to candidates who are rich or have financial backing. Then there are the costs to the party – the Conservatives' postal primary in Totnes cost £38,000 which is well beyond what most constituency parties can afford, and not even national parties will be able to fund many primaries at that sort of cost. Thus primaries, whatever view is taken of their merits, are likely to remain rare exceptions rather than the norm.

Parties and public engagement

Other than the political exchanges people hear or read about through the media, parties' contact with electors is generally confined to election campaigns in which they are asking for votes. In seeking support they may argue that their policies are better than their opponents, but this form of contact falls far short of real engagement with the electorate.

For democracy to work well, there is a case for parties having a stronger role in helping people to understand how politics works, the nature of current issues and the choices which their political representatives have to make. Parties may claim they already do this, but they do it only in the context of seeking support for their own, predetermined, views. What is needed is not political propaganda but political education. It is a job that cannot be left to the

THE REFORM DEBATES

media which too often has its own biases and prejudices, and it cannot be entrusted to Government agencies which would tend to favour the Government's perspective. Parties would of course present issues from the perspective of their own values, but as neutrality is not possible in politics and political ideas are never values-free, it appears that political parties may be best placed to undertake this type of activity.

Parties exist, however, to compete in elections for the power to implement their ideas. Their members cannot be expected to raise funds for anything other than running their parties and campaigning in elections. Any wider work in political education would therefore need to be publicly funded. For some, this might be controversial, but there is a national interest in having an effective democracy and therefore no good reason why public funds should not be used in this way. Moreover, such funding would only be an extension of the state support parties already receive for the freepost delivery of leaflets in major elections, free television time for party political broadcasts and support for their research work at Westminster. There would, of course, need to be strict controls on what parties could do with money as few electors would want to subsidise election campaigns.

Here there are lessons to be learnt from Germany where each major party has an associated foundation. These foundations are not there to seek party support or votes (at least not directly) but

> to motivate citizens to concern themselves with political matters and provide a platform for the discussion of political issues that is accessible to all citizens[7]

The work they do is guided by their values (social democracy, Christian democracy, etc.) but is independent of the parties. They hold conferences and events (not just for party members), conduct research and publish reports aimed at increasing public understanding of current affairs. The German parties, like their UK counterparts, need their own money to fight elections, so the money for the wider educational role of their foundations comes from the German government.[8]

There is surely a case for UK parties having similar, associated foundations. While some might protest at the use of public money in this way, the cost of building a democracy of more knowledgeable and more engaged electors must be seen against the billions that can be misused or wasted if a poorly informed electorate elects a government that pursues bad policies.

However, even if British political leaders are not as prepared as their German colleagues to be bold and imaginative, there is a strong case for state support for British parties, tied to activities which reach out to more people, stimulating an interest in politics and engaging people in real debate rather than just telling them why the policies of one party are better than those of its opponents. Not only could it transform perceptions of parties, but it would be good for politics.

Recommendations for political parties

- Parties must change their cultures. If they are to be part of a democracy which engages people in politics, they must be more attractive and engaging themselves. They must demonstrate their acceptance of democratic values, and in the conduct of their affairs they must show tolerance and respect. While they need to reach clear positions on policy, they must recognise that they are coalitions of people united in their values but with different views on how their objectives might be achieved.

- To help achieve a change in culture, parties should introduce codes of conduct for members and politicians and make it clear that disrespectful or abusive behaviour will not be tolerated.

- Parties must involve their members more on policy matters and not just treat them as just leafleters, door-knockers and local fundraisers. Telephone calls to members should not just ask for money, but should seek the opinions of members on policy alternatives. More use should be made of the internet, not just to tell members what the party is doing but to get their views on what they think the party should be doing.

- Local party branches should be encouraged to organise programmes of events that are attractive as well as stimulating, where appropriate involving the wider public, local organisations and community leaders. While there is a limit on what can be asked of hard-working activists, they could be assisted by providing models of good practice (and there are already some local parties whose practices are good).

- Nationally and locally, parties should do more to increase the involvement of all parts of society and people of all ages. Although parties have national sections for youth and students, women, BME and LGBT members, these should be better integrated with local party activities.

- Parties must do more to ensure that their candidate selection procedures for all tiers of government are fair and are seen to be fair. Local parties should be free to choose their own candidates, subject only to national parties' legitimate interests in not having candidates who are manifestly unsuitable and any measures to promote the representation of women. Where necessary, support should be given to candidates to ensure that those without money or institutional backing are not disadvantaged, and encouragement should be given to potential candidates from under-represented groups.

- Consideration should be given to publicly funding parties (or educational foundations linked to parties) to enable them to play a wider role in developing the electorate's understanding of political issues.

---

[1] Quoted by Tim Bale in J Garland and W Brett, *Open Up: the future of the political party*, Electoral Reform Society 2014

[2] L Baston and K Ritchie, *Turning out or turning off?*, Electoral Reform Society, 2004

[3] D and M Kogan, *The Battle for the Labour Party*, Fontana, 1982

[4] Patricia Hewitt, quoted in P Gould, *The Unfinished Revolution*, Little, Brown and Company, 1998

[5] J Strafford, *Political Parties and Democracy*, The Reform Foundation, 2015

[6] Research by Pippa Norris found 'women proved almost twice as likely to be elected under proportional as under majoritarian electoral systems'('The Impact of Electoral Reform on Women's Representation', in *Acta Politica*, Vol 42, no, 2)

[7] http://www.kas.de/wf/en/71.3712/ (Dec 2015)

[8] The resources provided by the German government are substantial – of the order of £200m p.a. This, however, covers activities not strictly necessary for the purposes for which funding is proposed in this chapter and for the UK a much more modest budget would suffice. The Konrad Adeneur Foundation's website

THE REFORM DEBATES

(http://www.kas.de/wf/en/71.3712/) explains the rationale for state funding as follows:

> Political discussions and political decisions ... are predicated on information and an ethical political orientation. Freedom can be asserted responsible only by persons educated along these lines. Consequently, political education is a necessary counterpart of political freedom.
>
> From this, we may conclude that political education is one of the constitutional mandates of a liberal state ...

3-10 An elected head of state

Surprisingly little attention is given to the position of the monarch in debates on our democracy. The conventional wisdom is that the queen is above politics and has nothing to do with the way the country is governed. She is seen as merely figurehead, brought out to add a little pomp to ceremonial occasions, to greet foreign dignatories, to award honours and titles, and to add a little feel-good factor to the nation. She is identified with things that are good and worthy and does not need to be associated with the grubby and controversial business that politics can often be, and consequently she has escaped from the derision heaped on politicians.

Why, then, should we even think about reforming an institution that appears to be harmless and a constitutional irrelevance? There are three questions we need to ask: firstly, is the influence of the monarchy really as weak and benign as some would have us believe; secondly, is it appropriate in a twenty-first century democracy to have a hereditary head of state; and thirdly, are there better ways of fulfilling the monarchy's functions.

In past, our monarchs were all-powerful. They claimed a divine right to reign and ruled the country more or less as they liked, and those who stood in their way generally ended up in the Tower or with their heads on the block. Much of the history of our country is usually described in terms of the exploits of kings and queens, the battles they fought and ways in which they exercised their control over unruly subjects. However, as we moved towards

THE REFORM DEBATES

a more modern age and the institutions of the state became more sophisticated, the role of monarchs was reduced and the more complex business of running the country put into the hands of the parliament. Nevertheless, our government remains 'Her Majesty's Government', and even the opposition is 'Her Majesty's Loyal Opposition', and before taking their seats, MPs must swear an oath of allegiance to 'Her Majesty, her heirs and successors'.

Although monarchs now appear to leave government to the politicians, it does not mean they are without power. Not only can the Queen refuse to agree to legislation passed by parliament, but if she doesn't like what politicians are doing she can dissolve parliament and appoint a new Prime Minister of her choice – that means she has the power to be a tyrant if she wants to be one. She can declare a state of emergency, take command of army, and issue proclamations which the police and magistrates would be obliged to enforce – formal powers that despots around the world must envy.

These powers are, however, to some extent theoretical. To use them, other in the most exceptional circumstances, would provoke a constitutional crisis which would probably bring the monarchy to an abrupt end. That, however, does not mean that the Queen is without power – as Tony Blair noted, our monarchs 'still have the power to keep us in our place'. However, although the powers of the monarch may in practice be limited, the monarch nevertheless has influence.

Each week, the monarch summons the Prime Minister for an audience. Successive Prime Ministers have maintained that these meetings are not just formalities but meetings of substance, but what substance? We are not allowed to know, as the affairs of the royals are exempt from the Freedom of Information Act. The mon-

AN ELECTED HEAD OF STATE

archy's own website tells us that the Queen has 'a right and a duty to comment on the affairs of government', so it must be assumed that she expresses views and that Prime Ministers must at least take account of them. Indeed, John Major has revealed that on some occasions government policies were changed following his meetings with her Majesty. Some may argue that these audiences are only part of our tradition, but if they are meetings at which Prime Ministers are either advised or held to account, is it right that the audiences are with someone of immense wealth and privilege who has no experience of the problems facing her subjects and who is not accountable to ordinary citizens?

Nevertheless, even many who are opposed to the monarchy accept that our present Queen has played her hand carefully. The same cannot be said for her heir-in-waiting, Prince Charles. Charles has not been shy in letting government ministers know his views, and on many occasions he has used his position to influence, or attempt to influence, governments of the day. He has lobbied in support of alternative medicine (persuading the government, against all medical advice, to divert a £300,000 of the health budget to his Foundation for Integrated Health)[1]; he supported fox hunting during government moves to ban it; he has opposed GM crops; he has argued in favour of grammar schools; and he has been critical of modern architecture, intervening with the Qatari royal family to stop a proposed development of Chelsea barracks.

As well as having had numerous meetings with government ministers in recent years, he has frequently sent his 'black spider letters' (so called because of his handwriting) expressing his views to government. In 2005 a Guardian journalist made a Freedom of Information request for the release of some of these letters and the

THE REFORM DEBATES

Guardian conducted a long legal action to have them made public, but the royals claimed they were exempt from the FOI Act. Although the Guardian won its case in an FOI tribunal, the then Attorney General, Dominic Grieve, used a power of veto to overturn the decision. He argued that 27 letters, written over a seven-month period, were 'particularly frank' and if disclosed would compromise the Prince's political neutrality, suggesting of course that the letters were not politically neutral. The matter then went to the Supreme Court which, in March 2015, decided in favour of the Guardian.

The letters that were released showed the extent of the Prince's lobbying. He had, for example, urged a badger cull, called for the replacement of Lynx helicopters in Iraq, objected to EU legislation 'outlawing the use of certain herbal extracts' (Prime Minister Blair assured the Prince he would seek to delay implementation until 2011), attempted to save Armagh gaol, asked the government to bend the rules so that heritage funding could be used for Scott and Shackleton's the huts in the Antartic and he even called for the protection of the Patagonian toothfish. In one letter he asked the Health Secretary to accelerate redevelopment at a hospital site in which his architectural charity was involved, with the warning that 'chickens will come home to roost' if action was not taken. If such letters had been sent by a member of the public they would, at best, have been disposed of with a polite acknowledgement but, coming from the Prince, ministers felt obliged to take account of them.

We do not know if the Prince continues to lobby in this way because the Freedom of Information Act has been amended to include an 'absolute exemption' on all matters relating to the Queen or Prince. However, in 2015 research by Republic, which campaigns for an elected head of state, showed that since 2010 the Prince had had 87 meetings with government ministers, opposition leaders and senior civil servants.

We may agree with Charles on some things and disagree with him on others. The issue, however, is not whether he is right in his views, but whether it is right that he should use his position to exert pressure on elected politicians. If our aim is a society in which all citizens have an equal voice, allowing someone who is unelected and unaccountable to have such influence runs counter to democracy. Some maintain that Charles will act different when he becomes king, but others fear that after years of lobbying ministers he will find the habit hard to break. Moreover, there have been reports that he intends to be a more interventionist monarch than his mother.

That we are no longer allowed to know about the Prince's lobbying is just one facet of the cloak of secrecy which surrounds the royals' affairs. It is not new. In the nineteenth century the political commentator, Walter Bagehot, wrote: 'When there is a select committee on the Queen the charm of royalty will be gone. Its mystery is its life. We must not let in daylight upon magic.'[2]

But can it be right, in the twenty-first century when we demand transparency in the affairs of government and our national institutions that we are not permitted to know what our royals are up to? Democracy demands that people know what their leaders and representatives are doing as without that knowledge they cannot make informed judgements. Our head of state, and his or her entourage, should not be shrouded in 'mystery' and a select committee on the monarchy might be no bad thing.

The 'Queen's and Prince's Consent' is another constitutional device by which the Monarch or Prince of Wales can, at least theo-

THE REFORM DEBATES

retically, have influence on government. Any proposed bill which would have implications, and generally that means financial implications, for the monarch or Duchy of Cornwall (which provides income for the heir) needs the consent of the monarch or Prince of Wales before it can even be debated in parliament. Bills for which consent has been required include ones as mundane as the High Hedges Bill, the NI Contributions and Statutory Payments Act, the Work and Families Bill, the Planning Bill, the Civil Partnership Act and the Wreck Removal Convention Act. While there is no evidence that the monarch or Prince of Wales have prevented parliament from discussing issues (other than in 1999 when the Queen, on the advice of ministers, vetoed a private members bill which would have given parliament, rather than the monarch, power to authorise air strikes against Iraq), what we do not know is which bills have been amended in order to gain consent even before they were put before parliament.

Like the Queen's and Prince's Consent, Royal Prerogative powers, which allow decisions to be taken in the name of the monarch, allow ministers to act without the approval of parliament. Again, while there is no evidence that the monarch has used these powers on her own initiative, the existence of the monarchy gives ministers a way in which they can bypass parliament. For some, this is wholly undemocratic.

Similarly, the Privy Council takes decisions without the opportunity for parliamentary debate and scrutiny. The decisions taken are decisions of ministers, but it is the monarchy which allows ministers to take them. Many decisions of the Council are on matters that are not contentious, but some are – it was, for example, the Privy Council which removed the trade union rights of workers at GCHQ, and which ordered the eviction of 2000 people from

AN ELECTED HEAD OF STATE

their homes on the Chagos islands to make way for a US-UK military base. It is the power vested in the monarchy which allows such things to happen without the consent of our elected representatives.

However, even if the political neutrality of the monarch and her family could be guaranteed, and even if the costs of the royals were not a major concern, their very existence may be seen as incompatible with a society in which everyone, whatever their wealth or the circumstances of their birth, are, as citizens, equal. Does the monarchy perpetuate the notion that we are not all equal and there are some who, for no reason other than their parentage, enjoy a status and privileges of which others can only dream? Is it right that not just we, but also our most senior political representatives, must show deference to members of a family whose status is based merely on the positions held by their ancestors? The protocols which surround the monarch - such as bowing and curtseying, addressing the queen as 'Ma'am' and not speaking unless spoken to – are surely out of place if we want a society in which all citizens should be treated with the same dignity and respect. If, as we have argued, true democracy requires a political culture in which it is the people who are sovereign, a sovereign monarch appears to be an undesirable leftover from a past era when some were born important and the rest of us had to know our place.

If we were to abolish the monarchy, what would we put in its place? In a democracy in which it is the people who are ultimately sovereign, it seems clear that the head of state should be chosen by them and should be accountable to them. The constitutional powers of the head of state should be defined and limited, and the head of state should be impeachable should powers be misused.

THE REFORM DEBATES

What powers of the head of state should, and what role he or she should play, have raises the question about the sort of head of state we want. We can even ask whether we need a head of state, but there is an argument that in the event of a constitutional crisis, for example if the political parties found themselves unable to agree who should form a government, then there should be a single person to break the deadlock. However, constitutional crises are, fortunately, exceedingly rare, and while it may be desirable for a head of state to have wide powers, there seems no need for a head of state exercising these powers other than in the most exceptional circumstances. While an executive president on the US or French models is an option, it would mean a radical, and probably unwelcome, change in our political system. For the UK we need look no further than Ireland for an appropriate model: the Irish president is directly elected for a fixed term and does not get involved in the business of government (and Irish presidents have enjoyed levels of popularity of which politicians can only dream).

There are also ceremonial roles for a head of state to play – even under a republican system there is a place for ceremonies that add dignity to the affairs of state and engender a sense of national identity and pride. Ceremonies, however, should reflect the prevailing culture and not harken back to the days of empire or attempt to glamorise our imperial past.

A head of state should also be able to act as the representative of the nation in a broad, apolitical way. A head of state chosen by the people would surely be able to speak for citizens with more legitimacy than a monarch whose wealth and privileges makes her so remote from the lives and concerns of her people. The queen's website maintains that she "acts as a focus for national identity, unity and pride", but a monarch who heads the Church of England in a multi-faith/non-faith society and who, at least for the foreseeable future will be white in a multi-racial society, is hardly well-placed to be a unifying figure. A head of state elected by us all, ideally by a method such as the Alternative Vote to ensure majority support, would surely be better able to fill this role.

Only the most fervent and optimistic republicans, of course, believe that the monarchy can be replaced quickly, but that is no reason for not setting a direction of travel. Although public opinion, so much shaped by an establishment-controlled media, is not quite ready for the monarchy's abolition, there are nevertheless steps that can be taken to limit the monarch's role (and, of course, costs). These include:

- Opening up the affairs of the royals to public scrutiny through removing their exemption from the Freedom of Information Act, thereby allowing us to know if and how the royals are using their influence and resources;
- Changing the oath of allegiance which MPs and others are required to swear: MPs should be accountable to us so, rather than swearing allegiance to a hereditary monarch, they should swear that they will faithfully serve their constituents and country;
- Ending the Queen's and Prince's Consent: if the people are sovereign, their elected representatives should not be restricted on what they can debate and on what they can legislate;
- Ending weekly audiences with the Prime Minister (whilst recognising the need for a head of state to be kept informed about the nation's affairs): our Prime Ministers surely have better ways of using their time;

THE REFORM DEBATES

- Changing the way in which the monarchy is funded by giving it a budget which, just like any government department, must be justified and must take account of overall spending priorities;
- Ending the Royal Prerogative so that all decisions of the government are subject to the scrutiny of parliament;
- Removing the monarch's role as head of the Church of England (the 'established church'): while royals should be free to follow whatever faith they choose, having a monarch heading a particular branch of a particular religion is incompatible with society in which people of all faiths, and of no faith, are deemed to be equal.

Although opinion polls show that only a minority favour the immediate abolition of the monarchy, there is a majority who believe the monarchy will not last for ever. When the time comes to replace it, what will the new head of state look like and how will the transition be made?

While it is clearly desirable that any head of state should have a good understanding of politics and constitutional issues, he or she need not be a politician. As the head of state should be above and outside party politics, there is a case for barring serving politicians from standing in order that the head of state is not seen as being aligned to one party or another. By using the Alternative Vote method to elect the head of state, the successful candidate would need to have the support of over 50% of the voters (after the elimination of candidates who cannot achieve this), and that means having support from people of several parties. Election, however, would be for a fixed period rather than for life, and there could be a provision for removing a head of state if there was

AN ELECTED HEAD OF STATE

widespread and serious dissatisfaction over how they were performing their duties.

Unlike a monarch, elected heads of state could have clearly defined job descriptions, with powers limited to upholding and protecting the constitution. It may make sense for them to have other roles, such as head of the armed forces, but they don't need medals or fancy titles to do that, and while they would have ceremonial duties, these could be performed without all the trappings of pomp which could undermine their position as a representative of all people. Again unlike the monarchy, the head of state would not be a family business with junior princes and princesses being regarded as minor soap opera celebrities, but would be a person elected, on his or her merits, to do a job.

An elected head of state could come from any part of society – they could be of any ethnic group, religion or sexuality. They could be academics, writers, people who have made their name in culture, business leaders or trade unionists, or just plain ordinary – the thing that is important, however, is that they should have been chosen by the people. And having been chosen, they, unlike hereditary monarchs, would have legitimacy when speaking about people's hopes and aspirations.

The British, rightly, have no stomach for revolutions and few would wish to see the monarchy overthrown in the manner that some monarchies elsewhere have come to an end. It is not impossible, however, to envisage a peaceful transition in which the powers and privileges of the monarch are gradually removed until a point is reached when the royals are no longer of any great importance and could be offered a respectful exit into retirement, making way for the first election of our head of state.

THE REFORM DEBATES

On attending Barak Obama's first inauguration, Gary Younge, the Guardian columnist, spoke of children wearing T-shirts printed 'When I grow up I want to be President'. Only when we change to an elected head of state will it be possible for British children to aspire to holding the most senior position in the country.

---

[1] A charity which closed in 2010 following allegations of fraud and money laundering.

[2] Quoted in Peter Hennessy, *Establishment and Meritocracy*, Haus Publishing, 2014

3-11 Engaging young electors

Younger people are less likely to be engaged in formal politics than those who are older. It is not good for them that their voices are not heard as strongly as they might, but neither is it good for others. Our national debate needs the involvement of all parts of society, and particularly of people whose outlook has not been conditioned by decades of political frustration and disappointment: what the young lack in experience may be compensated for by a greater openness to new ways of doing things. The younger generation of electors also has more than its fair share of people who face the uncertainties of how they will earn their livelihoods, where they will find a place to stay and how they will be treated by the unsympathetic bureaucracy of the welfare system, and these are people with a greater need for a political voice than most. That younger electors are relatively less engaged in politics than their elders must therefore be a concern for us all.

In elections, the turnout of electors in the 18-24 age group is lower – often much lower – than the overall average, and the problem is compounded by the registration rate for younger people being lower. In 2005 the turnout for this group was only 38% and although it improved in subsequent elections (estimates for 2015 vary widely – see chapter 1-2, page 13), the views of young electors remained seriously under-represented.

In November 2015 when the government published its Autumn Statement, the Chancellor was criticised for policies which favoured the elderly over the young. Whether or not the allegations that the government was being nicer to those more likely to vote (and more inclined to vote Conservative) can be justified, there is a danger that those less likely to exercise their democratic rights will not receive the political attention they need and deserve.

This chapter therefore explores why younger people are less likely to vote and what needs to be done to more fully engage them in politics.

Young people's views of politics

Young people, Russell Brand asserted, 'do not give a fuck about politics'. If by 'politics' we mean voting in elections and joining political parties then, allowing for a comedian's overstatement, he has a point. But that does not mean that young people don't have political views or that many are not politically active in other ways. The problem is that they don't see the formal institutions of politics working for them.

Young people are as concerned about political issues as their elders. Many must worry about whether they will find a decent job, where they will find a place they can afford to live, how the state of the economy will affect their prospects, etc. (and for some there are concerns about tuition fees and the consequent debts). Their views, often shaped by social media, tend to be more socially liberal – they are less likely to feel threatened by multiculturalism, immigration and terrorism,[1] and more concerned about issues of social justice, rights and the environment. Thus while they may be concerned about the same things as those of older age groups, their priorities are often different, perhaps contributing the view that 'political parties aren't interested in the same issues that concern young people' (a view expressed by 64% of a sample of young people in 2011[2]).

They are also at least as willing as others to express their concerns through political actions: many sign petitions, go on demonstrations and observe boycotts, and they are more likely to get involved in volunteering and local campaigns. However, unconvinced that party politics either can or wants to change things, many use their political energies outside mainstream politics and are more likely to get involved in single-issue campaigns.

Although these forms of political activity are very laudable, they nevertheless leave many young people disconnected from the discussions and debates that lead to decisions on things that are important to them. While the political system, from councillors' surgeries and party branch meetings to Westminster debates and party conferences, should be something they can use in working for the causes they feel strongly about, they tend to be less interested in formal politics, less confident in their knowledge of it and consequently less likely to use it to promote their interests.

However, in spite of this relative lack of interest, there is evidence that young people's views are not always as negative view as those of older age groups, perhaps because they have not accumulated the same years of experiences of politics' failures and disappointments. Research by Gerry Stoker[3] suggests that:

> if the politics on offer got better, or perhaps worse, many citizens, but younger citizens in particular, would shift to becoming more politically engaged.

What we most need to engage young people more fully with politics is therefore a different style of politics. Their knowledge of politics, and particularly how to get involved in it and how to use it, must be improved, but we also need a change to a form of politics that attracts them because they see it as being relevant and effective.

Citizenship education

It is not surprising that many young people (and many of their elders) don't know much about how our democracy and our system of governance work. Most of them are not taught much about it.

Although 'citizenship' has been part of the core curriculum in England[4], it has too often been a neglected part. We insist that people leaving school should know how to count, read and write, but we do not put the same emphasis on requiring them to understand their rights and responsibilities as citizens. Citizenship is not an examinable subject in the same way as arithmetic and English, and consequently it can find itself a low priority in schools concerned about their places in exam league tables.

To make matters worse, there is no obligation on 'academies' and 'free schools', which are not under local authority control, to follow the citizenship curriculum (at present around a quarter of schools are academies). In March 2016, the government announced that it wanted all schools to become academies, a move that would effectively abolish the entire national curriculum in England. If we want an electorate that understands politics and their role in it, citizenship education must be something that all schools are required to provide.

Citizenship was added to the national curriculum in 2002 following the recommendations of the Crick Report[5] in 1998 which asserted that:

> the teaching of democracy ... is so important both for schools and the life of the nation that there must be a statutory requirement on schools to ensure that it is part of the entitlement of all pupils.

In the years that followed, many schools developed imaginative approaches, but Ofsted reports referred to weaknesses, particularly in the area of political literacy, with problems arising from the lack of specialist teachers and teachers' reluctance to tackle areas of political controversy.[6] Nevertheless, although Ofsted reported in 2010 that citizenship education in half of the schools inspected was good or outstanding, a survey in 2011[7] found that even of those who had taken a GCSE in Citizenship Studies, 64% claimed it had done little or nothing to increase their understanding. The Hansard Society's 'Audit of Political Engagement'[8] found in 2013 that only one in 5 of the 18-24 age group (the only age group to have 'benefited' from citizenship education) perceived themselves as knowing at least "a fair amount" about politics. By 2014[9] this had risen to 34%, but even that figure was much lower than the number for any other age group, and well below the 50% average.

Following the change in government in 2010, there was a proposal to remove citizenship education from the curriculum. After much lobbying, it was retained, but with a revised curriculum which, as David Kerr has noted, gave 'more weight ... to civic knowledge and the prominence of financial and social citizenship at the expense of the political' and that, in spite of an increasing

THE REFORM DEBATES

need for young people to be politically literate, since 2010 citizenship has experienced a 'drop in prominence in political and educational terms'.[10] Although parties are a key part of our political system, the word 'party' does not appear even once in Department of Education's three-page document of the citizenship curriculum: it requires students to be taught about the roles played by public institutions and voluntary groups, but not parties.

Although the national curriculum still aims to ensure that all students 'acquire a sound knowledge and understanding of how the United Kingdom is governed', too many leave school without an adequate understanding of politics and the institutions of government. That far too many young people seem to have little idea of how elections are conducted was confirmed by a survey conducted by a Member of the Youth Parliament which found:

> Only 48% of the young people we survey had been taught how to vote, but some 80% wanted to be taught that ... Only 30% have been taught about petitions and how to engage in direct democracy[11]

It should not be difficult to introduce students to voting in elections, from the completion of registration forms (which for appropriate age groups could include completing actual forms), applying for postal votes and how to vote in a polling station.

Citizenship education should not, however, be just about dry facts – it should be something that excites and inspires. The stories of the courage of those who fought for the right to vote need to be told to instil an appreciation of the value of democracy and political liberty. Democracy should not be taught as just the mechanics of how governments are chosen and how decisions are taken, but as something that empowers people, giving them a voice in shaping the society they live in.

If we want an engaged electorate, students must be taught how to use the opportunities that democracy provides. As citizens they are not completely powerless, but organising, campaigning and lobbying are all skills that students must be helped to acquire. Some schools arrange talks by local politicians and visits to local councils to observe how they work, but citizenship education must go further, providing practical opportunities for students, as citizens, to engage in real lobbying and campaigning.

Citizenship education must include an element of political education to develop students' understanding of the broad themes of political debate - for example, the extent to which the state should provide services and how it raises funds to pay for them, where the balance between public ownership/control and private enterprise should lie, where the boundaries between state and individual responsibilities should be drawn, etc. This does not need any theoretical discussion of competing ideologies, but it should enable students to recognise some of the policy choices that can be made and help them understand where parties stand on issues. For some, this raises a fear that citizenship education may become politically partisan but, while there must be safeguards against the promotion of one doctrine over another, citizenship education that does not expose students to the debates and controversies of real-life politics would be sterile. Through discussion and debate, citizenship education must help young people develop their own views and the confidence to engage meaningfully in politics (and mock elections, which many schools and colleges already hold, are one way in which this can be done).

THE REFORM DEBATES

Whatever political views students form, it is important (as the curriculum acknowledges) that they develop skills in critical thinking. For democracy to work well, people must have the ability to weigh up arguments and make their own, individual judgements. They need to be able to assess the claims of politicians with a sceptical mind (but not with cynicism) and to distinguish between fact and prejudice in media reporting. In France, a compulsory part of the baccalaureate is philosophy, an exam in which students needed to demonstrate not their knowledge of the ideas of others but their ability to think for themselves: even if we are not inclined to go as far as this, there is something worth considering in the French argument that education is as much about developing citizens as producing people to meet the country's economic needs.

The authors of the Crick report on citizenship education aimed at 'no less than a change in the political culture of this country both nationally and locally'. If citizenship education is to fulfil its potential in contributing to that goal, it must be given more ambitious objectives and a more central position in curriculum.

How to engage young people

No matter how much citizenship education is provided, we cannot expect young people to fully engage in politics unless politics engages them. If politicians are not talking about things relevant to them, or if they appear unconcerned about the things young people care about, then we cannot be surprised if young people show little interest. The unnecessary acrimony of much of our political debate, which is off-putting to people of all generations, may be even more off-putting for the young who have not spent so much time watching political battles and who are likely to have more interest in issues than in party warfare. Attracting a new generation to politics needs a new style of politics.

There are, however, practical steps that can be taken even if little else changes.

What local authorities can do

We have already noted the relatively low levels of electoral registration for the 18-24 age group, and the problem could become very much worse with introduction of Individual Voter Registration (IER – see 3-12). As young people tend to spend less time at home, and as they may move home more often for their studies or employment, the risks of electoral registration forms not reaching them are higher than with other age groups. We therefore need special efforts by local authorities to make sure a disproportionate number of young people are not disenfranchised through not being on the electoral register.

For those in education, there is an easy answer. Schools and colleges should be required to work with local authorities in ensuring that all their students above the age of 16 are registered (other, of course, than any who are ineligible for reasons of nationality). Some universities already do this, but the majority take the view that it's not their job. That must be changed – if necessary by making public funding for colleges and universities at least partly related to registration levels, and giving Ofsted a remit for assessing their efforts in registration.

Although registration is not the same as voting, the two are related. In chapter 1-2 we noted that turnout for the 18-24 group in the 2015 general election was much higher than predicted. One explanation is that the efforts made in the months running up to the election to get young people registered also served to stimulate their interest in the election itself. That suggests that the work of organisations which promote registration, such as Bite the Ballot, has had real value and there is surely a case for encouraging them to repeat their efforts for future elections (and funding is the encouragement they most require).

Local authorities have responsibility not just for compiling registers but for promoting participation in elections. Not enough is done, however, to reach younger electors through schools and colleges, clubs and pubs and other places where they are likely to congregate. The strategies which Electoral Registration Officers use to meet their objectives are assessed by the Electoral Commission: there is a case for requiring EROs to develop specific strategies for reaching younger people.

Local authorities have a statutory duty to involve local people in decision-making. Where decisions have a particular relevance to young people, it should involve them, and even those who have not reached voting age. Many local authorities already have youth councils (sometimes called youth forums or youth parliaments) which are elected by young people (generally school students) themselves, and there are others which have 'young mayors', often supported by a group of elected 'young advisors'. While some youth councils and mayors may be little more than ornaments which allow local councils to claim they are attentive to young people's needs, in others they have been given real roles in work of councils and their committees.

Youth councils fully involved in decision-making can bring to local councils, generally dominated by people who are at least middle-aged, the views of a much younger generation – generally people who have not yet reached voting age. There are, however, difficulties in that the democratic mandates of youth council members are often bad, even compared with those of local councillors: it is important that youth councils speak for all young people and have resources to enable them to know what young people want them to say. Nevertheless, at their best youth councils and young mayors are, or could be, ways of giving young people a real voice in local affairs, and that in turn could stimulate longer-term interests in the workings of local democracy. There is therefore a case for requiring all local authorities to have youth councils with rights to participate in decision-making (but without formal voting rights on matters on which elected councillors must take responsibility). Such youth councils should be elected not just in schools and colleges but also by all those of the relevant ages (including, for example, those who are already on the electoral register) to make youth councillors as representative as possible, and they should be given budgets to allow them to consult with all young people in their area.

What politicians can do

If we want young people to engage with politicians, politicians must engage with young people. They must talk to them, but in language they will understand and without being patronising, and, more importantly, they must listen. That may mean going to schools and colleges from time to time not to lecture but to conduct surgeries, and colleges should be required to offer them (and their political opponents) the necessary facilities.

Many young people and many politicians communicate by social media, but rarely do they use it to communicate with each other. Nevertheless, here there appears to be loads of potential for online exchanges to allow young people to tell politicians what they think. Politicians, however, must adapt to the style of the medium and, of course, the content of what they have to say must be relevant and engaging. Long blog posts on the worthy things MPs have been doing will not excite young people – what they want to know is what the politicians are doing for them and on the issues that concern them.

What political parties can do

All parties have youth sections, many of them with groups around universities and colleges, even if the numbers involved are often disappointing (the other opportunities of university life perhaps appearing more attractive for many students). Nevertheless, in many of these groups the enthusiasm for politics is encouraging, and it is through them that many get their first experiences of politics.

Parties have been less successful, however, in reaching out to young people who are not in tertiary education. They need to be encouraged to get involved in politics where they live, but few of them will want to participate in meetings dominated by older generations discussing issues that are unlikely to excite them. Local parties therefore need to find ways of supporting younger members in developing their ideas, campaigning on issues that are important to them and organising activities more attractive to their own age group.

That, of course, does not mean that young people should not be encouraged to play active roles in the affairs of local parties as full and equal members. The model constitution for a Constituency Labour Party (CLP) requires the appointment of a Women's Officer as one of the CLP's five officers, but there is not even a mention of a Youth Officer – only the possibility of a 'co-ordinator' with responsibility for youth issues: the equivalent constitution of the Liberal Democrats gives a place for representatives of youth and student groups, where they exist, on the executive committee, but that the Conservative Party does not even mention youth. If the constitutions of local parties required them to ensure the representation of younger members on their committees and, where appropriate, to consulted them on plans, it might send more of a signal that local parties that do not manage to engage with younger people are unacceptable.

Votes for 16 and 17-year olds

At present only those who are 18 or over can vote, although the arguments for changing this have raged for years. In Scotland 16 and 17 year olds were allowed to vote in the 2014 independence referendum, but a move to let them vote in any referendum on Britain's membership of the EU was defeated in December 2015.

There will always be a voting age, but whatever age is chosen there will be those who think it should be lower or higher. Deciding when people can vote must be a matter of judgement based on the arguments, and there is no shortage of arguments. Those who favour votes at 16 can point to the things 16-year olds are already entitled to do, such as joining the army, earning wages on which they must pay tax, and having sex. Their opponents can counter that soldiers must be 18 before they can fight in the front line, that between 16 and 18 they are required to be in education or training, and that until they are 18 they need their parents' consent to marry (unless they decide to get married in Scotland). They can also argue that there is little debate around 17 being the minimum age for driving a car, or 18 for drinking alcohol in a pub. Thus there is no single age of maturity.

THE REFORM DEBATES

These arguments are not, however, about democracy, and we need to consider what voting age serves democracy best. Here the case for votes at 16 appears strong. While opponents maintain that few 16 year-olds have the experiences of life or knowledge of politics to make reasoned decisions, many of them know what they want from life and, if citizenship education were effective, they would know more about politics than many of their elders. Although not all 16-year olds may have sufficient understanding to make informed judgements, if it is accepted that many of them do then it would appear unreasonable deny a vote to those capable of using it responsibly.

Citizenship education provides one strong reason for reducing the voting age to 16. If it is about training people to participate in democracy, it would seem perverse to deny them the opportunity to participate when they have finished their course. An election would be an opportunity to learn through engagement, and with the current cycle of elections it is almost certain that all will have an election of some sort when either 16 or 17.

There is another reason, perhaps even more compelling, for reducing the voting age to 16. If people had the opportunity to vote at 16 when most will still be in full-time education, the education system can encourage them to vote, ensuring that they understand what the election is about, assisting them with registration and postal vote applications where necessary, and allowing them time to get to their polling stations. Without this encouragement, some will not vote, and the more often people don't vote the greater the chance of them becoming habitual non-voters.

Reducing the voting age to 16 has for many years been the policy of the Liberal Democrats, the SNP and Plaid Cymru and the Green Party, and Labour, in its 2015 manifesto, promised to make the change by May 2016. It was the Conservatives, however, who won the 2015 election. Although there are prominent Conservatives who favour a reduction (including the Conservative leader in Scotland), their party does not, and there is little sign of it changing its position. Nevertheless, if the momentum of the campaign for a change in the voting age can be maintained, this is a reform that will surely be made as soon as an opportunity arises.

There are nearly 6 million people in the 18-24 age group – that is just over 11% of the population of voting age – and a further 1.6 million are 16 or 17. Unless our politics engages them, our democracy will be incomplete. The measures proposed in this chapter:

- a renewed commitment to citizenship education covering the practice of politics as well as an understanding of its institutions;
- action by local authorities, politicians and political parties in promoting the involvement of young people; and
- a reduction in the voting age to 16;

all have the potential to make a difference, but what we also need is a change to a style of politics to which young people, and others, can relate.

---

[1] Matt Penn and Nick Foard, *Young people, political participation and trust in Britain*, paper presented EPOP conference, 2011.

[2] ibid

THE REFORM DEBATES

[3] Gerry Stoker, 'Political citizenship and the innocence of youth', in A Mycock and J Tonge (eds), *Beyond the Youth Citizenship Commission: Young People and Politics*, Political Studies Association, 2015

[4] In other parts of the UK, 'citizenship' does not appear in the curriculum as a subject, but many of the issues are covered under other headings. A review of the curriculum in Wales has recognised the need for active citizenship and an understanding of democracy and even social justice (http://gov.wales/docs/dcells/publications/150225-successful-futures-en.pdf), while Scotland's new 'Curriculum for Excellence' and Northern Ireland's curricula also recognise the role of the education system in producing 'responsible citizens'. Other than in England, however, the guidance is non-statutory (although any requirement for citizenship education in England may disappear if, as the government proposes, all schools become academies).

[5] *Education for citizenship and the teaching of democracy in schools: Final report of the Advisory Group on Citizenship*, Qualifications and Curriculum Authority, 1998

[6] David Kerr, 'Enhancing the political literacy of young people', in A Mycock and J Tonge (eds), *Beyond the Youth Citizenship Commission: Young People and Politics*, Political Studies Association, 2015.

[7] Matt Penn and Nick Foard, op cit.

[8] *Audit of Political Engagement 10*, Hansard Society, 2013

[9] *Audit of Political Engagement 11*, Hansard Society, 2014

[10] David Kerr, op cit.

[11] *A Curriculum for Life*, British Youth Council, 2013 (survey by Matthew Otubu, MYP)

3-12 Running better elections

Only about two out of every three electors vote in general elections, and only around third bother to do so in local elections. There is clearly something wrong with our democracy when so many people don't turn out to have their say on who represents them in parliament or on their local councils, but might more people vote if we ran our elections in a different way? This chapter looks at some of the changes that should be considered.

However, at the outset it needs to be recognised that most non-voters don't vote because they don't see sufficient reason to do so. In a survey of people who did not vote in the 2010 general election:

- 27% didn't believe their vote would make a difference;
- 25% thought the parties/candidates were all the same;
- 19% were not interested in politics, and
- 18% did not have enough information/knowledge to choose.

The way elections are conducted is not, therefore, the main reason that turnouts are low. People are not staying away from polling stations because it has become harder to vote – back in the years when turnouts were over 80%, fewer people had postal votes, polling stations were not open for so long, and most worked longer hours than they do now.

Nevertheless, in the same survey, 9% of non-voters said they were not able to get to a polling station or get a postal ballot. If we take them at their word (it is possible that, for some, difficulty in voting was an excuse rather than a reason), it suggests that over 1.4 million additional people might have voted if voting had been easier for them, and that number of people could easily have changed the outcome of the election. Thus, although improvements in the way elections are conducted can only be a small part of what is needed, they well worth considering.

Registering to vote

In Britain you cannot vote unless on polling day your name appears on the electoral register, so electoral registration is a first issue to consider.

In 2011 the Electoral Commission published research suggesting that 6 million people otherwise entitled to vote were not on the electoral register - a figure nearly double the previous estimate. It meant that around 12% of potential voters would not be able to have their say in elections. Work by electoral registration officers, parties and and other organisations may have reduced this number before the 2015 election, but it is likely that the number of people not registered to vote was two to three times greater than the difference between the votes received by the two major parties.

In the past the register was compiled through forms which a member of every household had to complete giving the names of those eligible to vote. With concerns over electoral fraud, 'Individual Electoral Registration' (IER) started to be introduced in 2014, requiring every voter to complete a form with their National Insurance number and date of birth. With fears that the change would result in many names being removed from the register, as an interim measure it was agreed that those previously registered would remain on the register provided their names could be identified on other government databases. By October 2013, 35 million voters had been transferred to the new registers automatically, but that left about another 10 million who would only be registered if they completed a form. While many of them did, it must be assumed that many lost their right to vote in 2015 in this way.

The Government decided that the change to IER should be completed by December 2016, in spite of the Electoral Commission recommending that electoral registration officers should be given a further year to implement the change. There was outcry, but when the proposal reached the Lords, not enough peers turned up to force a delay. Labour was particularly concerned, expecting that those more likely to drop off the register would be disproportionately people in parts of society more sympathetic to Labour. Research by Hope not Hate in found that 8 of the 10 local authorities with the largest drops in numbers registered were in inner London, while the drop-off rate was much lower in the more affluent suburbs, thereby demonstrating that Labour's fears were justified.

Many of those who don't register may not be concerned as they have no intention of voting and, although registering to vote is compulsory, action to enforce it has so rarely been taken that the theoretical threat of a fine has little effect. There may be many others, however, who, when election day arrives, find they are disenfranchised because they forgot to register, or simply assumed their names would be on the register, or find that a change in address has left them without a vote.

THE REFORM DEBATES

An election in which millions are barred from voting simply because they are not on the register is far from satisfactory. There is no single or easy solution to the problem, but there are a several things that could be done to substantially reduce the extent of non-registration. For example:

- Electoral registration officers (EROs) need to be given the resources to do an effective job in ensuring that registers are as near complete as possible. Some do better than others, but in cash-strapped local authorities there may not be the funds needed for additional visits to homes where none are registered. The work of EROs is important, but we cannot expect them to provide an adequate service without adequate funding.
- When we know that people exist, they could be added to the register without the need to complete a form. Those not registered are often known to the authorities - most pay council tax, many are on benefits, some live in local authority or other forms of social housing, and some have driving licences and/or passports. As we know who they are and where they live, surely there is an argument for automatically putting their names on the register. The official objection to doing this is that they might not all be entitled to vote – e.g. they may be of nationalities not allowed to vote in all, or some elections. However, the number in this category is likely to be small, and in many cases people's nationalities will have been recorded in other databases available to the election registration offices. Rather than disenfranchising a large number of people, it would make sense to assume that people have an entitlement to vote unless there is evidence to suggest that they don't.

- Schools could be required arrange the registration of their senior students. Some might not be of a voting age, but at least they would be on the register, making it easier for registration officers to follow them up to ensure they remain on the register. Some, of course, may leave home or decide that they have no interest in voting and hence in re-registering, but for many it would ensure that they do not inadvertently find they are denied the opportunity to vote.
- Voting day registration is something which should be considered. This is used in a number of states in the US where anyone turning up at a polling station is allowed to vote, whether or not they are on the electoral register, provided they can prove their eligibility. If there is doubt, they may only be offered a 'provisional ballot' and their votes will not be counted until their credentials have been confirmed. There seems little reason why a similar procedure could not be used in the UK.

These measures, and no doubt others, are needed if we are to reduce the number of those unable to vote because they are not registered. The change to IER, however, makes the need for new approaches to registration particularly important as it increases the danger that those not on the register are mainly people with a real need for a political voice – the young, those of ethnic minority communities, people in temporary accommodation, those who must often move home in search of work, those in multiple-occupation properties, people living on their own who may not be at home when local authority canvassers call with registration forms, etc. Unless we can get more such people registered, and voting, then our elections are likely to be skewed in favour of those who are home owners, more settled, and more comfortably off.

There is a further danger if we do not get our registers as near complete as possible. The government elected in 2015 has stated its intention to have constituency boundaries redrawn to produce constituencies of roughly the same number of electors.[1] At first sight the idea might seem reasonable. The problem, however, is that constituencies contain people who are not registered as well as those who are, and a great majority of the former, as noted above, are likely to live in the more deprived, inner city areas rather than the better off suburbs and rural areas. Not only might the proposal lead to even greater disparities in number of people in each constituency, but the larger constituencies (by population) would be those with a higher proportion of people needing the services of their MP. If democracy is to mean an equal voice for all citizens, then electoral registration is something we must do better.

The way we vote

Voting at polling stations

About three quarters of those who vote do it in the traditional way at a polling station and the remainder vote by post.[2] Some who vote at polling stations do so because it is the way they have always voted (and there are still people who regard going to the polling station as part of their civic duty), but for most others it is simply the default option. However, there is much to be said in favour of polling station voting: the secrecy of the ballot is ensured and, although 'impersonation' (i.e. people claiming to other than who they are in order to use another's vote) is possible, it is difficult on any scale as each vote requires a separate visit to the polling station. Moreover, polling stations are only open at the end of election campaigns, so there is no danger that people vote and then find, as a result of any scandals or unexpected policy statements from the parties, they would have rather voted for someone else. A disadvantage of voting at polling stations is, however, that those living close to polling stations are more likely to vote than those who need to travel some distance.

Postal voting

Postal voting is on the increase, with all parties trying to get more of their supporters to vote in this way. Until 2000 voting by post was only allowed if an elector could give a good reason for requiring one, but in an attempt to increase turnouts, that was changed and now any elector can ask for a postal vote without giving any reason. As a result, the numbers voting by post has increased rapidly.

What evidence exists suggests that postal voting does indeed increase turnout. This was demonstrated in a number of trials in local elections between 2000 and 2003 when 'all postal voting' (in which postal voting was not an option but the only way of voting) generally produced higher turnouts, and when all-postal voting was used in four regions for the 2004 European elections, turnouts in these regions were on average 5% higher than in other regions. In 2010, 83% of those who were registered for postal votes actually voted compared with 63% for those who were not (although the difference here is likely to be mainly because people who applied for a postal vote wanted to vote, while others not interested in voting would not have applied). Similarly, almost half of the 15% who voted in the Police and Crime Commissioner elections in 2011 were postal voters.

THE REFORM DEBATES

Getting people to vote by post has therefore become a major campaign tactic of the political parties. If people have a postal vote, it can be easier to persuade them to use it, and to do so well in advance of the election: parties can then have 'votes in the bag' before polling day arrives, thereby reducing the task they have in their 'get out the vote' activities, i.e. contacting potential supporters and making sure they get to the polling stations in time. The large increase in postal voting is therefore largely due to the efforts of candidates and their campaigners.

However, although postal voting may produce some increase in turnouts, it has its drawbacks. Most importantly, if we allow people to vote away from polling stations, the secrecy of the ballot is lost. There is no point in bribing electors who will vote in a polling station because, once in the polling booth electors can vote as they please and no-one will ever know, but if an elector votes by post they can vote in the presence of the briber and prove that they have delivered on the contract. Even if bribery is not involved, a dominant household member can gather others and tell them where to put their crosses, or a disinterested elector can simply pass a ballot paper to someone else for completion.

Following the introduction of postal voting on demand, there were also concerns that votes might be cast by people other than those to whom they were issued. Ballot papers, for example, put through the single letter box of a block of flats might be collected and completed by whoever gets to them first. This problem has been partly overcome by requiring applicants for postal votes to give a signature and date of birth which are also required to prove the legitimacy of a vote when returned, but the safeguard is not foolproof and can cause difficulties if people vary their signatures or (as some Returning Officers have reported) inadvertently enter the current date rather than their date of birth, thereby invalidating their votes. Moreover, it does not prevent fraudulent applications for postal votes with requests for the ballot papers to be sent to addresses other than those of the real electors.

Electoral fraud, which has been relatively rare in British elections, has become much more of a problem with postal voting. The worst case arose in Birmingham in 2004: police found three councillors in a warehouse in the middle of the night with hundreds of ballot papers and there were reports of intimidation, fraudulent applications for postal votes and threats to postal workers delivering ballot papers. In quashing the results of elections in two wards, the judge lambasted the procedures for postal voting and referred to 'evidence of electoral fraud that would disgrace a banana republic'. As a result of this and other cases, there are some who argue that postal voting, at least on demand, is too dangerous – even suspicion of fraud can undermine confidence in election results and therefore in democracy itself.

Internet and telephone voting

Online voting has many proponents. Many of us pay our bills and order our groceries online and, it is therefore argued, we should also be able to vote online, particularly as many organisations and trade unions already use online voting to save on postal costs. Although local trials of online voting in 2002 and 2003 did not produce any significant increases in turnout, there is every reason to believe that many people would find it easier to vote in this way and that new, larger-scale trials might provide different results. Moreover, as it would be easy for the voting software to offer links to webpages with details of the candidates, their parties and their policies, it could help voters to make more informed decisions before casting their votes.

THE REFORM DEBATES

However, as with postal voting, online voting has the problem that the secrecy of a vote cast outside a polling booth cannot be guaranteed.[3] Online voting requires no signatures to enable checks that those voting are the people to whom the votes were issued, and if the PIN numbers provided to voters were sold or bought by party campaigners it would be difficult to detect. Then there are the technical vulnerabilities: clever hackers might enjoy the challenge of interfering with people's votes, possibly to subvert an entire election or even changing the candidates voters have supported (there have been some notorious examples of this in the US). There are also concerns that people's votes may be recorded using software and on equipment provided by contractors with the risk that the data might fall into the wrong hands either by accident of through a deliberate leak. As a result, internet voting has never gone beyond the pilot stage in the UK, but it is still on the agenda.

Text messaging is the preferred means of communication for many young people, and some believe that many more of them would vote if they could use their mobile phones. However, the arguments around voting by mobile phones are similar to those on online voting.

Striking a balance

Making voting easier, through postal voting, internet or text message voting, could increase turnouts, and the more people who vote in an election, the more likely that the winning candidate will be the most representative of electors. Making voting easier, however, may make fraud easier. We therefore need to weigh up the advantages against the risks.

There is evidence that postal voting increases turnouts and, with requirement that has been introduced for signatures and dates of birth on postal vote applications, some of the risks have been reduced. There remains the problem that the secrecy of the ballot is compromised in that people can show others how they are voting. Warnings of draconian penalties for anyone found to have shown their vote to another might deter some, but the chances of a crime being detected are slim. However, for many people postal voting has become the normal way of voting, and it may be that the risk to ballot secrecy is something we need to live with.

These risks are greater in local elections where it may only need a few hundred votes, or less, to change an outcome - in a parliamentary constituency it is more difficult to know how many fraudulent votes might be needed to affect the result, but the number is likely to be in the thousands and fraud on that scale without detection is difficult. Even with local elections, however, incidences of fraud need to be kept in perspective. In the vast majority of wards there have been no suggestions of any impropriety, and the Birmingham case arose within a particular ethnic community where understanding and respect for electoral rules were far from what they should have been.

If we assume that all-postal voting could increase turnouts in local elections by 5% it would mean about an extra 2 million people voting, and even if the increase from postal voting on demand is more modest, it would seem perverse to reduce the opportunity for these people to exercise their political voice because of the danger of a very few unscrupulous people trying to cheat, particularly now that postal voting has become the norm for many people.

THE REFORM DEBATES

Internet and text-message voting is another matter. Although early trials in 2002 and 2003 did not show much increase in turnout, it is reasonable to assume that these voting methods could be particularly attractive to younger electors. However, the risks of a major cyber attack or the leak of data on how people voted being, either deliberately or inadvertently, are significant. Unless and until ways are found of reducing these risks to a point at which they are near negligible, internet and text message voting would appear to be a step too far. Some, however, will disagree, and there is space for debate.

When we vote

In the UK we vote on Thursdays. It has not always been so – until 1935, elections were held on different days of the week. There were Christian objections to Sundays and Jews did not want Saturdays; for many Friday was pay day and some might head for the pub rather than the polling station (and those who did get around to voting might then have impaired judgement); in many areas Thursday was market day and consequently a day when many would be in the towns where the polling stations were situated. However, what logic there might have been for choosing Thursday is now long lost. Every day is now a shopping day and the numbers with religious objections to voting on a holy day are too small for it to be a determining factor.

But is there a case for holding elections on a different day? Across Europe, Sunday is the most common day for elections although there is not a single day of the week that is not used for elections by one or more countries. There is some evidence that countries that vote at weekends have higher turnouts, but research on countries that moved their elections from a weekday to the weekend found that it made little difference. In the UK there is an argument that at weekends fewer people are at work and more will therefore have time to cast their votes, but whether more would is another matter. Nevertheless, there is nothing sacrosanct about Thursdays and anything that might improve turnouts is worth a try.

In England there have been two experiments with weekend voting. In 2000 Watford was allowed to hold its local elections at a weekend, but turnout dropped. This was not too surprising: all other local elections had been held on the previous Thursday and by the time the elections were held the media coverage was of elections that had already taken place. Electors in Watford could be forgiven for thinking that by the time the weekend came they had missed the boat. Two years later Camden held elections on the weekend before other London boroughs, but again the London-wide media coverage of the coming Thursday elections may have led some to believe that election day had not yet arrived and the change did not produce any benefit. These trials do not therefore provide any real indication of whether weekend voting would help.

Thus, while a change in the day we vote is only likely to have a very slight impact on turnout, there is nevertheless a case for a full, nation-wide trial of weekend voting. It may mean having polling stations open on both Saturdays and Sundays to overcome religious objections but, given the importance of democracy, if weekend voting made a real difference, the extra costs would be a price worth paying.

If weekend voting is to be tested, an obvious place to start would be European Parliament elections (and the local elections

THE REFORM DEBATES

often held at the same time). European elections cannot be counted until Sunday evening when voting has finished across Europe for fear of election results in one country influencing voting in another (although the risks of this happening would appear minimal). Weekend voting would allow votes to be counted immediately after the close of polls, avoiding the need for ballots to be stored for three days and putting candidates and campaigners out of their misery without a three-day wait.

Some, however, have suggested a more radical change. If election days were made into bank holidays, few would be prevented from voting by work commitments. There would, of course, be the danger that some would use the opportunity for, say, a trip to the seaside rather than staying at home to vote, and with polling stations open from 7 am to 10 pm, work commitments may be more often an excuse rather than a reason for not voting. A polling day holiday, however, would have the effect of making election days a little more special - elections would rank higher in public consciousness and few could argue that they had simply forgotten that an election was being held. If we are to have more bank holidays, then this idea certainly seems worth a try.

Another option worth considering is 'early voting'. Instead of voters needing to wait to polling day when they may have other engagements, they could be given the opportunity to vote several days beforehand. While this has only been piloted on a very small scale in the UK, in the US it's big. Before the 2012 Presidential election day arrived, as many as a third of electors may have voted, and in Colerado it was estimated that an astonishing 85% might have voted early. If polling stations in the UK were open several days before an election, voters could choose which days and times suited them best: if commitments on election day were like to be a problem, a voter could vote beforehand without the need for a postal vote.

Having polling stations open for several days rather than just one would, of course, significantly add to the costs of elections and, however passionate we are about democracy, that is not something for which we can argue unless there are clear benefits.

If early voting simply meant people could vote at their local polling station on a different day, it might not make a great deal of difference in the final turnout. However, the real potential of early voting might lie in the opportunities it could provide for voting not at the normal polling stations but in places that many electors would find much more convenient.

Where we vote

Unless voting by post, an elector can only vote at the designated polling station for the area in which she or he is registered. Generally that means the area where an elector lives, but even in urban areas the polling station may be some distance away – in some cases a mile or more – and not every polling station is on a bus route. For some, voting therefore requires a bit of effort, and those who spend much of their day away from home before getting back to eat, put children to bed, etc., may not feel inclined to make the trip to a polling station.

If people could vote where they do their shopping, at their railway station or near their office, it is possible that more might do so. With early voting, this is perfectly possible. Polling booths could be set up in convenient places, with electoral registers for a whole local authority area, allowing people to vote without need to make a separate journey to do so.

THE REFORM DEBATES

Some have argued that people should be allowed to vote at any polling station, even on election day. This would, however, require all polling stations to be online to prevent multiple voting, and the risks of a technical malfunction appear to be too great to justify any benefits.

Improving the voting experience

Voting is perhaps the most important form of democratic engagement, yet we often ask people to vote in dingy community centres, draughty church halls and school classrooms. No major company intent on keeping its clients would treat people in this way – they would be welcomed to plush offices, offered comfortable seats and offered a cup of tea or coffee. Why should it be different with voting? Those voting are citizens fulfilling a civic duty, and treating them with the respect they deserve need not be a huge cost compared with the cost of elections.

The late Robin Cook often remarked that voting is probably the only time most people use a pencil and even that pencil is tied to the desk in the polling booth. No company in the twenty-first century would promote its activities using stubs of pencil - not only would they offer the use of a pen, but they would invite people to take away the pen as a reminder of their visit.

Companies employ marketing agencies to devise the images and messages that will attract people to their products, but we don't market democracy. The Electoral Commission does some good work, but the resources it has are mere fraction of the advertising budgets of large companies. (In its earlier years the Commission had a responsibility and a £7.5 million budget for increasing participation in politics, but this was removed in 2007 after a report by the short-sighted Commission for Standards in Public Life.)

Returning Officers now have a responsibility for encouraging turnout: some are innovative and creative in doing so, but there are some who do little, perhaps because they have not been given the budgets they need, but in some cases because they don't think it's as a priority for them. They are obliged to send cards to electors, informing them of coming elections and telling them where they can vote. These cards, printed in black, often look more like invitations to a funeral than to a wedding – it has been remarked that 'most dentists are able to make a summons to have a tooth out more welcoming that the invitation to vote'.[4] The main cost is in delivering the cards rather than in printing them, so why not use colour and, even if there is statutory wording that must be used, add more enticing messages about why the election is important?

Democracy is something we should celebrate. Whether or not we make election days into bank holidays, there is a case for more of a carnival atmosphere. Our elections have become very low-key affairs and it is not surprising that some don't vote simply because they forgot an election was being held. Elections should be occasions when all flags are flown, when announcements are made on station tannoys, when poster vans with loudspeakers tour the streets and radio programmes commemorate the sacrifices of those lost their lives or liberty to win for us the right to vote. Election days should not just be like other days – there needs to be something special about them to remind us of the importance of exercising that right.

THE REFORM DEBATES

[1] It is a proposal which the Conservatives made in the previous government, but it failed when their Liberal Democrat coalition partners refused to support it

[2] Figures for the 2015 general election from the Electoral Commission

[3] Some online voting systems partly overcome the risks of bribery by allowing people to change their vote at any time before polling day. There would be then be little point in pressing, or bribing, a voter to vote in a particular way as the voter could easily recast their vote later for the candidate they really wanted. However, such systems do not protect against the risks of PIN numbers being bought or sold.

[4] L Baston and K Ritchie, *Turning out or turning off,* Electoral Reform Society 2004

3-13 Should voting be compulsory?

If we want more people to vote, should we not just make voting compulsory, fining those who do not do so? It's a debate that has been around for many years, and as recently as November 2014 the House of Commons Political and Constitutional Reform Committee recommended that it should be considered at least for some types of elections. A survey conducted for the Committee found public opinion very evenly divided on the question.

It is fairly safe to assume that the threat of a fine would get many more people to the polling stations. In countries in which voting is compulsory turnouts are much higher than in the UK, for example over 90% in Australia and nearly 90% in Belgium (even although the legislation is rarely enforced there). When voting was compulsory in Austrian Presidential elections the turnout was always above 90%, but after 1980 when compulsion was removed it started to fall and was only 54% in 2010.

Higher turnouts mean that election results reflect the views of a higher proportion of the electors, and that is what we want in democratic elections. There are, however, other arguments made by proponents of compulsory voting:

- Political parties have little interest in overall turnout – all they want to see is a high turnout of those who support them. Elections can be won and lost not on the attractiveness of parties' policies but on which party is best able to get its supporters to

vote. Party campaign organisers often talk more about 'Get out the vote' (GOTV) activities than about getting reluctant electors to appreciate the merits of their messages. If voting were compulsory and it had to be assumed that nearly everyone would vote, GOTV campaigns would become redundant and election campaigns would need to focus on policies rather than mobilising potential supporters. Canvassing simply to identify who to target on election day would no longer make sense – instead canvassing would be about engaging with voters on policy issues.
- If electors know that they must vote, some argue that they are more likely to take an interest in what the parties are offering so that they can decide how to use their votes.
- Democracy gives people political rights, but it should also give them political responsibilities. We have accepted compulsory registration (in theory if not in practice) and there is a compulsion to serve on a jury if summoned. Compelling people to vote need not therefore be seen as an authoritarian measure.

There are, however, drawbacks and dangers. At present voting is an act of political engagement, but would it be so if people were only voting to avoid a fine? A high turnout with compulsory voting would not indicate that people are more interested in politics – many might be even more resentful of a political class that compels them to do something they would prefer not to do. While turnout is not the only measure of political engagement, there is a danger that compulsory voting would merely hide the extent to which people are alienated by politics.

This problem could be partly overcome by having a 'None of the above' box on the ballot paper, allowing voters to express their disapproval of all candidates on offer. Some have argued strongly for this but, while compulsory voting should not mean compelling people to make a choice (a voter can after all simply leave the ballot paper blank), a vote for 'none of the above' seems to miss the point of an election. One of the candidates will be elected, and the ballot paper does not ask which candidate the voter thinks is wonderful, but which of the candidates the voter thinks would be best, or least bad.

There are also practical difficulties. Compulsory voting would make little sense without compulsory registration and, while we have that in principle, it is not something that has ever been enforced. It would be perverse to fine those who did not vote but who took the trouble to register, but not those who did not even register. The number of people liable to be fined could be huge: if compulsory voting had produced, say, a turnout of around 90% in the 2015 election, the number who were registered but did not vote added to those who did not even register would have been over 10 million. Is it conceivable that a government would attempt to fine 10 million people? What would happen if there was mass civil disobedience on a poll-tax scale? It could have our court rooms working overtime for years to come. Even if people were not to take to the streets, the scale of the resentment against compulsion could be fatal for any government. It is therefore something that none could contemplate introducing unless there was strong cross-party support for the measure, and at present that does not exist.

Some of these problems could be overcome with 'incentive voting' – a carrot rather than a stick approach. Those who vote could be offered a small reduction in their council tax (which is not much different from a council tax supplement – a form of fine - for

THE REFORM DEBATES

those who don't), and some have suggested that the names of those who vote should be entered into a prize draw, but there seems something distasteful about making voting into a free lottery ticket.

From a democratic perspective, however, the political objections to compulsory voting are more important. We want to create a political culture that engages people, and that requires the whole raft of reforms considered in this book. We cannot compel people to be interested in politics and to see it as their opportunity to shape the society they live in – we need to change to a style of politics that makes people want to vote. Rather than truly engaging more people in politics, there is a danger that fines for non-voting would increase political alienation.

Nevertheless, the debate over compulsory voting is likely to continue.

3-14 Defending rights and liberties

Robbie Parkin with Ken Ritchie

A democracy without protection for the rights of all citizens could merely be the tyranny of the majority over minorities – it could be, as Thomas Jefferson put it, 'nothing more than mob rule, where fifty-one per cent of the people may take away the rights of the other forty-nine'. Democracy and rights must therefore go hand-in-hand.

This chapter looks at what our rights are and how they have developed. It argues that although our rights have been expanded and strengthened over the years, we are now facing new challenges which could undermine them. Rights, by their very nature, place limitations on what governments can do, and unless citizens are vigilant in defending them there is a danger that governments will over-ride them when they find it expedient to do so.

What are 'rights'?

While we often talk about 'our rights', the concept of 'human rights' refers to only one very specific body of rules, as encapsulated by the Universal Declaration of Human Rights and the European Convention on Human Rights. What many of us think of as 'human rights' is something rather more vague and fundamental. Legal historians, indeed, often prefer the term 'Fundamental Rights' for the broader idea that there are some

THE REFORM DEBATES

rules so important that no government should be allowed to break them, even if it would be otherwise legal, beneficial for or popular with the public.

The concept of human rights goes back a long way: as a legal concept it probably originated in medieval common law. Magna Carta, the Bill of Rights 1689, and the Act of Settlement 1701 all said much the same thing, in various ways. The American Bill of Rights, and the French Declaration of the Rights of Man and of the Citizen, both 1789, updated these schemes and were largely inspired by them.

The United Nations was established after the horrific experiences of the Second World War and the Nazi persecutions. Its founding Charter 'reaffirmed faith in fundamental human rights' and these rights were then set out in its Universal Declaration of Human Rights which was adopted in 1948. The rights it described were regarded as 'universal' in the sense that they are entitlements and protections that everyone should have, irrespective of the country in which they live.

The Council of Europe went further with its own European Convention on Human Rights which came into force in 1953. What made the Convention different from the UN Declaration, however, was the creation of the European Court of Human Rights to enforce it and hear cases brought by those who considered their rights had been violated. The rights defined in the Convention were broadly similar to those of the UN Declaration (although many were qualified by clauses allowing governments act, for example, in the interests of national security or to preserve the rule of law), but it took the form of a code of conduct for governments, stating that:

- Governments cannot kill anyone, except where death results from the use of minimum possible force in self-defence or the defence of others, used in carrying out a legal arrest or preventing escape, or in quelling a riot or a rebellion. They must make efforts to prevent unlawful killing, and investigate murders which do take place.
- Governments cannot use torture, inhumane, or degrading treatment, regardless of extenuating circumstance.
- Governments cannot enslave anyone, or use forced labour (but with exceptions such as prison work and military service), and must make positive efforts to prevent slavery or forced labour.
- A government cannot imprison anyone except for the purpose of punishment of crime, arrest, school detention, for public health reasons, or for immigration enforcement. Any detained person is to be made aware of the reasons for his detention, promptly tried or bailed, and can apply to court for bail. A wrongfully arrested person must be compensated.
- Any trial must be fair[1], and the results publically announced unless there is a sufficiently good reason not to. The accused is presumed innocent until proven guilty.
- Governments must respect the right to privacy and family life, the right to freedom of opinion and religion, the right to free speech and other expression, and the right of free assembly. These rights can be restricted in so far as is proportionate and for a good cause.
- A government may not prevent people from marrying except by reason of imposing a minimum age of consent. This includes same-sex marriage, but that has only been recognised since 2015.

THE REFORM DEBATES

A series of protocols introduced since 1952 updated the original text with certain additional rights: the right to own property; the right to education; the right to vote freely; the prohibition of debtor's prisons; only proportionate restrictions on movement within one's country and the right to leave one's country; a prohibition of expelling people from their own country and a requirement that migrants only be expelled legally; a right to appeal against criminal convictions; compensation for miscarriages of justice; a prohibition of double jeopardy; and a prohibition of gender discrimination between married partners.

The Convention requires governments to apply these rights equally to everyone regardless of race, nationality, religion, gender, or other defining characteristics, and, since 2000, that rule applies to any act of law, whether part of these rights or not.

The purpose of most of these provisions is plain enough. From the time the Convention was drafted in the middle of the last century, Europe has seen dictatorial and repressive regimes, many of them using the same collection of techniques to prop up their power. Political opponents have been subjected to extra-judicial killing or torture, or kept as slaves in concentration camps; even where there has been a functioning legal system, people have been arbitrarily arrested, imprisoned without trial or subjected trials that are manifestly unfair. There has been large-scale spying on the public. Religious and ethnic minorities have been persecuted and openly discriminatory laws passed. Opposition political parties have been outlawed as have been public demonstrations. The Convention makes such actions illegal.

Britain, thankfully, has not suffered from such repression, at least in its recent history, and prior to the ratification of the European Convention not many people in Britain would have had concerns about being killed by their government, tortured or enslaved. Nevertheless, the provisions of the Convention have provided standards which national legislation must meet and have thereby helped bring about changes from which many people benefited. For example, no longer is it permissible to discriminate on grounds of sex or race, there are protections for people with disabilities, and while members of LGBT communities might not yet have all the rights they want, we have come a long way from the days in which they could prosecuted even for what they did in private. It does not mean that discrimination has been banished from our society, but at least the law is now there to provide some protection from it.

Many of these developments in our rights did not, however, come about just because our government ratified a convention – they were fought for. It needed the spirit of women, such as those who staged a strike at Ford's plant in Dagenham in 1968 to win the right of equal pay for equal work; racial equality was not achieved without years of anti-racist campaigning; and it is very unlikely that we would have seen such progress towards LGBT rights without the courage of the gay rights activists.

Thus while democracy may have waned since the middle of the last century (see chapter 1-4), our rights have been considerably strengthened. They may of course have been extended even without the stimulus of international conventions, but in Britain, in the absence of a written constitution, it is these conventions which entrench rights and which should, at least in theory, protect them from erosion by national legislation.

However, while the development of rights in Britain has been broadly a good news story, our rights are now facing new challenges. In particular:

- We have a government that is, astonishingly, considering abandoning the European Convention on Human Rights (without necessarily abandoning many of the rights it provides) and rejecting the authority of the European Court of Human Rights to rule on rights issues in the UK;
- The need to combat the threat of terrorism has resulted in challenges to many of our rights as a consequence of our government's efforts (which are quite understandable) to protect society from attacks.
- Our ability to protect our rights (and to hold our government to account) has been reduced by cuts in funding for legal aid and legal advice, increased fees to applying to employment tribunals and changes to the judicial review system.

The remainder of this chapter looks at each of these threats in turn.

The threat to the European Convention on Human Rights

Countries that are members of the Council of Europe are not just required to respect the Convention abstractly – they must accept that, if they fail to comply with its terms, their citizens may sue them in the Strasbourg-based European Court of Human Rights.

When the Court rules against a government, it is not surprising that politicians feel resentful at what they may see as interference in their national affairs. To assuage such concerns, the manner of implementation of the Rights is largely left to the member states. Many constituent nations have found ways to ensure that the bulk of such decisions are made in home jurisdictions rather than Strasbourg. The UK did this in 1998 via the Human Rights Act which allows British Courts to interpret the Convention and make judgments on it. It makes it illegal for a public body (such as a government department or an NHS Trust) to act in a way which is incompatible with Convention Rights. If parliament passes laws which breach Convention Rights, certain courts can declare Acts of Parliament incompatible with the convention but must still follow parliament's wishes. Parliament, however, normally amends legislation in response, but does not have to.

The Human Rights Act does not then, as the Conservatives claimed before the 2015 election, 'undermine the role of the UK courts'[2]. In fact, the opposite is true- it allows British courts to apply Convention Rights without referring the cases involved to Strasbourg. Nor does it 'undermine the sovereignty of Parliament'- it expressly preserves it. It, contrary to what is commonly claimed, is far more generous to the government than equivalents in other countries[3].

Nevertheless, this has not prevented a barrage of criticism of the European Court of Human Rights from many Conservative politicians, no doubt fuelled by a suspicion of all things European (although the Council of Europe and the EU are quite different things). The Human Rights Act has also been a target of sections of the tabloid press, but claims that it allows prisoners access to pornography,[4] required police to give a suspected car thief Kentucky Fried Chicken[5] and enabled a prisoner on probation to kill, are all bogus. The Act has been criticised for not allowing Britain to deport advocates of terrorism to countries where they might not receive a fair trial, but this prohibition arises from international obligations other than the European Convention, and, contrary to a claim by Home Secretary, Theresa May, the Act has never prevented the deportation of anyone because of caring responsibilities for a cat.[6] Perhaps more controversial has been the European Court's ruling against Britain's blanket ban on prisoners voting,

THE REFORM DEBATES

but the case for allowing prisoners on short sentences to vote has been strongly supported by those concerned with prison reform and the rehabilitation of offenders.

Very few decisions affecting the UK are made in Strasbourg. Between 1998 and 2013, there were 202 findings that the UK had breached Human Rights out of 13,515 complaints, about 13.5 per year and a UK success rate of about 98.5%. That rate is improving at present, being about 99.1% in 2013 and only 8 findings. There is almost complete agreement between the UK courts and Strasbourg as to the application of Human Rights.

It is not the case that only criminals or migrants benefit from these decisions. Strasbourg has attacked sectarian discrimination in Northern Ireland, forced an investigation into the murder of the family of a schoolboy by a teacher who had stalked him, and prevented an NHS trust from refusing to resuscitate a severely disabled child without familial consent, among many others.

The process is far less costly than often claimed. Between 1998 and 2013, the UK paid about £1.7 million in compensation as a result of judgements in Strasbourg. That may sound high but, for example, the 15 year total is only about 1% of the amount paid by the Criminal Injuries Compensation board in the financial year of 2013-2014 in Scotland alone - a relative drop in the ocean.

These distortions are particularly lamentable because they miss legitimate controversies. No one seriously denies that murder, torture and slavery are bad things, or that freedom of speech, a responsible police force, fair trials and equality before the law are good things. The difficult moral questions concern balancing legitimate rights and interests. There will always be controversy and different opinions.

DEFENDING RIGHTS AND LIBERTIES

Proposals for Reform

The Conservative Party fought the 2015 election with a commitment to 'reform' rights legislation. They were opposed to the status quo, i.e. membership of the European Convention enforced in the UK via the Human Rights Act, but they did not propose withdrawal from the European Convention entirely or the abolition of fundamental rights altogether. Instead the present government favours a halfway house - continued membership of the European Convention, but with the Human Rights Act replaced with a 'British Bill of Rights'.

These proposals, while creative, are not so much wrong as incoherent. The idea that the repeal of the Human Rights Act, while remaining a member of the Council of Europe and a signatory to the European Convention of Human Rights would decrease, not increase, the influence of Strasbourg in the UK is completely misconceived. Replacing the Human Rights Act by passing convention rights as an act of Parliament would, in practice, either have exactly the same effect as the Human Rights Act, or radically strengthen the role of Strasbourg.

Other Conservative proposals include:

- Regarding European Court judgements that UK law is incompatible with the Convention as simply advisory: this, however, would be beyond the government's powers while the UK remains a signatory to the European Convention and the government would find itself being sued in Strasbourg, probably successfully, on nearly every occasion it refused to act on a judgement;
- Regarding the Convention as applying only to 'serious matters'- whatever that means: again, the government has no

THE REFORM DEBATES

power to do so and would find itself being forced to backtrack every time it is challenged;
- Limiting the reach of human rights to prevent cases being brought against British armed forces overseas, effectively allowing them to commit human rights violations abroad: even overlooking the abhorrence of such a desire, the government, once again, would swiftly find itself unable to resist legal challenges to that position.

In fact, the only important question is whether or not the government would preserve the right of British courts to make decisions on issues of Human Rights in all cases, or not. A person who complains today that the UK violates their Human Rights can take the offending government department to court to test their claim. The local court will make a decision and, if the complainant wants to contest that decision, they can appeal to the European Court of Human Rights. If that does not change, the government's approach would essential be window-dressing. If, however, the complaint could not be heard in a British court and that person had to apply directly to the European Court of Human Rights in Strasbourg to make their complaint, the UK courts would lose the right to make any Human Rights decisions at all, a complete perversion of the principle that these decisions should normally be made in the UK.

Whatever the consequences of Britain rejecting the jurisdiction of the European Court might be in Britain itself, the international consequences would be enormous. Britain had a central role in creating the Court. The Convention was drafted largely under the supervision of a British lawyer, Sir David Maxwell Fyfe, and Britain was the first country to ratify it. The Court has been far from toothless in its dealings with genuinely unstable or dictatorial governments (by far the worst offenders have been Russia and Turkey with Romania and Ukraine not far behind[7]), but British withdrawal would seriously weaken it.

In Russia, judgments of the Court prevented acts of ethnic cleansing by Putin's government in Georgia and Moldova, the use of torture to force confessions to crimes, and forced the government to actively protect its citizens from sexual trafficking. It seems inevitable that the Putin government's appalling approach to the war in Ukraine, or its treatment homosexuals, will be subject to similar judgments in the near future. In Turkey, judgments similarly prevented the use of the death penalty and show trials against the non-violent advocacy of secession, countered the use of violence by the government against peaceful demonstrators and state efforts to suppress the identity of the Alevi religious minority. In Romania, the government was prevented from using corrupt debt avoidance practices; in Ukraine, from using a form of torture which caused blindness in order to criminal force confessions, in Hungary, from the arrest of peaceful anti-government protestors. The list could go on and on. Human Rights violations are alarmingly frequent, horrific, and closer to home than we might like to suppose.

The European Convention is by no means a perfect solution. But it does manage to collectively impose on these countries ideas, laws and values ultimately originating in the UK, and, in doing so, does solve horrific humanitarian crises. It is an enormously strong soft-power tool to project the UK's moral and legal influence throughout Europe. It would hardly be in the UK's overall best interests to sacrifice that influence in return for a more favourable result in a handful of cases.

THE REFORM DEBATES

Removing the UK from the Convention would grievously undermine the moral authority of the ECHR. What would prevent Russia, or Turkey, or any other government with a poor human rights record from following the UK's example? The consequences for the overall stability of European international relations could be dire.

Rights and the threat of terrorism

The attacks on New York's 'twin towers' in 2001, in London in 2005 and in Paris in 2015 demonstrate too vividly the dangers we now face from international terrorism. Faced with the threat of such atrocities, governments must act to protect lives and security, and they are indeed obliged to do so by the European Convention. In doing so, it is not unreasonable that they should seek extra powers to detect and apprehend those it believes may be planning further attacks.

Protecting society, however, may sometimes require actions that restrict the rights and freedoms we enjoy in more normal circumstances, but drawing the line between what is necessary and what would constitute an unacceptable withdrawal of rights that underpin our freedom may not be easy.

The British government's response to the 7/11 attack was a proposal that those suspected of terrorism could be held without charge for up to 60 days. It met with fierce opposition – if there was sufficient evidence to justify arrest, why should it take 60 days to bring charges? After much debate in the Commons, a 28 day period was agreed (in 2011 it was eventually withdrawn). A further measure allowed for the indefinite detention without charge of foreign nationals suspected of terrorism who could not be deported (e.g. because of the dangers of them facing unfair trials or worse in their home countries): this, however, was rescinded following a challenge by the European Court and replaced with 'control orders' restricting suspects' movements and contacts.[8]

In their efforts to thwart terrorist attacks, it is understandable that security forces should want to use all the means at their disposal, and the advent of the internet and digital communications gave them an enormously powerful tool. The extent of the American and British government's collection of information on our internet usage and e-correspondence only became public knowledge through the disclosures of Edward Snowden in 2013.

These revelations produced outrage and much debate over what was legitimate and proportionate, but our government was not deterred. The Conservatives' initial plans were blocked by the Liberal Democrats when they were coalition partners, but the Conservatives' victory in 2015 allowed them to announce a bill that would require 'communication service providers' (CSPs) to retain information of what websites we visited and with whom we communicated (by email or phone), and to provide that data, on request, to police or intelligence officers without even the need for a warrant. With a warrant from the Home Secretary, the CSPs would be required to give information not just on with whom we spoke, but what we said. This proposal for what has been dubbed a 'snoopers' charter' has been widely criticised, with Liberty commenting that the move from targeted surveillance to the blanket surveillance of everyone 'transforms us from a nation of citizens into a nation of suspects'.[9]

Extraordinary circumstances may require extraordinary measures, but are the provisions of this bill a proportionate response to the threat of terrorism? Under the European Convention all suspects are entitled to a fair trial and to not be detained without trial, and we are all entitled to privacy which faces grave abridgement. Rightly, few people would sympathise with those who commit or attempt terrible crimes, but those rights are there for good reason – they provide innocent people protection from wrongful imprisonment and prevent unnecessary government prying into our private lives.

Striking a balance between giving our security services all the tools they want and protecting our rights is difficult. It raises many complex and controversial issues and different people will take different views. This chapter does not offer specific proposals on where the line should be drawn, but a question that must be addressed is how decisions on such matters should be made and who should have the right to make them. If we aspire to be a society in which citizens are sovereign, it does not necessarily mean that citizens collectively should take such decisions – they are far too complex and require specialist knowledge – but they should be taken in a way that is as transparent as possible and takes account of our opinions, and they should be taken by people who are, directly or indirectly, accountable to us.

The cost of justice

As citizens, we all have equal rights, but that equality is rather theoretical while we do not all enjoy the same access to the justice system. While the rich can employ lawyers to argue their cases, for most citizens going to court is prohibitively expensive, unless the nature of the case and a person's circumstances qualify them for legal aid.

DEFENDING RIGHTS AND LIBERTIES

Entitlement to legal aid, which was introduced by the 1945-50 Labour government to ensure equality before the law, has, however, been drastically reduced. As a result of massive cuts in 2013, there is no longer any entitlement to legal aid in family cases (such as divorce and custody of children), personal injury and some aspects of employment law, immigration (other than asylum cases and where a person is in custody) and some debt, housing and benefit issues. Even when cases qualify for aid, it is not available to people with assets of more than £8000: thus only the very poorest can receive any help at all.

These changes were, of course, fiercely resisted by many politicians and the legal profession. The government, thanks to our defective voting system, was able to get its proposals through the Commons, but in the Lords it was defeated 14 times before a vote was tied and, following convention, the government was considered to have won.

Labour ministers, Charlie Falconer and Willy Bach, writing in the Guardian in January 2016 noted that even Britain's most senior judge, Lord Thomas of Cwmgiedd, believed that 'our justice system has become unaffordable to most'.[10] They went on to observe that:

> In Britain, in the 21st century, a growing number of people can't afford to defend themselves and make sure their rights are respected. The facts are startling. In 2009-10, more than 470,000 people received advice or assistance for social welfare issues. By 2013-14, the year after the government's reforms to legal aid came into force, that number had fallen to less than 53,000 – a drop of nearly 90%.

THE REFORM DEBATES

The number of cases taken to employment tribunals also fell by 60% after application fees of up to £1,200 were introduced in 2013.

There are of course organisations like Citizens' Advice Bureaux and local law centres which provide free advice, but their funding, often dependant on cash-strapped local authorities, have suffered swingeing cuts and many centres have closed. Moreover, while they can provide advice, they cannot meet the costs of legal actions.

Judicial review is a procedure by which individuals or organisations can challenge whether decisions by government or other public bodies were properly taken. It has been described by Martha Spurrier, a human rights barrister, as 'a fundamental constitutional safeguard that allows individuals to hold the state to account and prevent abuses of power'.[11] In 2012, however, David Cameron promised his government would 'charge more for reviews so people think twice about time-wasting', and in 2015 changes were indeed made to increase the potential costs of bringing an action. Restrictions placed on courts' ability to issue cost capping orders[12] mean that some who wish to contest government decisions are unable to do so because of prospect of financial ruin if their actions are not successful. We are all still entitled under the law to apply for judicial review, but in many cases only the wealthy can afford to take the risk.

The government attempted to justify its draconian actions on the grounds that it must protect tax payers from rising legal costs, but tax-payers are also citizens and legal system is there to protect their rights. However good our laws and the international conventions that specify our rights, we cannot claim that we are all equal

DEFENDING RIGHTS AND LIBERTIES

in our citizenship while much of the legal system is essentially the preserve of the wealthy.

Many of the chapters in this book are about changes needed to improve our democracy. When it comes to rights and justice, however, the need is for opposition to changes, some of which have already been made and some of which are under discussion, that threaten to unravel the systems that have been developed over more than half a century to protect our rights and ensure that all have access to justice.

---

[1] In a criminal trial, the accused must be aware of the charges against him, have time to prepare a defence, must be entitled to legal advice, have the right to challenge witnesses, and to have the use of an interpreter. No one can be punished for actions which were legal at the time they were committed, or subject to a heavier punishment than was applicable at the time.

[2] *Protecting Human Rights in the UK: The Conservatives' Proposals for changing Britain's Human Rights Laws*, Conservative Party, 2015.

[3] The claim that German basic law takes priority over the convention is wrong, and a misreading of <u>Gorgulu v Germany c21/2004</u>. The German government, in fact, lost the case.

[4] Claimed by a prisoner but dismissed summarily,: http://webarchive.nationalarchives.gov.uk/+/http:/www.dca.gov.uk/peoples-rights/human-rights/pdf/full_review.pdf

[5] One of a number of ludicrous claims that have been made about the Human Rights Act given in Liberty's excellent Human Rights Act Mythbuster webpage: https://www.liberty-human-rights.org.uk/human-rights/what-are-human-rights/human-rights-act/human-rights-act-mythbuster

THE REFORM DEBATES

[6] A truly spectacular misreading by the Home Secretary of *Anon. (Bolivia) v SSHD* [2008] IA/14578/2008. http://www.bbc.co.uk/news/uk-england-15174254

[7] In 2013, the Court found Russia guilty of 119 violations, Turkey of 118, Romania of 83 and Ukraine of 65.

[8] In 2012 control orders were replaced with 'Terrorism Prevention and Investigation Measures', described by Liberty as 'control order-lite'.

[9] https://www.liberty-human-rights.org.uk/campaigning/other-campaigns/no-snoopers-charter

[10] Quoted by Charles Falconer and Willy Bach in The Guardian, 16 Jan 2016

[11] The Guardian, 3 April 2015

[12] Cost capping orders (CCOs) set a limit on the defendant's legal costs which may be recovered from the claimant.

3-15 A Written Constitution for the UK

Dr Andrew Blick

The United Kingdom (UK) is famous for lacking a written constitution. There is a longstanding debate about whether we should obtain such a text. Arguably the cause of bringing about this outcome has achieved added impetus in recent decades. But what actually is a written constitution? What are the arguments for and against it? How would we go about getting one? What would be in it? And is it ever likely to happen? And should it happen? The following chapter considers these questions.

When it is said that the UK has an 'unwritten constitution' a common retort often follows. Much of the UK constitution is in fact written down. Documents from *Magna Carta* up to more recent Acts of Parliament such as the devolution statutes and the *Human Rights Act 1998* (though now under threat) contain some core constitutional arrangements in them, relating to how government is organised and the relationships between government and the governed. But it is correct to say that the UK lacks a document or group of documents that has the label 'Constitution of the United Kingdom' expressly attached to it. Many other democracies comparable to the UK do possess such a text. Typically the judiciary is entrusted with upholding these written constitutions, and declaring actions and legislation that conflict with them to be void. They are generally also subject to special amendment procedures, making it harder to alter the written constitution than it is to change regular law, with requirements such as a supermajority in the legislature or agreement through a referendum having to be met before constitutional modification is possible.

In lacking a written constitution as described here, the UK is in select company, alongside Israel and New Zealand. What does the UK have instead? Traditionally, a defining doctrine of the UK constitution, rather than it being written in a special text, has been that at its core is the concept of parliamentary sovereignty. According to this principle, the Westminster Parliament possesses legally unlimited law making power. It is not formally subject to any constitutional text, and can if it chooses alter the constitutional arrangements of the UK as it sees fit. The only curbs upon the UK Parliament, according to this thesis, are the self-restraint of parliamentarians, and the practical plausibility of those measures it tries to implement. Many core aspects of the UK constitution, things we take for granted, exist only as conventions – that is, rules lacking in direct legal force. For instance, nowhere on the statute book are there firm legal requirements that the Prime Minister should be a member of the House of Commons, and that the leader of the party that has won a General Election outright should be appointed Prime Minister. These rules, critical to our democracy, are left to convention, with the assumption (in this case reasonable) that the Queen and her advisers know what to do.

But should we care? Some hold that the UK benefits from having an unwritten constitution. They say that there is no public demand for a change that would prove to be a gruelling task, likely to trigger divisive arguments over whether a written constitution is needed at all, and what should be in it. The existing constitution, they claim, is more flexible and able to adapt to changing times; while a written constitution would be problematically rigid and resistant to necessary modification. The values prevailing at the time it was drafted could be frozen forever. A further defect that opponents of the written constitution idea claim to identify is that it would place excessive power in the hands of unelected judges. Courts, lacking a direct popular mandate, would nonetheless be responsible for making crucial decisions about how the constitution should be implemented. Judges would, in the process, have the opportunity to interpret the constitutional text in accordance with their own proclivities, potentially wielding an inappropriate degree of personal discretion and influence. For those who advance this criticism it is proper that Parliament, containing an elected and preeminent chamber, the House of Commons, should, given its democratic mandate, be in a position of constitutional supremacy, rather than subordinacy to the judiciary. For those who share this outlook, parliamentary sovereignty appears to be preferable to a written constitution.

A further component of the argument against a written constitution for the UK is the idea that, whatever the drafters of a constitution may seek to achieve through the words they write, actual practice often differs from the prescriptions set out in the text. Cultural factors, it is sometimes held, are the key to a well-functioning democracy, not the contents of a document. The UK has coped without a written constitution, the argument runs, because it has a healthy political culture. It therefore has no need for a text, which would at best make no difference, and at worst could undermine a delicate equilibrium. A related view is that it is a mistake to resort to artificial instruments and blueprints as the basis for a polity. According to this school, it is the gradual accretion of practice and tacit assumptions over time that provides for a functioning social system. Once again, a written constitution could be seen from this perspective as redundant or undesirable.

But there is another side to the argument. The concept of a written constitution for the UK has its advocates. One point they advance is that, without a written constitution, it is very difficult for members of the public, or even participants in the governance of the UK, to know what the rules of the system and the rights of individuals within it are. In a democracy this lack of clarity is seen by some as a serious shortcoming. A written constitution, then, might set out clearly in one place the core principles and regulations, potentially bringing about greater public understanding of the constitution. Furthermore, supporters of a written constitution for the UK hold, it could provide greater protection for some of the fundamental values of our society from arbitrary alteration. The doctrine of parliamentary sovereignty, some fear, creates vulnerability. The government of the day can potentially use its Commons majority to force through Acts of Parliament that may compromise key principles such as the rule of law. A written constitution would make major constitutional change subject to a higher degree of consensus than it is at present, through the amendment procedure the text itself created. It could also create a protective barrier against legislation that violated the constitution, through the practice of constitutional review by the judiciary. Through these safeguards, the position of individual freedoms, and of institutions such as the devolved legislatures, might be protected against the possibility of interference from Westminster and Whitehall.

For some, a written constitution should seek to codify the constitution as it is at present. But for others, it would be a means of achieving a specific constitutional reform, or perhaps a set of changes. In such accounts, it might, for instance, expand the powers of the devolved settlements, and possibly introduce a Parliament and executive for England, or a group of English regional assemblies. It could offer a chance of bringing about electoral reform, or changing the composition of the House of Lords, perhaps making the second chamber of the UK Parliament directly elected, or providing a place for the devolved systems to participate in UK decision-making. A written constitution could bolster the status of local government; or entrench a UK Bill of Rights. A number of these reforms taken in combination could lead the UK increasingly to become a federal state, with powers clearly shared between the different territorial layers of governance. This option has of late frequently been floated as a means of averting the possibility of a break-up in the UK led from Scotland.

Another subject which has received heighted attention recently is the idea of a UK constitutional convention. Accounts of the need for such a process often note the long-term decline in traditional forms of political participation in the UK. They also tend to draw attention to other supposed forms of malaise, such as dwindling public trust in the system, inappropriate influence on the part of corporate interests, the uncertain future of the Union, and pronounced disagreements over such matters as human rights and European Union membership. A constitutional convention, it is argued, could help resolve some of these problems. It might enable a thorough consideration of the constitutional future of the UK and propose ways forward. It could promote wider public ownership of the constitution. Its output could be a written constitution.

There are examples of conventions from around the world that we can follow, in countries ranging from Canada to Iceland to Ireland. One form of good practice that might be taken into account is the idea of incorporating ordinary members of the public chosen at random. This method, known as sortition, dates back to the Ancient Greek democracies. An advantage it could bring would be that constitution-building might not seem purely an exercise dominated by professional politicians and officials. The democratic legitimacy and credibility of the end product, the constitution, might be enhanced. However, constitutional conventions that did possess this inclusive membership base have not always been successful, especially when the elite was not fully bought into them. Alan Renwick, now of the Constitution Unit, has made this point convincingly. For this reason it will probably be necessary to include at least some politicians in a constitutional convention.

I will declare my position now and say that I am in principle a supporter of a written constitution. I do not believe it will solve all our problems. It will probably not, for instance, trigger an instant rise in public confidence in the political system. Anyway, claims about a growing malaise requiring drastic remedial action should always be treated with a degree of caution. And while we may in some areas be over-dependent in the UK on nebulous conventions to regulate our constitution, these types of rules would continue to exist in some form even under a written constitution. Nor would devising a written constitution for a mature democracy be an easy task for a constitutional convention to undertake.

One of the best reasons for trying to introduce a written constitution would be that it could finally and decisively bring about an end to the doctrine of parliamentary sovereignty. As a matter of principle, the ultimate source of sovereignty should be the people, not an institution. The parliamentary sovereignty concept has always presented some intellectual challenges, and only the most

A WRITTEN CONSTITUTION FOR THE UK

ingenious of scholars can make it appear plausible after close inspection. Aside from whether it is viable in theory, parliamentary sovereignty now faces practical challenges. Membership of the European Union, the passing of the Human Rights Act and devolution all in their own ways serve to challenge the idea of parliamentary supremacy. It is unthinkable today that the Westminster legislature would seek, for instance, to abolish the Scottish Parliament. Indeed, at the time of writing, a bill passing through Parliament contains a clause that would declare the Scottish Parliament (and government) to be a permanent part of the UK constitution. In some ways, this stipulation resembles the type of provision that might be found in a written constitution. Nonetheless, if one wishes – as the UK government always does – to continue to assert the doctrine of parliamentary sovereignty, then Parliament would not be bound by this clause protecting the Scottish Parliament any more than it is any other normal Act of Parliament. Parliament could presumably either repeal the section expressly, or simply ignore it and legislate contrary to it anyway. Tying ourselves into intellectual knots over matters that are of far more than mere theoretical significance is not a good idea. We should admit that if we want to perform the functions associated with a written constitution, then we should introduce a written constitution.

A further problem with parliamentary sovereignty is that it can appear to be a standing invitation to government to seek to use their Commons majorities to perpetrate constitutional abuse. Earlier governments have used parliamentary sovereignty for such nefarious purposes as introducing mass internment without trial on security grounds; and – less dramatic, but important nonetheless – to continuously interfere with the business of local government. A recurring threat in recent times has been the possibility of the passing of a statute that imposed severe restrictions on recourse to judicial review of the decisions of public authorities. Such legislation would be within the terms of the doctrine of parliamentary sovereignty, but would compromise the rule of law. In recent years, Parliament has passed important constitutional measures – such as the introduction of five-year fixed terms for Parliament, and alterations to the number and electoral size of parliamentary constituencies – in the face of substantial controversy. It might amend or repeal the Human Rights Act on a similar basis. Major alterations to the way in which government functions, or to our rights, should surely require a higher degree of agreement than normal legislation. A written constitution would be the best way of ensuring that they do. The amendment procedure this text imposed need not be so demanding as to prevent change ever from taking place. But it could ensure that there was careful consideration, discussion, and some kind of cross-party or cross-territory agreement before it happened.

Giving the courts a role in upholding these principles, moreover, would not be a violation of democratic principle. No party wins a General Election with a majority of votes cast, and the overall trend is towards smaller shares for the victor. It is difficult to sustain the view that the group that controls the Commons has an irresistible right to govern. Moreover, a primary function of the courts under a written constitution would be to adjudicate between different tiers of governance, each with their own democratic mandate, rather than to impose the rule of the unelected on the elected.

But are we ever likely actually to get a written constitution? Among political players and commentators, there is much ingrained resistance, lack of interest or even absence of comprehension regarding this possible change. I was fortunate enough, during the 2010-2015 Parliament, to be adviser to a parliamentary body, the House of Commons Political and Constitutional Reform Committee, that carried out the first-ever official public inquiry into the possibility of a written constitution for the UK, under its chair, Graham Allen MP. As the first effort in this area, the inquiry was an important historic event, whatever the outcome. But some seemed to think that even to investigate this subject was somehow misguided, or even irresponsible, or a diversion from more important and more practical matters. For its pains, the committee was abolished in 2015. But the written constitution issue it had investigated as part of its overall workload could not simply be willed out of existence.

Some hold that only a major crisis is likely to trigger the outcome of a written constitution; and that such a crisis is never likely to happen in this country. I would be wary about signing up to either of these propositions. Constitution-building often takes place in the wake of serious disruption such as revolution or foreign occupation. But it does not have to. Patriation of the Canadian constitution in the early 1980s was not a consequence of any major crisis. Furthermore, it is important to avoid uncritical acceptance of the notion that the constitutional history of the UK and its national sub-components is a tale of only gradual, peaceful change. English constitutional documents such as *Magna Carta* in 1215 and the *Bill of Rights* in 1689 came about at moments of turmoil, of which there are many other examples.

In more recent decades, dramatic and seemingly unending constitutional transformation has been an inescapable fact. In the period since the end of the Second World War we have signed up

THE REFORM DEBATES

to the Council of Europe and the European Convention on Human Rights; created Life Peerages and admitted women into the House of Lords; created the Law Commission and the Parliamentary Ombudsman; joined what is now the European Union; seen substantial expansion in the role of judicial review; altered the system of local government on numerous occasions; established referendums as a means of taking or ratifying major public decisions; introduced devolution and freedom of information; used multiple electoral system other than first past the past post at various levels in the UK; passed the Human Rights Act; excluded nearly all hereditary Peers from the House of Lords; created a UK Supreme Court supplanting the Law Lords; reduced the scope of the Royal Prerogative powers; introduced five-year fixed term parliaments; and created directly elected Police and Crime Commissioners.

This list is exhausting, but it is not exhaustive. After such a bewildering procession of constitutional change, perhaps a written constitution could act as a stabilising measure. It certainly does not seem to be a completely implausible outcome. No-one in 1945 would have given credence to this itinerary of constitutional transformation. To rule out the chances of a further change might therefore be unwise. Indeed, there have since the 1970s been a number of efforts by individuals and organisations to propose their own versions of what a written constitution for the UK might be. Most recently, Professor Robert Blackburn of King's College London produced three options for the Graham Allen committee.

There is a particular way of enhancing the plausibility of such a project. If we think of a written constitution as a vast, all-embracing document, every article of which must be thrashed out in a convention, then agreed by some other method such as a referendum, we might understandably become dubious about the chances of success. However, it is more appropriate to think in terms of a mechanism by which we can provide certain systemic provisions which we consider of exceptional importance with the special status they merit. We already afford a higher level of protection to one legal rule, the five-year maximum length of a Parliament, which remains subject to absolute veto by the House of Lords under the Parliament Acts of 1911 and 1949. If this provision needs safeguarding, then why not some others that are also core to our democratic system, and why not by a means more satisfactory than relying on the Lords, an institution lacking in democratic legitimacy? An agreement between the UK Parliament and the devolved legislatures could list provisions - including the Human Rights Act, *European Communities Act 1972*, and the devolution legislation – that could only be altered by the consent of a majority of those legislatures, or perhaps with unanimity. This text could assert its supremacy over even the UK Parliament. If it could command sufficient public support, and acceptance among the elites of the UK within the different executives, legislatures and the judiciary, it could succeed in supplanting the doctrine of parliamentary sovereignty. Courts would be entirely justified in upholding this instrument if threatened. The UK would then have formed the embryo of a new legal source for its fundamental systemic arrangements, that might one day grow into something more substantial. The select international club of democracies without written constitutions would have lost its largest member.

3-16 An agenda for debate and action

This book has examined what is wrong with our democracy and the chapters of Part 3 have made proposals on how we need to change it. Political power needs to be shifted away from money, corporate interests and the political elite, and towards citizens who, collectively, should be in charge. The UK should belong to them and, although they elect politicians to run the country, those politicians should be there to serve the interests of, and only of, those they have been elected to represent.

A different type of politics is needed – a politics which engages people and gives them real influence over decisions which affect them. The previous chapters have presented some of the aspects of our political system which are in need of reform and they have made a number of recommendations for change. None of these recommendations would on their own produce the politics that are needed, but individually or taken together they would do much to enhance our democracy and affirm the collective sovereignty of citizens. Not all readers (or even contributors) will agree with every change proposed, and they are not an immutable package. As potential elements of a reformed constitution, however, they provide an agenda for debate and action. They cover:

1. A change to an electoral system for the Commons (and where necessary, local government) which would be fairer, would

AN AGENDA FOR DEBATE AND ACTION

offer voters more meaningful choices, and would provide representation to a wider range of views.
2. Measures to remove, or at least restrict, the influence of money and corporate power through better controls on lobbying and the non-parliamentary earnings of politicians, and reform of the funding of political parties.
3. Measures to ensure the accountability of politicians to those they represent, including the right of electors to 'recall' their representatives in exceptional circumstances.
4. An upper house in which there is no place for political patronage or unmerited privilege, which represents all parts of the country and society, and which is wholly or largely elected by us.
5. A press that is free but which serves democracy in a responsible manner, and more effective regulation to uphold standards and provide redress for those whom it wrongs.
6. A strong commitment to public service broadcasting, reform of the governance of the BBC to protect its independence, and measures to make all broadcasting organisations more accountable to those they serve.
7. Greater devolution of powers from Westminster to English regions and local government in order that decisions are taken closer to those affected by them.
8. Recognition that, while democracy must offer citizens opportunities to express their views, any moves towards so-called direct democracy could impair the important and valuable processes of deliberation that good democracy requires.
9. Changes to the way political parties operate in order to make them more engaging and more inclusive, and democratic in their internal affairs.

10. The ending of hereditary privilege, and moves to dismantle the monarchy and replace it with a head of state elected by all citizens
11. Greater efforts to engage younger electors in politics, including through a better quality of citizenship education, targeted actions by local authorities, politicians and parties, and a reduction in the voting age to 16.
12. Improvements in the way we run elections aimed at making voting easier and more attractive, while not compromising the integrity of the process.
13. A recognition that greater participation in elections requires better form of politics and that compulsory voting is not the answer.
14. The protection of our rights, respect for the international instruments which underpin those rights in Britain and elsewhere, and a legal system in which access is not determined by wealth.
15. A written constitution, protected from amendment by requiring more than a simple parliamentary majority to amend it, which defines where sovereignty and authority lie and which provides a framework for the rules by which the country is governed.

That is the agenda for a better democracy set out in this book. It is not claimed that these are the only changes required, and some readers may well have alternative ideas on how achieve the transformation of politics that is needed. What is even more important that the specific recommendations, however, is that we have a national debate on the issues.

AN AGENDA FOR DEBATE AND ACTION

As the country needs a form of politics that engages people and serves their interests, the debate on how we get there should itself involve as many of us as it can. It must not just be a debate for the political classes, but one for us all. In chapter 2-3 it was argued that the debate might be best led by a constitutional convention – a representative group of citizens, working with politicians and constitutional experts, with the task of preparing proposals for reform – but we are unlikely to get a sufficiently wide-ranging convention without a strong popular demand for one, and, for a convention to have the political weight to challenge the interests of the privileged and politically powerful, it needs to be connected to wider debates of citizens in all parts of the country and all sections of society.

This book is therefore a call to action. As citizens, we all have a responsibility for the state of our democracy and, if we don't like it, it is up to us to call for reform. We are not powerless: we can make demands of our politicians, argue our case in the media and build support for our ideas through our everyday conversations with friends and colleagues. Each of us in our own community can be a champion for change.

Individual action is important – even essential – but to be effective we also need to organise. In chapter 2-3 we referred to the 'reform lobby' – those organisations that are already campaigning for a better democracy. They can offer opportunities for collective, concerted action, and can provide the facts and arguments that are needed to make the case for change. These organisations need support – and in some cases they also need to be encouraged to recognize that real reform will only come about through action on a broad front and not just on their own specific issues. Some of the

THE REFORM DEBATES

key organisations are listed in the appendix, together with information on how to contact them.

This book has been written in the hope that those who read it will want their voices to be heard in redesigning politics and that it will help to make the reform debates happen. If all readers are prepared to assert their rights as citizens in demanding a better form of politics, then we may all look forward to an increased prospect of achieving real reform.

Appendix

Organisations engaged in the reform debates

The Reform Foundation, the publisher of this book, will welcome feedback on the issues raised in the book on its website and Facebook page.

Website: www.reformfoundation.com
Email: enquiries@reformfoundation.org.uk

The Reform Foundation is a small and relatively new organisation established to promote debate on constitutional reform. It seeks a form of politics in which citizens are sovereign, which engages people in decisions that affect them, and in which politicians are accountable to them.

There are many organisations in Britain already campaigning for democratic reform, some concerned with specific issues and others with wider agendas. This appendix lists some of the organisations working on the issues raised in this book and able to provide further facts, information and arguments for those who want to get involved in the debates on how democracy should be renewed.

All of the organisations on the list do excellent work, but the list begins with five which have particularly important roles in debates on reform – the Electoral Reform Society and Unlock Democracy because of the breadth of their interests and their campaigning capacity, and the Campaign for Press and Broadcasting

THE REFORM DEBATES

Freedom, Liberty and Republic which are leading organisations in fields not covered by the first two.

Electoral Reform Society

ERS has been campaigning for electoral reform since 1884, and that remains the focus of its work. However, ERS increasingly sees electoral reform as just one of the changes needed to create a better democracy, and its interests include Lords reform, 'votes at 16', political party reform, party funding and the conduct of elections.

Website	www.electoral-reform.org.uk
Email	ers@electoral-reform.org.uk
Phone	020 3714 4070
Address	2 – 6 Boundary Road, London, SE1 8HP

Unlock Democracy

Campaigns for a vibrant, inclusive democracy. Formed from a merger of Charter88 and the New Politics Network, its work has included most of the issues covered by this book - electoral reform and Lords reform, cleaning up politics, parties and party funding and the case for a written constitution. It has groups around the country whose members campaign locally.

Website	www.unlockdemocracy.org
Email	info@unlockdemocracy.org.uk
Phone	020 7278 4443
Address	5th Floor, 9 King Street, London, EC2V 8EA

APPENDIX

Campaign for Freedom of Information
Seeks to improve and defend the Freedom of Information Act, advising people about their rights under FOI and related laws.
Website   www.cfoi.org.uk
Email   admin@cfoi.demon.co.uk
Phone   020 7324 2519
Address   c/o Article 19, Free Word Centre, 60 Farringdon Rd, London EC1R 3GA

Liberty
Formerly the National Council for Civil Liberties, Liberty campaigns to protect basic rights and freedoms through the courts, in Parliament and in the wider community.
Website   www.liberty-human-rights.org.uk
Email   (via website)
Phone   020 7403 3888
Address   Liberty House, 26-30 Strutton Ground, London, SW1P 2HR

Republic
Republic campaigns for the replacement of the monarchy with a head of state who is elected by, and is accountable to, all citizens and who has a clearly defined constitutional role. It has a number of active local groups and works with organisations of supporters within the main political parties.
Website   https://republic.org.uk
Email   enquiries@republic.org.uk
Phone   020 7608 5742
Address   Suite 14040, 145-157 St John Street, London, EC1V 4PY

THE REFORM DEBATES

Other organisations which can provide information on the issues of the 'reform debates'

Bite the Ballot
A campaign to encourage young people to register to vote and engage in politics
Website www.bitetheballot.co.uk
Email (via website)
Phone 0330 1138428
Address First Floor, 78 Duke Street, London W1K 6JQ

British Youth Council
Seeks to engage young people in politics and community activities.
Website www.byc.org.uk
Email (via website)
Phone 020 7250 8374
Address CAN Mezzanine, 49-51 East Road, London, N1 6AH

Campaign for a Democratic Upper House
A grouping of Labour parliamentarians and members who support a second chamber which is wholly or mainly elected.
Website www.democraticupperhouse.org.uk
Email democraticupperhouse@gmail.com
Phone 07947 616921
Address 4 Brookway, London SE3 9BJ

Citizenship Foundation
An educational charity which helps young people understand the law, politics and democracy.

APPENDIX

Website www.citizenshipfoundation.org.uk
Email info@citizenshipfoundation.org.uk
Phone 020 7566 4141
Address 50 Featherstone St, London, EC1Y 8RT

Conservative Action for Electoral Reform
Makes the case for electoral reform within the Conservative Party
Website www.conservativeelectoralreform.org

Constitution Unit
Based in University College London, the Unit conducts research and produces reports on constitutional issues.
Website www.ucl.ac.uk/constitution-unit
Email constitution@ucl.ac.uk
Phone 020 7679 4977
Address 29-31 Tavistock Square, London WC1H 9QU

Fawcett Society
The Society promotes gender equality and women's rights at work, at home and in public life. Its concerns include the need for a much better gender balance in political institutions.
Website www.fawcettsociety.org.uk
Email info@fawcettsociety.org.uk
Phone 020 3598 6154
Address Unit 204, Linton House,
164-180 Union Street, London, SE1 0LH

Hacked Off
Created at the time of the Leveson Inquiry, campaigns for a system of regulation to protect people from mistreatment by the press while safeguarding freedom of expression.

Website	www.hackinginquiry.org
Email	campaigns@hackinginquiry.org
Phone	020 3735 8844
Address	Southbank House, Black Prince Road, London SE1 7SJ

Hannah Mitchell Society

A cross-party campaign for devolved, democratic government in the North of England.

Website	www.hannahmitchell.org.uk
Email	paul@hannahmitchell.org.uk
Phone	07795 008691
Address	Bank Top, 90a Radcliffe Road, Golcar, Huddersfield HD7 4EZ

Hansard Society

A charity which promotes democracy and the strengthening of parliament through its research reports and educational work.

Website	www.hansardsociety.org.uk
Email	contact@hansardsociety.org.uk
Phone	020 7710 6070
Address	5th floor, 9 King Street, London EC2V 8EA

Labour Campaign for Electoral Reform

Campaigns for electoral reform within the Labour Party

Email	lcerinfo@yahoo.co.uk

Labour for a Republic

An organisation of Labour members supporting republicanism.

Website	www.labourforarepublic.org.uk
Email	enquiries@labourforarepublic.org.uk

APPENDIX

Liberal Democrats for a Republic
As Labour for a Republic within the Liberal Democrats
Facebook　　Liberal Democrats for a republic

Open Rights Group
A digital campaigning organisation working to protect the rights to privacy and free speech online.
Website　　www.openrightsgroup.org
Email　　info@openrightsgroup.org
Phone　　020 7096 1079
Address　　12 Tileyard road, London N7 9AH

Operation Black Vote
Works for greater racial equality by encouraging the involvement of BME communities in public institutions.
Website　　www.obv.org.uk
Email　　info@obv.org.uk
Phone　　020 8983 5430

Spinwatch / Public Interest Investigations
Investigates the way that the public relations (PR) and lobbying industries and government propaganda distort public debate and undermine democracy.
Website　　www.spinwatch.org
Email　　info@spinwatch.org

The Democratic Society
A membership organisation promoting participative democracy through project work.
Website　　www.demsoc.org
Email　　hello@demsoc.org
Address　　Werks Central, 15-17 Middle St, Brighton BN1 1AL

The Reform Foundation

The Reform Foundation promotes public debate and greater public understanding of the need for political reform. It believes that all citizens should be able to participate in politics as equals.

The Foundation's purposes are:

- To promote popular debate on democratic reform by championing the concept of popular sovereignty;
- To promote greater understanding of the need for democratic and constitutional reform through its publications and events.

The Reform Foundation is a non-profit organisation and is independent of all parties.

All profits from the sale of this book will be used to support the work of the Foundation.